The Paradox of Hope

The Paradox of Hope
Theology and the Problem of Nihilism

By JUSTIN D. KLASSEN

CASCADE *Books* · Eugene, Oregon

THE PARADOX OF HOPE
Theology and the Problem of Nihilism

Copyright © 2011 Justin D. Klassen. All rights reserved. Except for brief quotations in critical publications or reviews, no part of this book may be reproduced in any manner without prior written permission from the publisher. Write: Permissions, Wipf and Stock Publishers, 199 W. 8th Ave., Suite 3, Eugene, OR 97401.

Cascade Books
An Imprint of Wipf and Stock Publishers
199 W. 8th Ave., Suite 3
Eugene, OR 97401

www.wipfandstock.com

ISBN 13: 978-1-60899-770-1

Cataloging-in-Publication data:

Klassen, Justin D.

    The paradox of hope : theology and the problem of nihilism / Justin D. Klassen.

    viii + 254 p. ; 23 cm. — Includes bibliographical references and index.

    ISBN 13: 978-1-60899-770-1

    1. Philosophical theology. 2. Postmodern theology. I. Klassen, Justin D. II. Title.

BT40 .K54 2011

Manufactured in the U.S.A.

Contents

Acknowledgments / vii

Introduction / 1

1 Contemporary Theology and the Turn to Rhetoric / 9
    Introduction: The Urgent Situation / 9
    The Modern Separation of "Religion" from "The Social" / 11
    Overcoming Postmodernism's Ontology of Difference / 32
    Persuasion/Inscription: Christianity as Social Mechanism / 46
    Conclusion: Rhetorical Narrative, *Sittlichkeit*, and Desire / 52

2 Language and the Fear of Death / 57
    Introduction / 57
    The Sophistic "Gesture of Security Against the Void" / 60
    Modern Spatialization / 66
    Necrophilia / 76
    Hart and Levinas on Time and Infinity / 85
    What is Christian Urgency? / 94

3 Consummation or Complication? / 104
    Introduction: Immediate Oppositions / 104
    Lingering Resonances: Milbank's Persuasive Absurdity / 110
    "Difficulty" in the *Postscript* / 121
    Incarnation and Christian Difficulty / 135
    The Invitation: Kierkegaard's *Practice in Christianity* / 148
    Conclusion / 154

Contents

4 Cultural Logic and Christian Sociality / 157
    Introduction / 157
    Milbank's *Altera Civitas* / 159
    Desire and Sacrifice in Girard / 173
    Milbank's Rejection of Girard and its Consequences / 193
    Conclusion / 197

5 Love's Obstinate Hope / 201
    Introduction / 201
    Erotic Love and Friendship in *Works of Love* / 203
    Love as the Crucifixion of Preference / 218
    Love as Expectancy of the Good / 230
    Conclusion: Christianity as a "Way" / 242

Bibliography / 247
Index / 253

Acknowledgments

I AM GRATEFUL TO THE Social Sciences and Humanities Research Council of Canada for the CGS Doctoral Scholarship that funded the initial research for this book, and to McMaster University, which provided significant financial assistance during my tenure as a graduate student in the Department of Religious Studies.

I am deeply grateful also to the people who made my time at McMaster so rewarding and memorable—faculty, support staff, and fellow students. Specifically I thank Travis Kroeker, whose encouragement, able guidance, and keen ability to spot the crucial questions ignored or evaded in any argument made the book better than it would have been without his assistance. In addition, I remain grateful for his enduring friendship and support. Thanks also to Peter Widdicombe and Stephen Westerholm, both close readers of this text in an earlier form and vocal and engaging questioners of its author.

Many current and former doctoral students at McMaster, all friends, played direct or indirect roles in shaping and refining the questions that animate this book. To Justin Neufeld, who continues to challenge and inspire me to think more deeply about what I read but also how I live, I am deeply grateful. David Penner provided a constant source of lively skepticism about the merit of this project, and thus improved it, along with teaching me a great deal about Heidegger and Kierkegaard over beer at the Phoenix. Greg Hillis, Carlos Colorado, Nathan Colborne, Darren Dahl, Leo Stan, and Paul Doerksen were all in diverse ways willing contributors to the outcome of this project.

To the faculty and students at Austin College, where I spent the last two years teaching, I owe a significant debt of gratitude. Specifically I thank Phil Barker and Nate Bigelow for making work a place where true friendship can burgeon and thrive alongside lively discussion, argument, and pipe-smoking. Thanks also to Todd Penner for chairing a Religious Studies Department that attracts such challenge-ready students. And thanks to those many students, specifically the brave souls who endured (with style!) an upper-level seminar on Kierkegaard, and to the brothers and affiliated sisters of Chi Tau Chi.

To my families, both Klassen and Bohn, I owe much gratitude for unwavering encouragement and support. To Melissa Klassen I owe that much and more, for not only enduring but also alleviating over many years the stresses that result from undertaking a project of this magnitude, and more significantly, for skillfully and lovingly deflating the self-aggrandizement with which such stresses are often alloyed. Finally I thank my daughters, Clara and Gracie, for their patience with their dad's work, but also at times for their blessed oblivion to it. Would that I might one day return their favor of joyful distraction.

Introduction

How should Christian theology respond to the increasingly prevalent force of "secularism" in the modern West, which threatens to make suspicion of religion a required component of human rationality? One possible response is offered by "Radical Orthodoxy," which suggests that both suspicion and faith are less rationally justified than we often imagine. Christian faith has always known this, of course, since by definition it admits a lack of objective certainty about reality, yet chooses nonetheless to trust that creation is rooted in love and peace. By contrast, "secular reason" finds reality to be fundamentally manageable and objective, leaving no room for faith's appeal to mystery, and no need for a "subjective" relation to truth whatsoever. Radical Orthodoxy claims provocatively that this conclusion is not a genuine discovery of reason but the result of individuals' resistance to entering into the mystery of creation on its own terms. That is, where modern suspicion sees a fundamental opposition between faith and reason, Radical Orthodoxy interprets a contrast between faith and fear.

Some of the most provocative theological responses to the current popularization of suspicion, such as those of David Bentley Hart, Terry Eagleton, and at least to some extent, Charles Taylor, have benefitted from precisely this Radical Orthodox reconfiguration of the poles in the debate about faith and reason.[1] Yet many readers familiar with conversations surrounding the so-called "new atheism" remain unacquainted with the original imperatives of Radical Orthodoxy, which provide an essential backdrop to such discussions. Among other things, this book seeks to address this gap. Thus, one of its guiding questions is this: How exactly has Radical Orthodoxy re-cast the apparent dilemmas facing the

1. See Hart, *Atheist Delusions*; Eagleton, *Reason, Faith, and Revolution*; and Taylor, *A Secular Age*.

proponent of religious faith in the present age, an age in which instrumental rationality seems to exert a stranglehold on the domain of the "real"?

Specifically and uniquely, in the chapters that follow I describe the innovations of Radical Orthodoxy in this regard as the accomplishment of an "existential turn" in Christian thought. The character of this turn is not entirely novel, in that it owes much to Søren Kierkegaard's account of temporality and faith, as we shall see below. Yet until now, Radical Orthodoxy's debt to Kierkegaard has been difficult to characterize with any precision, since while the two parties agree on the "existential" nature of Christian truth, they seem to diverge in their understandings of how Christian faith moves the subject through life. Apparently at odds with Kierkegaard's iconoclasm, Radical Orthodoxy construes the continuance of faith as a matter of rhetorical persuasion. Interestingly for this book, John Milbank has sought recently to mitigate this seeming conflict, suggesting that Kierkegaard's reputation as an "iconoclast" is not entirely deserved, and that the Kierkegaardian "paradox" is in fact perfectly compatible with Radical Orthodoxy's attempted synthesis of *eros* and *agape*.[2]

In large part, the reader will find in what follows a sustained critical rejoinder to this claim of compatibility between Radical Orthodoxy and Kierkegaard. I argue at length that Kierkegaard's account of love implies a mode of expectancy that must remain "unauthenticated" by any rhetorical appeals to preferential desire. But I offer this argument not simply to trace and clarify intellectual lineages, which would only try the reader's patience. More provocative, I hope, is my broader, Kierkegaardian contention in the face of contemporary suspicion of religion that only Christian faith's eschewal of persuasion in favor of hope's inexplicable *resolve* can provide adequate resistance to the subject's despairing desire for an objective "identity." To put this another way, I argue throughout the book that only a refusal to dance with the human subject's fear and suspicion leaves room for banishing it, and that this refusal is the hallmark of the essentially Christian, which Radical Orthodoxy would do

---

2. See especially Žižek and Milbank, *Monstrosity of Christ*, a debate between an atheist and a theist in which each thinker's fidelity to Kierkegaard becomes an important point of contention. Milbank had already gone some distance toward construing Kierkegaard as a forerunner of Radical Orthodoxy in his 1997 article, "The Sublime in Kierkegaard." I treat this article at length in my third chapter.

better to heed, even on its own logic. Thus the critical point of contention that underlies the diverse waypoints charted in the following chapters is relatively simple, though I hope the reader will find that its subtlety and depth warrant traversing some complex terrain along the way.

My basic claim, that Radical Orthodoxy effects an existential turn in Christian thought, stems from the Radical Orthodox construal of the "objectification" of truth as the common root of modern and postmodern suspicion of religion. That is, for Radical Orthodoxy, both modern and postmodern thought generate skepticism about the possibility of a religious life because they are faithful to certain *a priori* conclusions that "life" as such is not possible as a temporal way of being. On the one hand, for modernity's sense of time as empty and predictable, the human being cannot become a true "agent" in history, but remains the object of a spatialized logic of causation. On the other hand, postmodernism's acute sensitivity to temporality as unpredictable "flux" nonetheless implies that the subject is "sacrificed" at each successive moment to an arbitrary measure of difference. Either way, what is ruled out is the possibility that the human being might be related in time to the "distance" of the future as something that is both mysterious and yet nonetheless traversable, via the measure of *caritas*. What is excluded, in other words, is the Christian supposition that the true form of creation, through which it may be reconciled to its creator, is not a "thing" but a "way," a way whose temporal articulation is analogous to the eternal "differentiation" of the Trinitarian God.

The theological response to the objectifying tendencies of Western thought advocated by Radical Orthodoxy is to defend Christianity in a "metacritical" fashion. That is, theology must not appeal to better yet equally objectifying definitions of the religious life, but to a real tradition of historical action that accords with its supposition that temporal transitions may be lived according to the mystery of *caritas*. Making its appeal not in an "explanatory" but in a "rhetorical" fashion, theology thus calls into question the very objectifying premises on which modern and postmodern suspicion of religion is based. By extension, for Radical Orthodoxy, a theological rhetoric alone safeguards the human being from objectification, in that it does not tempt the subject to define himself or herself as a thing, but "woos" that subject into becoming a self only by *participating* in the temporal movement of love. In this sense, or so I shall argue below, Radical Orthodoxy implies that theology must respond to our present philosophical milieu by reemphasizing the character of the Christian life as inexorably existential—concerned not with "what" one is, objectively speaking, but with the "how" of one's living.

In the first place, this book will work toward a demonstration of how the existential conception of truth that underlies Radical Orthodoxy's theological imperative speaks to its largely unacknowledged Kierkegaardian heritage. This heritage becomes clearest once one comes to grasp the account of temporality that justifies Radical Orthodoxy's supposition that theological communication must not presume upon the false certainty of a "metaphysical justification." Radical Orthodoxy eschews such justifications largely because it makes the radical historicist assumption that the existing subject can never gain access to a truly extra-historical vantage point. Despite the offense taken by some Radical Orthodox theologians at Kierkegaard's relentless iconoclasm—a reaction we shall explore in detail in the work of Catherine Pickstock and David Bentley Hart—I argue that one can discern a significant resonance between this refusal of "metaphysical justifications" and Kierkegaard's suggestion that Christianity "must not be defended." Both theological moves, one rhetorical and the other dialectical, relate to a common goal—that of preserving the existential character of the Christian life.

Clarifying the Kierkegaardian resonances of Radical Orthodoxy's theological rhetoric will lead to the more significant pursuit of this book, which is to adjudicate the relative adequacy of "rhetorical" and "dialectical" communication to the subjectivity of Christian truth. (And by "subjectivity" here I mean simply the idea that Christian truth is not indifferent to the transformation of the human person, or that one cannot "know" this truth apart from becoming a self in accordance with it.) Thus our guiding question shall be something like the following: If the objectifications of secular reason result from subjective *doubt* that the "sublime" distance of the future's impendence can be traversed by a peaceful measure, then ought theology to provide a "persuasion" to the effect that such a traversal is possible? The answer of Radical Orthodoxy, and especially of John Milbank, is an unequivocal "yes." On Milbank's account, any refusal to "adorn" the distance of the sublime with the persuasive possibility of *caritas* leaves the anxious and insecure subject paralyzed before the uncertainty of temporal change. Thus Milbank, despite his denigration of metaphysically justified communication, wages a battle against those who acknowledge Christianity's unique affirmation of a peaceful reconciliation of time and eternity, but without appealing directly to a positive historical "content" in order to confirm and so persuade us of that possibility. My own answer to the question, however, is that there is ultimately too much in rhetoric that aligns with the objectifying tendencies of secular reason, which Radical Orthodoxy otherwise so helpfully targets. I argue, then, chiefly via a reading of Kierkegaard's *Works of Love* in the final chapter, that only a Christian ethic whose appeal is utterly indirect vis-à-vis human "preferences" is adequately attuned to the connection between human *eros* and the despairing self-protection that seeks a secure but paralyzing objectification of truth. Let me briefly spell out the trajectory of this proposal.

The first chapter, "Contemporary Theology and the Turn to Rhetoric," provides a full-scale interpretation of John Milbank's *Theology and Social Theory* (1990), a book that has proven to be the most important contributing factor in the rise of what is now called Radical Orthodoxy. The chapter focuses on Milbank's articulation of "meta-suspicion" as a possibility unique to theology, and considers Milbank's deployment of such meta-suspicion against ancient, modern, and postmodern thought. There we will come to see that for Milbank, the ultimate nihilism of these forms of thinking is rooted in their shared tendency to "hypostasize" and separate the immanent from the transcendent. This separation pretends to a "metaphysical justification," on the basis of which it becomes seemingly impossible to wager that history is anything but calculable routine (Weber) or arbitrary flux (Heidegger). What history *cannot be*, on the basis of such a boundary between the immanent and the transcendent, is something like "mysterious continuance." Theology's essential distinction from other modes of thought must therefore reside in its superlative *historicism*. That is, for Milbank, theology can avoid the metaphysics of presence upon which all secular thought runs aground in virtue of its rhetorical preference for a particular historical tradition as the persuasive analogical "breach" of secular reason's boundary between transcendence and immanence. The chapter thus arrives at a clear sense of the origins of Milbank's advocacy of a necessarily rhetorical form of communication for theology.

In the second chapter, I follow Catherine Pickstock's argument in *After Writing: The Liturgical Consummation of Philosophy*, which builds upon Milbank's critique of secular reason by articulating a distinction between the subject's inscription in truth as mediated in "writing" or in "speech." Pickstock begins by suggesting that Plato's suspicion of the written is theologically pertinent insofar as it implies that the truth of reality cannot be "had" in abstraction from the movement of time. Orality is therefore preferable for Plato not because it is somehow closer to the timeless, immemorial origin of being, but because it beckons a temporal enactment analogous in its movement to the infinite's own erotic interval of temporalization. Pickstock then argues that Christianity provides not so much the refutation of a philosophy destined to give birth to the nihilism of secular reason, but the *consummation* of a Platonism that had already gone some distance toward understanding the relationship of the human being to infinite truth in "existential" terms. The Christian "addition" consists for Pickstock in its Trinitarian conception of the origin of all being, such that any tragic dimension to the Platonic "othering" of an originary unity is decisively overcome. Yet precisely by reducing the Christian distinction from Platonism to this speculative difference, I argue that Pickstock also brings the possible irony of any rhetorical advocacy of Christianity into view for us. That is, when Pickstock elevates the importance of retrieving a medieval Christian *construal* of the reconciliation of time and eternity, she ultimately allows the properly Christian urgency of *living* that reconciliation to slip from view. The work of David Bentley Hart is instructive on this point as well, in that Hart suggests that the only danger a properly historicist theology cannot abide is an attack on the aesthetics of its truth. Thus, Hart goes on to argue, theology must above all seek to overcome the possibility of persuasive aesthetic "offenses" at the Christian account. I devote considerable space in the chapter to rehabilitating some of the thinkers who most offend Pickstock and Hart in these areas, notably Martin Heidegger and Emmanuel Levinas.

In the third chapter, I turn to an alternative interpretation of the uniqueness of the essentially Christian, arguing specifically that Kierkegaard's account of Christianity as an infinite complication rather than a speculative consummation of all other forms of religiousness better captures Christianity's unique evasion of the objectifications of secular reason. In contrast to "Religiousness A"—which I suggest ultimately includes Radical Orthodoxy—for Kierkegaard's Christianity the eternal is not everywhere present and hidden, but becomes historical in a particular man. The "essentially Christian" thus proclaims that Jesus wants to make the human being eternal, in time, which means by extension that even in one's inclination to offer the best "construal" of the eternal's kinship with the temporal, one is and has been forfeiting the condition of such kinship. For Kierkegaard, only a "Religiousness B" that undermines all possible security, even in a rhetorical construal of kinship with the divine, adequately preserves the religious life as inexorably enacted. Therefore, only a Christianity that is not directly communicable fully outstrips the objectifying tendencies of secular reason—the tendency of all broken human thought to allow the human subject to evade the genuine but security-shattering reconciliation of the eternal and the temporal *in a life*.

In the third chapter, we shall also be introduced to what I will argue is the essential core of Radical Orthodoxy's rhetorical imperative. Specifically, we will see that Radical Orthodoxy is premised upon an account of the human being's temporal situatedness in which the uncertainty of the future inevitably provokes subjective anxiety. For Milbank, this account gives rise to a Kierkegaardian "skepticism" about the possibility of temporal continuance. Crucial to Radical Orthodoxy's overcoming of postmodern nihilism is therefore the task of reconciling such skepticism with "fideism." In returning to our analysis of *Theology and Social Theory* in the fourth chapter, we will find that this task of reconciliation requires a rhetorical construal of the "gap" of temporal differentiation as possibly traversed according to the measure of *caritas*. In that chapter I offer a close consideration of the work of René Girard, whom Milbank singles out as particularly deficient in this regard. I argue that what Milbank misses in Girard is his account of the function of all cultural "significations" in justifying human desire-as-violence, which explains Girard's reticence to communicate the uniquely Christian possibility of peace in a directly persuasive "idiom." I further demonstrate how Milbank's critique of Girard on this point is connected to his dismissal elsewhere of what he calls "Protestant" differentiations of the purity of *agape* from the fundamental corruption of human *eros*, and conclude with Milbank's corresponding suggestion that the Christian ethic can only be a possibly *enacted* way of living if it integrates the universality of *agape* with the particular "charms" that woo human *eros*.

This last point leads directly into the fifth chapter, in which I offer a reading of Kierkegaard's *Works of Love* that is meant to provide a final resistance to Radical Orthodoxy's fundamental claim that only the metaphysically unjustified persuasion of rhetoric can animate an existential Christian sociality. I argue that Kierkegaard's account of love, which refuses to appeal to a "hope" that is authenticated by any rhetorical exemplars, more adequately captures the Radical Orthodox imperative to Christianity as an existential *way* than does any rhetorical appeal. On my reading, Kierkegaard provides an account of love as giving rise to a unique mode of expectancy—a hopeful comportment to the future as the possibility of the good whose distance from even a "rhetorical" justification alone saves the subject from the despairing desire for a conclusive "identity," and thus keeps that subject in motion through faith's inexplicable *resolve*.

Ultimately, then, I think what the reader will find here is a unique account of, and sympathy for, the fundamentally existential concerns of Radical Orthodoxy, crowned by a subtle yet crucial resistance to the Radical Orthodox claim that those concerns are best addressed by a theology that *persuades*. Instead, as I hope to have demonstrated by the end of the book, even rhetoric must be eschewed if theology hopes to oppose the objectification sought by doubt's despairing suspicion; trying to "convince" the doubting subject ultimately only wastes time validating his doubt. Without further ado, then, let us begin by turning to Milbank's *Theology and Social Theory*.

1

Contemporary Theology and the Turn to Rhetoric

Introduction: The Urgent Situation

IN THE INTRODUCTORY ESSAY to their edited volume, *Radical Orthodoxy: A New Theology*, John Milbank, Catherine Pickstock, and Graham Ward suggest ominously that "for several centuries now, secularism has been defining and constructing the world."[1] The authors are especially concerned that secular reason has constructed a world in which "the theological" has no ultimate relevance. That is, they worry that ours is a world in which theology is not free to propose an alternative to the predominant, immanentist construal of human "social" reality, and instead must accept the position of "a harmless leisure-time activity of private commitment."[2] Radical Orthodoxy, which Milbank has more recently described as "an ecumenical theology with . . . a set of specific recommendations,"[3] asserts the urgency, in the late stages of secular reason's reign, of reclaiming theology's supremacy as a discourse, especially in the domain of "social theory." Thus Radical Orthodoxy is, at the outset, positioned critically vis-à-vis any so-called theology that acquiesces to secular reason's assertion that the religious life is essentially personal or private.

1. Milbank et al., "Suspending the Material," 1.
2. Ibid.
3. Milbank, "Alternative Protestantism," 25.

If theology has lost its grip on the world in the secular age, it is also true that secular reason "grips" the world more tightly than theology ever needed to. We will explore this below when we consider secular reason's pretension to a metaphysical justification, which theology proper does not require, according to Radical Orthodoxy. But secular reason's tight grip is now faltering, Milbank et al. suggest, and it is reaching its self-destructive end. For a secular world-construction implies the supposedly liberating detachment of finite reality from its former eternal situatedness, and the nihilistic consequences of this severance are becoming more and more blatant—for example in Las Vegas, where all self-grounded and apparently free objects of desire are but thin facades upon a barren desert. It is in the midst of contemporary Western culture's provision of such dead-end destinations that Radical Orthodoxy offers an "ontology of participation," in which lies the sole possibility of once again "allowing finite things their own integrity."[4] Thus, as the finite objects that secular reason sought to liberate now melt into the desert sand, Radical Orthodoxy intends through its alternative, rhetorically justified ontology, to "reclaim the world"[5] itself.

In order to be better able to assess the "radicality" to which this reclamation calls all theology and even all thinking, we must first explore in greater depth why, for Radical Orthodoxy, all secular reason is nihilistic, and then consider why a specifically "rhetorical" theology might be uniquely well-equipped to address and correct this pervasive trend in Western thought. Accordingly, in this chapter I will offer a reading of John Milbank's *Theology and Social Theory*, a book that is comprehensive in scope—i.e., it relates "all" of modern, postmodern, and antique reason to Milbank's unique theological alternative—and which has had an undeniably seminal influence upon more recent Radical Orthodox imperatives. My sense is that some readers will balk at this prospect nonetheless, since Milbank has an established reputation for intractable writing,[6] and because more recently it has become fashionable in the "blogosphere" to dismiss Radical Orthodoxy on account of its bombast. I think neither of these criticisms is wholly baseless; but I also think they can serve as strategies for avoiding the hard work of mounting a serious engagement of Milbank's oeuvre. Whether or not it warrants unqualified

---

4. Milbank et al., "Suspending the Material," 3.
5. Ibid., 1.
6. See Janz, "Radical Orthodoxy and the New Culture of Obscurantism."

agreement, I hope at least to show in this chapter that *Theology and Social Theory* deserves close and serious attention, not least for having changed the manner in which contemporary theology may respond to suspicion of religion. I hope also that the reader will find some of Milbank's most notoriously complex arguments clarified here.

I aim to cover several sub-topics over the course of the chapter, the structure of which runs parallel with Milbank's book itself. First, we shall see how Milbank's advocacy of theological "meta-suspicion" in the face of all sociological critiques of religion is intended primarily to undermine the "boundary" that modern thought posits between "religion," on the one hand, and "the social," on the other. Undermining this barrier has become the primary tactic of all Radical Orthodox theology. Second, I will demonstrate that Milbank's "for" and "against" readings of Hegelian and Marxian dialectics hinge on the possibility in such thought of a genuine *Sittlichkeit*, which is to say, a conception of virtue that unites the universal good with the particular, customary instance, and so refuses the boundary upon which secular reason is staked. Third, we shall see that Milbank's hostility to postmodern thought is due, perhaps strangely for a theologian, to the reluctance of such philosophy to be sufficiently historicist, sufficiently *post*-modern, in its account of social genesis. Finally, I shall attempt to clarify, with reference to Milbank's criticism of Alasdair MacIntyre's "dialectical" means of persuasion, why theology's overcoming of the secular finally requires a specifically rhetorical form of communication. In relation especially to this last point, I shall try along the way to problematize the possibility of communicating a seemingly *existential* Christian "identity" (for Milbank, to be Christian is not to be an objective substance but to enact a particular "movement") by means of rhetoric. These critical interjections will be fleshed out in later chapters. For now, let us try to get a handle on Milbank's account of how modern thought reduces religion to something that is entirely transparent to an objective sociological analysis.

The Modern Separation of "Religion" from "the Social"

Meta-Suspicion

Milbank tells us that *Theology and Social Theory* is "addressed to both social theorists and theologians"—especially to those theologians who assume that "a sensibly critical faith is supposed to admit fully the critical claims of sociology."[7] In this comment Milbank is targeting any theology that is, for supposedly "theological" reasons, too ready to agree with modern sociology's explanation of religion in terms of immanent, transparently "social" factors. In response to this kind of putatively sensible theology and social theory, Milbank's primary aim is to persuade us to adopt a theological "'meta-suspicion' which casts doubt on the possibility of suspicion [of religion] itself."[8] It may be helpful first of all to identify just what sort of theology Milbank imagines is ready to agree with sociology that religion is not a mysterious presence in history but only serves a transparent social function.

Milbank will often stress that the metanarrative of modern and especially Protestant theology tells of a "providential" emancipation of true, "personal" religion from the authoritarian grasp of institutional order. His identification of the problems arising from such a Protestant view of the inwardness of Christian truth and its purely negative or iconoclastic relation to social reality as it is actualized in history has remained at the center of even his most recent polemics.[9] According to Milbank, the belief that true Christian religiousness constitutes a transcendent interruption of the normal, "immanent" course of human action and history, an interruption that can only be maintained inwardly, immediately justifies secular reason's takeover of social theory. Of course, what makes such thinking still "theological" is the hope that its concession of the social domain to immanent explanations will be a "propaedeutic to the explication of a more genuine religious remainder."[10] That is, once we are disabused of the idea that our immanent social achievements and failures have anything to do with our participation in the economy of salvation, we will come into more certain possession of the true, inward locus of that salvation. But as Milbank is quick to remind us, if this remainder of the truly transcendent significance of religion "concerns some realm of 'private experience,' then we have every reason to believe that this does not really escape social mediation."[11] At precisely

---

7. Milbank, *Theology and Social Theory*, 1, 101.

8. Ibid., 102.

9. For example, see Milbank's debate with Slavoj Žižek, a seemingly unlikely representative of "Protestantism," in their recent co-authored volume, *The Monstrosity of Christ*.

10. Milbank, *Theology and Social Theory*, 101.

11. Ibid.

this point, then, when religion stands on the brink of being excised from the realm of human significance altogether, theology's response to sociological suspicion becomes critical. Here, the Protestant trajectory culminates in the so-called "neo-orthodoxy" of Karl Barth and his later interpreters. According to Milbank, such theology responds to sociological suspicion by becoming *equally* suspicious, insisting "on the absolute contrast between the revealed word of God and human 'religion,' which as a mere historical product can safely be handed over to any reductive analyses whatsoever."[12] This neo-orthodox suspicion would undermine *all* pretensions to religiosity from the "immanent side," be they those of ecclesiology or of the individual's "experience" of faith. Immanent human reality is manifestly unable to bear the weight of a transcendent causality, neo-orthodoxy ostensibly suggests, which implies, of course, that the immanent is entirely transparent to human reason.[13]

Milbank's own "meta-suspicion," by contrast, seeks to cast "doubt on the very idea of there being something 'social' (in a specific, technical sense) to which religious behavior *could be* in any sense referred."[14] That is, Milbank's suspicion calls into question the transparency of the immanent to human reason, and thus questions whether it should be understood as "immanent," or entirely unto itself, at all. And if theology does not call this essential premise of the secular human sciences into question, then it allows itself to be positioned by something other

---

12. Ibid.

13. Despite Milbank's suggestions in this regard, Karl Barth, for example, is anything but confident of the transparency of the immanent, and in fact allows the "sciences of man" their own integrity *only insofar as they do not become "dogmatic,"* or we might say in Radical Orthodox terms, only insofar as they do not try, scientifically, to justify any suspicion of religion: "The exact science of man cannot be the enemy of the Christian confession. It becomes this only when it dogmatizes on the basis of its formulae and hypotheses, becoming the exponent of a philosophy and world-view, *and thus ceasing to be exact science*. As long as it maintains restraint and openness in face of the reality of man [i.e., a finally irreducibly spiritual reality], it belongs, like eating, drinking, sleeping and all other human activities, techniques and achievements, to the range of human actions which in themselves do not prejudice in any way the hearing or non-hearing of the Word of God, which become acts of obedience or disobedience only in so far as they belong to individuals with their special tendencies and purposes.... To the extent that it remains within its limits, and does not attempt to be more or less than exact science, it is a good work.... Opposition is only required if it becomes axiomatic, dogmatic, and speculative." Barth, *Church Dogmatics III.2*, 24–25. Emphasis added. For a more recent take on Barth's critique of human religion, see Boulton, *God Against Religion*.

14. Milbank, *Theology and Social Theory*, 102.

than "the word of the creator God."[15] Should it accept secular reason's premise that the immanent is utterly transparent, then theology will find itself confined to a word already limited by this premise—a word that, precisely as a word of *God*, is defined as incapable of penetrating "the realm of human symbolic constructions without getting tainted and distorted," assimilated to the known mechanics of the immanent. Hereby the proper object of theology, the word of the creator, comes to be "*without impact upon the world.*"[16] Thus the importance, for Milbank, of regaining an orthodoxy more "radical" than "neo-," an orthodoxy characterized by a meta-suspicion whose goal is to undermine secular reason's legitimating narratives, first of all by exposing them as unnecessary conjectures rather than self-evident truths. It will be helpful to turn now to Milbank's critical reading of Max Weber in order to clarify how this theological meta-critique is to be applied. This consideration will prepare us to assess Milbank's more complicated additional claim that both theology *and* secular reason represent "metaphysically unjustified" wagers, and that theology's supremacy does not ultimately lie in the ability to overcome this apparent weakness, but in the capacity to abide it.

Applying Meta-Suspicion

Milbank includes Weber's work in the category of "neo-Kantian" sociology, which he says can be characterized by its claim

> to provide an exhaustive inventory of the essential aspects of our (social) finitude in such a manner as to make theological or metaphysical explanation of the content of this finitude impossible and redundant. At the same time, it repeats the Kantian identification of religion with the private, the subjective and the evaluative, in contradistinction to a public, natural or social realm of objective, but humanly meaningless fact.[17]

Milbank argues that this methodological premise, which isolates a rationally transparent "social" sphere from a totally inward/transcendent locus of "religious" significance, "both enshrines and conceals a particular history, namely the emergence of Protestantism."[18] Milbank is not

15. Ibid., 1.
16. Ibid., 101. Emphasis added.
17. Ibid., 76.
18. Ibid., 76, 77.

opposed to this narrative insofar as it emphasizes the unaccountable uniqueness of the redeemed sociality to which the Bible attests; the problem is that it also tries "to read this uniqueness as the always implicit presence in the west of a private realm of value."[19] In other words, the Protestant narrative reads the uniqueness of Christian sociality as implying its irreducibly negative relation to any actualizable social order, and thus its properly *private* domain. Neo-Kantian sociology takes from Protestantism not only this justification of religion's separation from the social, but also a certain hermeneutic strategy that assumes a possible "identity between the mind of the author and the mind of the interpreter,"[20] a strategy that sociology applies to the "reading" of history. That is, Milbank would like us to imagine this hermeneutic possibility as the "protest" of *sola scriptura* against the less manageable Catholic "traditional accumulation of meanings." When applied to history, such a Protestant hermeneutic implies a possibly discerned identity between agential intentions and tangible effects, and thereby justifies a methodological "concern to isolate and exactly describe a historical moment."[21] This approach to history Milbank calls "explanatory," and contrasts it at all points with "historiography," which he says pays more attention to the "narrative relation" between historical events than it does to a causal one. The crucial difference between these approaches is that the explanatory approach assumes that all of the data necessary for a totalizing explanation of history are available, while the narrative approach admits of mysterious dimensions to history that are only accessible to one already inscribed in its drama.

For Milbank, Max Weber takes an unfortunately "explanatory" approach to history, in that he "clings to the notion of an 'interior' subject, whose ideals and motivations can be 'compared with' the external course of events."[22] Weber assumes, in other words, that historical transitions can be understood immanently. This critical suggestion is complicated, as Milbank acknowledges, by the fact that Weber intentionally distances himself from those theories of history that read all historical transitions as manifestations of "laws of nature." That is, Weber specifically wants to allow for the possibility that *Wertrational* motives play a role in human

19. Ibid., 96.
20. Ibid., 78.
21. Ibid., 79.
22. Ibid., 83.

agency and social genesis, in addition to those motives that are oriented to "rationally transparent" ends. The task Weber sets for himself, therefore, is to show how one can register the effect of humanly meaningful, "religious" motivations in the immanent "social" sphere. Yet by assuming that this is the problem that sociology can solve, Weber of course only reifies the idea that religion and the social are inherently negatively related. Thus he concludes, according to Milbank, that one may attain objective knowledge of the effects of such *Wertrational* motivations "to the extent that one registers deviations from the 'ideal type' of means-end rationality."[23] And this implies, by extension, that "fully objective history (sociology) is *primarily* about economic rationality, formal bureaucracy, and Machiavellian politics."[24] In other words, it implies that history only *really happens* according to the immanently discernible logic of "economic rationality," such that *Wertrational* motivations must be understood as having their effect only within the terms of that logic, even if by (measurably) deviating from it. This is precisely the premise that Milbank's meta-suspicion seeks to undermine.

To clarify the preceding let us put it as follows: 1) in order for sociology to be able to refer reliably to "the social" and thereby justify its existence as a self-sufficient discourse, it must be able to "read" social history objectively, which implies the capacity to trace the effects of religion in immanent terms; 2) for Weber, this tracing is possible because one can read the historical effects of religion, which is inexplicably transcendent in itself, as a measurable "deviation" from the rational processes by which that world inexorably operates. The historical effect of religion can only be registered as a momentary deviation because Weber assumes *a priori* that there can be no such thing as an enduring interruption of generally transparent historical processes. This assumption is especially evident in the utter irreconcilability of Weber's categories of "charisma," on the one hand, and "routinization" on the other. As Milbank puts it, for Weber,

> any religious pattern of valuation which semi-permanently distorts the operations of pure means-end rationality cannot be acknowledged as a factual presence in terms of its symbolic ordering of the world; instead it can only be registered as an inertia, as a mechanical persistence [i.e., "routinization"] of the

---

23. Ibid., 84.
24. Ibid., 84.

effect of response to charisma, after the original charisma has passed away.[25]

Such is the inevitable conclusion of any "secular" social theory; even its apparently humble concession of the inexplicable transcendence of the religious event or "charisma" is revealed, in combination with its explanatory confidence vis-à-vis historical "routinization," as a hubristic "policing" of religion, such that the latter is prevented, *a priori*, from achieving a "factual presence in terms of its symbolic ordering of the world." The assumption that religion cannot positively determine and actualize a *different* logic from that of means-end rationality, which might nonetheless achieve a persistent historical presence, constitutes for Milbank the root of secular reason's problematic suspicion of religion.

Milbank's counter-suggestion is not that theology can make history *more* objectively transparent. In fact, quite the opposite—he claims that the sociological assumption that routinization is metaphysically inevitable must ignore the equally tenable claim that even in the most "routinized" of series, "one can never fully 'account for' what comes after in terms of what precedes," since "preceding conditions are only causally adequate at the point where they have already been superseded by the new circumstances."[26] Thus, for Milbank, the notion of a fully transparent objective history, which is required if sociology is to have a legitimate "domain," is, at the very least, not an inevitably discovered "fact" of human existence. Power, even "charismatic" power, can be operative in less tractable but more persistent ways than the "formal regularity" of Weberian history will allow, which means that historical transitions may be more appropriately (though not more "transparently") approached through "narration," by which Milbank implies a practice that remains embedded in the series it describes. Such a "historiographical" rather than "explanatory" reading of history refuses to decide beforehand that it will not find in historical transitions something more mysterious than "formal regularity," and in this very openness to history as it really happens, it undermines the purported "realism" of sociology's assumption that religion and "the social" are necessarily irreconcilable.[27] And if it is

---

25. Ibid., 85.

26. Ibid., 83. Note the parallel between this claim and that of Kierkegaard's Climacus in *Philosophical Fragments*, esp. 72–88.

27. Milbank will also suggest that some non-Western societies call sociology into question in this regard. As he says, "the more it is the case that the social order is totally

not, therefore, a sensibly critical realism that presupposes this boundary as an "ahistorical absolute," it may turn out that "there is nowhere in reality that Weberian 'society' can truly find a home."[28] In other words, if Weber's assumption of necessary routinization is not really the product of a serious attention to history, but only of an *a priori* decision, then it may turn out that even a nominally "secularized" society only "operates" by virtue of an ever-present permeation of the sociological boundary, an ever-recurring irruption into social life of "transcendent" factors, which objective social science simply decides to overlook.

If it turns out that the putative "boundary" between the religious and the social cannot be shown to be *necessarily* impermeable in the case of any particular event, then it is by no means required of theology to concede the reducibility of "this-worldly" manifestations of religion to "social factors." Indeed, it makes more sense for theology to give up the "metaphysical" authority of the Protestant metanarrative of the emancipation of religion from the "immanent."[29] This will also mean giving up on the Protestant hermeneutic with respect to social genesis, and maintaining, with Milbank and against sociology, that "social genesis itself is an 'enacted' process of reading and writing" that does not offer itself up to the search for an indisputably "rational" explanation.[30] In order to get at the truth of social genesis, beyond sociological reductions to *a priori* logics, theology must abandon the quest for "evidence" that is not another text. Theological meta-suspicion will therefore maintain that there

---

'inside' a religion, then the more the idea of a 'social factor' dissolves away into nothingness," and the more it becomes "impossible to give explanatory 'priority' to social causation over religious organization" (*Theology and Social Theory*, 89). In other words, in an Islamic society, for example, the near-identity of the "religious" and the "social" will make it difficult to separate out "charisma" from "routine," revelation from "social effect." The existence of such societies indicates that it may be quite possible to understand the "social" as always already inherently "charismatic."

28. Ibid., 92

29. Of course, there are some possibly genuine theological fears concerning religion's relationship to "social organization," such as those present in Søren Kierkegaard's claim that genuine Christianity will *always* constitute an offense to the "established order." For Kierkegaard, the polemical character of true religion vis-à-vis the "social" does not have to do with a metaphysical irreconcilability of "transcendent" and "immanent" realities, but instead with a connection between the establishment of "order" and sin, and by extension between an always active movement of "interruption" and *faith*. Milbank tends to ignore this possible reading of the "polemical" character of religion vis-à-vis the social for Protestantism. See Kierkegaard, *Practice in Christianity*.

30. Milbank, *Theology and Social Theory*, 114.

is no such thing as a wholly "social" action, and at the same time that all action is already both inscribed and inscribing. This means that theology cannot hope to attain an "explanation" of human sociality or history that is itself detached from actually *living* that very history; it cannot hope for a "knowing" or a "telling" that is not also and inescapably a "living." Milbank concludes that theology needs "to take more seriously the Biblical narratives, which often 'chronicle' rather than causally diagnose, and which presumably tell how things happened *in the very idiom adopted by their users for the making-of-things-to-happen*."[31]

It is this refusal to think that one can separate and describe historical happenings "objectively," apart from the narrative idioms that render them sensible to their participants, which constitutes theological "meta-suspicion." Such a narrative approach to history will of course fall far short of the totalizing accounts of any particular occurrence sought by secular reason. For this reason the approach seems to admit that it sees "less" of history than sociology's objective, bird's-eye-view promises. Yet the "meta-suspicious" nature of theology's approach here means that it will not admit that sociology's view is looking at anything more "real" than what it concludes about history apart from living it. So yes, the self-understanding of a religious society is not a metaphysically justified, ahistorical absolute. It both supports and arises from a particular way of *being in history*. Yet for this reason it is profoundly more realistic than the view that pretends to know everything without even seeing it. This latter (secular) view also makes a contingent wager that generates its putatively objective description, but in this case owning up to the wager would mean admitting a "choice of values with respect to the conjunction of an empty freedom with an instrumentalist reason," which "requires on the part of secular thought a *nihilist courage*."[32] Religious societies, on the other hand, are *more* able to admit the contingency "of their fundamental choices, for religions themselves acknowledge that these are not fully explicable, but wrapped up in mystery and the requirements of 'faith.'"[33] To admit contingency in this way means precisely to refuse the "boundary" of the secular, and to become instead theologically "meta-critical," which is to say, to remain, in faith, "wrapped up in mystery."

---

31. Ibid., 121. Emphasis added.
32. Ibid., 136. Emphasis added.
33. Ibid.

Let us turn now to Milbank's readings of Hegel and Marx, two possible "meta-critics" of the modern. That is, in the first place, Hegel's criticism of the Kantian detachment of "true" morality from the social sets in motion a possible meta-critique of sociology; and in the second place, Marx seriously undermines capitalism's pretension to utter secularity by revealing the necessity of commodity-*worship* for the operation of a capitalistic system of "valuation." But while Milbank is "for" these dialecticians in important respects, he ultimately finds them incapable of offering what he really wants to defend, which is an account of historical existence in terms of "baroque *poesis*," finally clarified, as we shall see, in Maurice Blondel's "concept of a self-dispossessing action."[34]

Hegel's Conservatism

Milbank begins his chapter on Hegel with an "expressivist" critique of Kant and of all modern philosophical "conservatism." Milbank's appeal to expressivism—chiefly to Hamann and Herder—is meant especially to challenge any philosophical attempt to isolate finite from infinite being. Whereas with Kant and neo-Kantianism one assumes a categorical separation between the humanly "meaningful"—i.e., the moral, the transcendent, or for Weber the charismatic—and the realm of immanent history that proceeds according to an inevitably "routinized" means-end rationality, for Milbank's expressivists, there is no such thing as a "transcendent" subjectivity that can be isolated from the historical. To be more precise, for these thinkers there is no such thing as a "thought" or a subjective consciousness that is prior to or outside of "the external, visible and audible modifications to matter made by human beings in 'art' (meaning all processes of 'making') and in language."[35] Therefore there is no possibility of separating a purely "moral" or religious subjectivity from its actual historical existence, or in Weberian terms, no possibility of separating a "charisma" from its "routinization." Milbank suggests that Hamann and Herder can make this "denial of priority to thought" because if we "only think in language, it is impossible even to disentangle the knowledge we have of ourselves from our knowledge of the world (or 'nature'), or vice versa."[36] This suggestion that language does

---

34. Ibid., 209.
35. Ibid., 149.
36. Ibid.

not refer to some prior, "real" meaning, but rather brings its own "new content" into being, implies that the truth about ourselves and the world alike is only accessible via an *aesthetic* discernment or reception of "expression." Thus we cannot any longer exclude the humanly meaningful, or "original charisma," from the supposedly routinized realm of human *poesis*. That is, we cannot pretend to give a description of "the historical" that is justified by a view from entirely outside of history, such as the view that assumes historical routinization to be an "ahistorical absolute."

Such are the implications of what Milbank calls the "post-Renaissance discovery that language creates rather than reflects meaning."[37] This is the discovery to which Hamann and Herder, as Milbank's representative expressivists, are faithful. Milbank admits that it is a terrifying discovery, that it opens up an "abyss" by suggesting there is no "meaning" outside the "endless flux of human operations on the world."[38] What Milbank means by philosophical "conservatism" is the effort in the face of this abyss to "establish a new pre-linguistic stability for meaning in the 'internal' domain of the 'subject.'"[39] This (fundamentally Cartesian) move is repeated in any philosophy that subjects the flux of "the human creative process, or history," to some more stable "logic" to which that process refers.[40] By contrast, for Herder and for baroque expressivism generally, the historical process itself is "simultaneously the divine revelation,"[41] which means, at least on the one hand, that historical events do not refer to a stable, pre-linguistic logic that the thinking subject can ascertain abstractly—i.e., in separation from the series of events in question. But on the other hand it implies that historical events *really do* offer something of eternal truth, provided that one deigns to become a knowing subject only by virtue of a trusting participation in the series. This is precisely the meta-critical gesture of expressivism vis-à-vis philosophical conservatism, the gesture of making it "less easy to draw the Kantian boundary between 'legitimated' knowledge of finitude, and illegitimate pretensions to knowledge of the infinite."[42]

37. Ibid., 150.
38. Ibid.
39. Ibid.
40. Ibid.
41. Ibid., 148.
42. Ibid., 151.

The fact that Milbank begins his chapter with this expressivist meta-critique indicates that he will evaluate Hegel's thought with respect to how well or poorly it avoids the "philosophical conservatism" that tries to reverse the baroque destruction of the "boundary" between eternally stable meaning and historical/linguistic flux. And it should probably be obvious already that Hegel will fail to evade Milbank's charge in this regard. That is, by virtue of his account of the historical process with reference to a mythical "logic" of negation, "Hegel once more subordinates the contingencies of human making/speaking to the supposedly 'logical' articulation of a subjectivity which is secretly in command throughout."[43] And yet, despite this obvious sense in which Milbank's "radical" theology cannot be fully Hegelian, he is willing to admit that Hegel approaches a "meta-critique" of the secular at certain points.

Of particular importance here is Hegel's attempt to reinstate *sittlich* ethics against Kantian *Moralität*. The basis of Hegel's opposition to Kantian morality, according to Milbank, is his realization that "supposedly perfect intentions become . . . collusive with the world's actual evil if they cannot be defined in terms of any actual practice of virtue. The 'beautiful soul,' who retains his purity of aim inwardly intact, is really the empty subject, and not the truly free subject, as Kant supposed."[44] On this Hegel and Milbank agree, and they also agree that the solution is to reinstate a "customary" ethics, which can unite morality and politics, or the "sublimity" of ethics with the "merely" social sphere. This reinstatement consists in elevating the importance of the unique dimensions of any given ethical situation in moral decision-making, rather than reducing these particularities via a bare appeal to the "universalizable." By emphasizing *Sittlichkeit*, Hegel therefore acknowledges the inextricability of morality and freedom from their actual social situatedness. Even more interesting to Milbank is that the "young Hegel" reads true *Sittlichkeit* as a fundamentally Christian invention, and reads Jesus as the (dialectically premature) revelation of the unity of spirit and nature, precisely in regard to the *sittlich* character of Jesus' ethics. As Milbank puts it, for Hegel,

> [Jesus'] command to "love one's neighbor" does not place restrictions upon the subject, but on the object of morality. *It is not really a command at all*, because instead of appealing to the

---

43. Ibid., 157.
44. Ibid., 161.

"ought" against murderous and covetous desire, Jesus appeals to the "fact" of our natural ties to the neighbor in family, locality, and even among strangers whom we may chance to meet . . . we only enter into perfection to the degree that we have really passed beyond a merely "moral" striving.[45]

In other words, for Milbank's Hegel, Jesus champions an ethic that is more in keeping with Aristotelian *praxis* than with Kantian deontology, since he refuses to appeal to a "purity" of will that is only possible in abstraction from any real human situation. Emphasizing instead our natural connectedness with those already present in our "situation," Jesus makes possible a new practical engagement therein. By reading Jesus against Kant in this manner, Milbank believes Hegel is being "profoundly true to the Gospel."[46]

Where Hegel begins to go wrong is in his inability "to accept the full contingency of Jesus' founding of a new sort of human community."[47] That is, despite his reading of Jesus' *sittlich* morality as a real, meta-critical enactment of the unity of spirit and nature, Hegel always subjects the fuller historical possibility of this unity to an *a priori* logic of historical becoming. More precisely, while Jesus discovers and lives the meta-critical truth that nothing in nature precludes one from attaining to a "crucial" proximity with spirit, Hegel strangely does not allow this to imply the possibility of a reconciled living *at every moment*, within the flux of *any* historical series. Thus Hegel ultimately "conserves" the stability of truth ("logic") from the flux of the historical, in the manner of all other secular reason. Jesus may witness to a wondrous reconciliation, but his failure to "realize his moral vision"[48] by transforming his own social order demonstrates to Hegel that this reconciliation finally *is not* an ever-present possibility, but must be brought about as an objective situation—not by Jesus, who failed, but by the greater sovereignty of a dialectical "logic":

> Thus while, at a certain level, one can transcend law [e.g., in the case of Jesus], there cannot, for Hegel, be a society without law,

45. Milbank, *Theology and Social Theory*, 165. Emphasis added. In light of Milbank's enthusiasm about this point, I cannot help referring to Matt 10:34–39, where it seems Jesus' call to discipleship really does go against "customary" desire.
46. Ibid.
47. Ibid.
48. Ibid.

a society where processes of forgiveness, contrition and expiation form of themselves a self-sustaining cultural process. Yet to deny that this is at least a *possibility*, is to deny that there can be complete salvation within the physical, bodily order. And this denial belongs intrinsically with Hegel's metaphysics, which posits a sphere of "indifference," a realm which self-expression must enter, yet whose sheerly contingent elements can never be sublated by the Idea.[49]

In other words, Hegel denies that the *Sittlichkeit* of Jesus, which spells reconciliation between spirit and nature, is a genuinely *sittlich* possibility.[50] For him, nature as nature is inadequate to spirit as spirit, at least until nature reaches a higher "stage," in which its "indifferent" elements will have been discarded. In Hegel, therefore, the hope of reconciliation as *Sittlichkeit* ultimately succumbs to a "gnostic" fidelity to the objective dictates of an *a priori* logic. Thus Milbank ultimately concludes that Hegel "only half-grasps Jesus's pragmatism: a full grasp would situate 'the kingdom' entirely within the realm of particular cultural practice, not in dialectical suspense between nature on the one hand, and the spiritual subject on the other."[51]

Marx's Secular Hope

Given Milbank's ultimate assessment of Hegel's philosophical conservatism, Karl Marx's materialism would seem to stand him in better stead

---

49. Milbank, *Theology and Social Theory*, 167. In *The Monstrosity of Christ*, Slavoj Žižek's "plea for the Hegelian reading of Christianity" offers a provocative rejoinder to Milbank's interpretation of Hegel. For Žižek, Hegel does not imagine that Spirit heals the wound of self-alienation by transcending all the "indifferent" material of history, but by "getting rid of the very full and sane body into which the wound was cut" (72).

50. There is a sense in which Milbank can be challenged here: Hegel *does* posit *Sittlichkeit* as a (future) social possibility, the possibility of a future objective situation that is not hostile to Jesus-like living. For Milbank really to go beyond Hegel, he ought not to hold up simply the possibility of a certain "society" of forgiveness, which, as a noun, will be defined just as objectively as Hegel's hope. Rather, Milbank would do better to suggest that the "present" possibility of *Sittlichkeit* lies in a way of living that *does not need to change over the objectivity of nature into something else, for example the church, but can live "the church" in every objective situation.* In other words, as I will suggest further in later sections, the possibility of a true overcoming of secular reason requires a certain "disinterestedness" in overcoming secular reason and in "transforming" society—not the building or narrating of a particular "community," but the enactment of a certain "commun*ing*" at every moment.

51. Ibid., 172.

with Milbank's meta-critique. That is, Marx's materialist view makes it less likely that he will be able to write off the possibility of "reconciliation" for the historical in virtue of nature's inadequacy to "spirit." But despite this difference from Hegel, it remains the case that Marxian dialectics subordinates the actual historical to an *a priori* logic of becoming. Moreover, while Marx too can be helpfully critical of the secular, he retains, as we shall see, a fidelity to the secular "as the buried natural 'origin,' which is to be regained at a higher level."[52]

Marx is primarily helpful to Milbank's project in virtue of his critique of capitalism with reference to "fetishization." Marx, quite like Milbank, takes an intentionally secularized logic, in which all immanent transactions are reduced to the purportedly transparent medium of "capital," and demonstrates that the operating mechanism in such processes is still something akin to worship. Capitalism claims it is able to interpret society and its operations with reference only to their immediate, "market" value, divesting all parties to exchange of any supposedly transcendent or "mythical" significance. This is why capitalism claims to be the defender of "brass tacks" realism—nothing "extra-immanent" is allowed to show up. Marx exposes this pretension as illusory by pointing out the "hieroglyphic" character of the capitalist commodity. A "hieroglyph" is construed by Marx as a "priestly" and therefore perverse linguistic invention, a mysterious symbol that alienates language from its original immediacy to its communicative purpose. The commodity can be called hieroglyphic "because it exists through the obliteration of its own genesis as a condition of its functioning; men forget that the 'value' embodied in the commodity expresses only the dispositions of power that persist within the human community."[53] This means that the value which capitalism ascribes to a commodity in virtue of its market "weight" is not a value immediate to the thing's true nature, but instead inheres on the basis of how power is disposed toward that thing—in other words, on the basis of *how that thing is worshipped*. Capitalist valuation is therefore not a stripping down to "the real," but a hieroglyphic symbolization on the basis of fetishization, hieroglyphic because it "involves treating as equivalent the inherently non-equivalent and incomparable."[54] Marx is helpful to

52. Ibid., 187.
53. Ibid., 184.
54. Ibid.

Milbank, then, because he says in effect that the ostensible "secularity" of capitalism is a ruse, just as Milbank says that "the secular" does not exist as a matter of course, and in fact it does not exist *as secular* at all.

Despite Marx's usefulness to Milbank on this score, however, there is a significant difference between the two that Milbank ultimately uses to exclude Marx from the rank of theological "meta-critic." Whereas Milbank criticizes the *pretension* of secular reason to achieve mastery over the finite through its illusory discernment of the immediate "weight" of things as objects, Marx criticizes instead the *failure* of capitalism to achieve this immediacy. In other words, Milbank argues that the fundamental mistake of secular reason resides in its claim to have made human immediacy-to-self possible (through various gestures of philosophical conservatism), and while Marx affirms capitalism's failure in this regard, he also retains the goal of overcoming this failure. This makes Marx, again like Hegel, a philosophical conservative. As Milbank has it, "Marx accepts too readily the notion of illusion, and fails to reflect that to be human, or to be a cultural being, is *necessarily* to inhabit a fiction."[55] That is, Marx takes the self-alienation inherent in capitalism and in all cases where human values are transferred to objects of worship to be fundamentally opposed to authentic human existence, which he therefore understands as immediate self-possession.

Milbank believes Marx's materialist myth in this regard is based on Feuerbach's theory of "projection," which rests not "on the idea that religion generates through [hieroglyphic] language a wholly illusory content, but rather on the idea that the content is displaced from its real site, man, to an imaginary site, God."[56] The human being's original immediacy to himself, or at least "the idea that original human meaning was natural, practical and free of religious illusion,"[57] ended for Marx with the division of labor: "A priestly class foments the illusion that theoretical activity has its own *raison d'être* apart from *praxis*, and so philosophy is born, and imaginary theoretical objects—the 'gods'—are granted objective existence."[58] With this first division of labor, the immediate relation of human meaning to human *praxis* is torn asunder, and the connection to what were once humanity's own self-possessions becomes

55. Ibid., 185.
56. Ibid., 180.
57. Ibid., 179.
58. Ibid.

entirely "hieroglyphic" and so self-alienating. Marx's own Hegelian debt, of course, means that for him this alienation occurs as a dialectically "necessary" means of increasing the scope of the human *proprium*, through both advances in technology and the attribution of superlative qualities to the objects of religious worship. The fruits of all such advances, he thinks, shall be reclaimed when the alienation of human subjects that they require reaches its apogee in utter self-contradiction, which cannot be sustained. The Marxian utopia therefore promises an explicit human immediacy-to-self of all of those possessions that comprise the original human *proprium*.

Milbank is therefore pleased, on the one hand, with Marx's realization that "religious logic is no more or less strange than cultural logic in general,"[59] but on the other hand he finds that Marx fails especially, as with Hegel, vis-à-vis post-Renaissance, expressivist insights about language. For Milbank, that is, it is never the case that the operations of a human culture mediated by expression could have achieved Marx's desired immediacy. Rather, this "alienation" is the condition of all human expressing and acting: "Right from the outset, we only have identity to the extent that we 'identify with' what is other to us, and therefore alien."[60] Thus Milbank especially cannot share Marx's idea "that capitalism necessarily and contradictorily produces a subject antagonistic to itself."[61] Instead, the real benefit of Marx's revelation of the fictitious character of capitalism's valuation is that it allows us to maintain the inherently fictitious character of *all* cultural arrangements, and thus the impossibility of "mastering" *any* of our expressions or creations. This allows us to suggest alternatives to capitalism that are not just putative "fulfillments" of its failed pretension to secularity. As Milbank writes:

> To acquiesce in the power of capital over labor is not, therefore, demonstrably "irrational." But for reasons belonging to a *different* desire, and a different fiction, one can still declare (as I would want to) that workers *should* construct themselves as subjects antagonistic to capital.[62]

---

59. Ibid., 187. This equivalence of religious (at least, if this includes the "essentially Christian" logics) and cultural logics will be heavily criticized by Kierkegaard and Girard, below.
60. Ibid.
61. Ibid.
62. Ibid., 193.

In other words, capitalism is not approaching, nor will any culture reach, some maximally irrational alienation of the human from its mythical "self-identity." Rather, every culture is already "religious," and as such, self-alienating: "any conceivable *culture* involves equivalence, which is necessarily 'metaphysical,' yet can be constructed as an ethical language of just exchange."[63] Therefore we can ultimately say that just as Hegel's proposed *sittlich* reconciliation of spirit and nature misses how this reconciliation is already possibly enacted in the flux of history, so Marx's return of the alienated "spirit" to the immediate possession of humanity misses how a genuine "appropriation" of the spiritual is already livable, not via revolutionary seizure but via just and faithful *praxis*.

Sittlichkeit *in Blondel*

The chapter that follows Milbank's discussion of Marx is of critical importance to his project as a whole, not so much for its (more or less nominal) focus on liberation theology as for its reading of Maurice Blondel, who, Milbank says, "more than anyone else, points us beyond secular reason."[64] The significance of dealing with liberation theology is that it represents a certain theological attempt at what was for Hegel the reconciliation of spirit with nature and for Marx the repossession of spirit by nature. That is, liberation theology takes from the second Vatican Council the notion of an "integralist revolution," through which any radical distinction between "nature" and "grace" is called into question, and tries to elucidate the social and political implications of such a revolution. As Milbank puts it, the reasonable claim of liberation theology is that, "if the whole concrete life of humanity is always imbued with grace, then it is surely not possible to separate political and social concerns from the 'spiritual' concerns of salvation."[65] But there are more ways than one to do integralism, and "whereas the French version 'supernaturalizes the natural,' the German version [preferred by liberation theology] 'naturalizes the supernatural.'"[66] For Milbank, in other words, the German version posits the "integration" of natural and supernatural by suggesting the presence of the supernatural in an already hyposta-

63. Ibid., 202.
64. Ibid., 219.
65. Ibid., 206.
66. Ibid., 207.

sized and putatively transparent "nature." Thus, for German and especially Rahnerian integralism, "the social is an autonomous sphere which does not need to turn to theology for its self-understanding, and yet it is already a grace-imbued sphere, and therefore it is *upon* pre-theological sociology or Marxist social theory, that theology must be founded."[67]

This notion of a sphere of pure nature, in which human action would occur according to the operations of a presumably measurable, immanent causality, is opposed, Milbank says, by Maurice Blondel's "concept of a self-dispossessing action," which alone can point the way "to a postmodern [and post-secular] social theology."[68] On Milbank's account, Blondel suggests that "the human will, from its most native desire, demands a completion that goes beyond its own resources," or that it "never finds any satisfactory resting place in any of its natural intentions or actions."[69] For Blondel then, the human subject is never immediate to herself insofar as she acts, for action as such requires the "superaddition" of something else, something "unintended"—namely, "supernatural grace." This grace can be "explicitly rejected," but it is always implicitly accepted, as a condition of the possibility of action; such is the requisite "transcendent completion" to even the will's most "immanent impulses." We can think of this as the pragmatic extension of the baroque/expressivist insight that all of our linguistically inscribed "doings" bring a "new content" into being, which we cannot wholly intend, and to which we are therefore never fully immediate. This does not imply a Hegelian or otherwise philosophically "conservative" reading of the meaning of history, according to which much of the content of our existence is a matter of indifference to the "logic" that underlies it. Rather, for Blondel, "an action is rational, a true 'event,' because 'it works,' and is a successful experiment which fits into reality and discloses a new reality."[70] It is *praxis* itself that works toward "understanding," in the sense that, *as* action, it does not express "a prior 'original' in thought," and therefore does not find its meaning only by virtue of its adequacy to an *a priori* principle—e.g., a myth of negation. Instead, "by acting/thinking we grope towards a synthesis which seems 'right' to us, and yet is not originally intended by us, but only 'occurs' to us out of the

67. Ibid., 208.
68. Ibid., 209.
69. Ibid., 210.
70. Ibid., 213.

future plenitude of being, and has implications that we cannot contain."[71] Therefore every action requires at the very least "an implicit faith that a new and 'correct' synthesis will be discovered," that our wills will somehow be brought "to self-agreement."[72] This means that all human actions have meaning only through their faithful (to varying degrees) tendency toward "an intuited harmony, the combining together in infinite unity of disparate elements."[73]

For Blondel, the human will has a philosophically discoverable tendency toward this harmony, which leads to the further discovery of being itself as "love." But for Milbank, insight into the meaning of action is only available on the basis of participation in a series or tradition of action that gives rise to and supports a particular meaning. And for precisely this reason, Milbank finds that he must resist Blondel's confidence in the ability of "philosophy" to arrive at the particularly Christian insight into the meaning of action. For Milbank, philosophy may discern the "logic of action," but "the logic of action alone cannot, as Blondel taught, decipher action as love."[74] In other words, philosophy can discover that in any particular act there is a "risking" of the self, in the will's alienation from its intended completion; yet this discovery cannot of itself lead us to the conclusion that to exist "truly" is to act with a loving tendency toward harmony. To make this insight available to *philosophy as such* would only undermine it, by lending it a too-metaphysical justification that would violate Blondel's baroque expressivism. Therefore Milbank emphasizes that only "allegiance to a particular series of actions, or a particular tradition," can lead us to anything like a "meaning" of action.[75] Without being situated in such a tradition, without being persuaded by a particular way of living the unity of thinking/acting, the mere logic of action might make *praxis* "appear to be nothing but violence and risk," to which one could quite easily respond with a nihilistic, despairing indifference to "harmony." Theology, on the other hand, which must remain a "thinking" that is inexorably embedded in a particular tradition of acting, can offer a genuine counter-persuasion to nihilism. Thus Milbank will say that even Blondel's superlatively critical philosophy only stands

71. Ibid., 214.
72. Ibid.
73. Ibid.
74. Ibid., 217.
75. Ibid.

insofar as it may be "reunderstood as theology,"[76] which is to say, insofar as it may be adequately situated within the Christian tradition, whose particular series of actions justifies the "discovery" of being as love.

The key to Blondel's ability to point us beyond secular reason, therefore, is finally his properly "theologically situated" account of being as "emanative *poesis*." Unlike the Cartesian identification of subjectivity with transcendent truth by virtue of a thinking interiority (here recall the philosophical "conservatism" that seeks to make truth a purely noetic category and thereby do away with the "problems" posed by expression and *poesis*), for Blondel's appeal to the supernatural, "our receptivity does not reside primarily in the possibility of contemplation: instead, we are receptive at the point of our greatest activity, our own initiative."[77] For philosophical conservatism, by contrast, we access the transcendent by referring to our own subjective capacity for thought, whose divorce from the merely "immanent" processes set in motion with expression and action is akin to that which secular reason posits between the infinite and the finite as such. But for Blondel, in keeping with Milbank's earlier construal of expressivism, our *action*, rather than our thinking alone, constitutes our openness to the divine. The transcendent ground of our being therefore *emanates* in all of our doing and expressing—in all human *poesis*, which always finds a completion it does not fully intend, but receives. Milbank concludes as follows:

> As mere thinkers, aiming to sum things up once-and-for-all, we are inclined to project God as ourselves, to make him in our own image. Yet as doers and makers, we *really do* invent a God we cannot control, so that we are all, as Blondel says, *theotokoi*, giving birth to the divine image in our conjecturing practice.[78]

For Milbank, then, Blondel's importance consists in the way his approach to history contests secular reason's ostensibly incontestable "explanatory" approach. That is, in Blondel's dispossessive logic of action we witness a specific employment of what Milbank calls theological "meta-suspicion," insofar as Blondel explicitly undermines any exclusion of religion from the social on the basis of a supposed "mastery" of the immanent (as doers, for Blondel, we are especially *not* "in control").

76. Ibid.
77. Ibid., 218.
78. Ibid.

When Blondel's "logic" speaks from within a real tradition of action-toward-harmony, moreover, the undeniable "risk" it posits at the center of every human action begins to appear traversable in "love."[79] And yet why adopt this triumphant tone with Blondel, we might ask, when we all know that postmodern historicism is the great leveler, capable of reducing all societal rhetorics—especially those of "love"—to a common dynamic of mere power? By asking such a question we anticipate what Milbank calls the most "virulent" form of secular reason, whose suspicion of theology is heightened by a fundamental "ontology of difference." To such virulence we shall now turn our attention.

Overcoming Postmodernism's Ontology of Difference

Confronting Postmodern Historicism

We ought to have the sense by now that for Milbank, historiography, or the practice of narration from a non-totalizing perspective, is the sole discipline adequate to account for human existence and sociality. Any discipline that is up to this task must be adaptable to "the peculiar fractiousness and innovative capacity of human behavior."[80] So while natural science, for example, is perhaps adequate to the investigation of isolated "parts" of human reality, the "innovative capacity" that characterizes humanity does not readily open itself to the view of such an objective reading. In order to approach "questions of the human as such," therefore, one requires not simply a "systematic" discipline, but one capable of contemplating "the transitions of systems."[81] Secular social science claims to be able to make such transitions rationally transparent by delimiting them to an exclusively "social" sphere, as we have seen. Theology opposes this account of the human with a reading of sociality as unavoidably permeated by an unpredictable "spiritual" or "religious" life, which makes human "transitions" irreducible to social-scientific explanation. In this regard, history is theology's ally: "written history, which produces

---

79. The question of whether one can indeed be wooed, rhetorically, into traversing the distance of uncertainty that stands before any temporal human action shall be addressed in great detail in later chapters.

80. Ibid., 259.

81. Ibid., 260.

exceptions to the supposed universal rule; lived history, which permits us always to enact the different."[82]

This insight into the supremacy of written and lived history among the human sciences is of course fundamental to what is called "postmodern" thought, which is characteristically "historicist." In his opposition of theology to postmodern thought, therefore, Milbank will need to deal with a suspicion that is more germane to theology itself. In particular, the Nietzschean turn to "genealogy" is not entirely dissimilar to Milbank's own advocacy of a "historiographical" engagement with the human. Postmodern suspicion of religion that follows from Nietzsche therefore does not claim to make religion transparent as "really social." In the face of religion, it "merely points to other 'truths,' and shows how these are suppressed or denied by a totalizing perspective."[83] In effect, then, postmodern suspicion puts "religion" exactly in the place of "secular reason" for Milbank. Its supposedly thoroughgoing historicism disallows the possibility of preferring a comprehensively theological reading of human reality, since without a vantage point outside of history, all readings must be judged equally valid/invalid. Theology, especially in its Radical Orthodox mode, will not want to justify itself in the face of this relativization with recourse to any sort of "foundationalism." Milbank has, after all, just done much to deconstruct any pretension to read history from the perspective of a conserved, abstract exterior. What then is to be done, from theology's perspective?

Interestingly and compellingly, Milbank suggests that it is precisely the utterly relativizing aspect of postmodernism's genealogical approach that reveals where it is not historicist enough. That is, for postmodernism, "the obvious implication of 'many truths,' or rather, 'many incommensurable truths,' is that every truth is arbitrary, every truth is the will-to-power."[84] In its certainty that any genealogical method will uncover "incommensurability," postmodern thought hereby reveals its primary faithfulness not to historicism but to an "ontology of difference." The Nietzschean response to Christianity is particularly telling in this regard, since Christianity, "uniquely, dissimulates the will-to-power,"[85] and the fact that Nietzsche insists on read-

82. Ibid.
83. Ibid., 261.
84. Ibid.
85. Ibid.

ing this as only a more cunning and subversive manifestation of the same will-to-power demonstrates that he will allow only a historicism whose narrative does not violate his finally "metaphysical" commitment to a certain logic of difference. And Milbank claims that even those postmodern thinkers who ultimately reject Nietzsche's fidelity to a Dionysian logic of becoming "in effect find the ontology of difference to be true, and yet not just; their questioning issues in a despairing refusal, a mode of gnosticism or, at best, Platonism."[86] This is where the difference of the Christian is most importantly emphasized, for Milbank, in that the Christian narrative allows for an account of reality as "peace" by virtue of its *more*-historicist willingness to believe a genuine unpredictability in historical becoming. This genuine historicism in turn makes possible a living by faith that *refuses* "ultimate reality to all conflictual phenomena."[87] Thus, while theology is disabled from *rationally* refuting the ontology of difference, it remains capable of revealing "this doctrine of perspectivism as itself just another perspective: the perspective of a paganism made aware of its worship of violence by Christianity, and then nakedly espousing such worship."[88]

To clarify: a characteristically postmodern genealogy suggests that every historical enactment, every human commitment to a particular tradition, is an equally *arbitrary* wager of the will-to-power, which is to imply that historical difference as such is "coded" so as to preclude the possibility of peaceful harmony. Milbank's Christianity suggests, by contrast, that this "code" itself can be no more than a contingent wager, one that is possibly refused—by reference to another tradition, based on a different wager. In this regard, the peculiarity of Christianity is its faith in the possibility of living a form of life that is "coded" by an ontology of peace, a faith that is justified not rationally but precisely by a *living participation* in a tradition of peaceful transition. Therefore theology's response to the postmodern suspicion that every historical series is a story of arbitrary conflict is to remain more historicist than this, to maintain that there is no sense in which the story, even of the church, can be "decoded" by a "moment of 'inner' understanding."[89] This latter is essentially the Nietzschean claim, which is that a proper (for Nietzsche,

86. Ibid.
87. Ibid., 262.
88. Ibid.
89. Ibid., 264.

"naturalist" or "psychological"[90]) reading, a really "subterranean" look at historical transition, will reveal its *a priori* "meaning" to be will-to-power. We should be able to see by now how in this respect Nietzsche duplicates the philosophical conservatism Milbank seeks to challenge. Instead of trying to "out-explain" Nietzsche, Milbank's theology remains historicist in the sense that it refuses to offer its contingent story to a comprehension that might transcend the narrative. From Milbank's baroque perspective, we are as knowers and doers inexorably *inscribed*, which means we cannot conclude *a priori*, as postmodern philosophy tends to do, that the meaning of historical existence is irreducible difference (just as we cannot claim anything else about this meaning on a purely "philosophical" basis).[91] A more properly historicist, *a posteriori* conclusion about such "meaning" will be particular to the tradition in which it is situated, and for Milbank the Christian tradition is uniquely capable, in its peculiar movement, of justifying wagers of "peace" in this regard. Thus, by offering its alternative genealogy, Christian theology does not offer an explanation to be contested rationally, but rather the possibility of an enacted participation in its narrative. "Interpretation" for any genuine historicism cannot be a knowing that is not simultaneously a "doing" of the very narrative it interprets. The Christian alternative therefore will not "resolve" into ahistorical comprehension, but it might be persuasive as a *way* of living/comprehending.

All of this implies that the crucial element in a meta-critical social theory is not its reference to what Milbank calls the modern "reflective distance" between human beings and the "fictions" they inhabit, nor to some immediacy to the "real" force behind ontic and cultural differentiation (as for Nietzsche's critique). Rather, meta-critique advocates the possibility of an unconscious, which is to say reconciled-in-thought-and-action *praxis* that is "better" or more persuasive than another. This is clarified by Milbank's engagement with certain critiques of capitalism, particularly that of the Frankfurt school, which suggests that the problem with capitalism is its reduction of human existence to an "unconscious" participation in a reality that is rendered as inexorably causal. The solution to such a problem is to recover the possibility of a conscious or unpredictable ("autonomous" in the Kantian sense)

---

90. See, for example, Nietzsche's interpretation of the ascetic in *On the Genealogy of Morality*, 93–94.
91. Milbank, *Theology and Social Theory*, 265.

way of living. For Milbank, by contrast, "the real question is that of the *quality* of the 'unconscious' processes."[92] Because Milbank believes that an "unconscious," habituated sociality actually inheres nowhere as the utterly calculable "routinization" that Weber claims to identify, there is no reason to oppose it to an utterly autonomous subjectivity. To do so in fact ignores the adaptability of capitalism to every "deterritorializing" and so apparently autonomous input.[93] That is, capitalism need not care when whole sets of social values (particular ways of being conscripted to the market) are rejected in an apparent show of autonomy, because this display only justifies the proliferation of what is marketed. Thus Milbank concludes that capitalism is totally "indifferent to anything but power," and suggests critically that "to say 'freedom' is to say power."[94] A meta-critical posture emphasizes instead that *all* supposedly autonomous (Weber would say "charismatic") decisions "persist into the future in a relatively unconscious way," and therefore that this in and of itself cannot "signify moral deterioration." Against such a gnostic conclusion, meta-critique maintains that certain "routinizations," in distinction from others, may "mean the development of a desirable habit."[95] The quest for emancipation from the "heteronomy" of culture therefore is not ultimately helpful, because it pits the cultural, or the inescapably inscribed, against an empty subjective "freedom." The real problem with capitalism, from theology's perspective, is not simply that it inscribes us in a narrative, but that its narrative is a bad one, based on a wager that human sociality is most "naturally" coded "without reference to principles of just distribution," and instead with reference to the "indifferent" proliferation of power.[96] A truly meta-critical claim, then, would be to suggest that human society can be (equally) "routinized" (but) according to a different wager, that it can take shape as a living that does not totally eschew prediction and control, but which proceeds nonetheless according to a different ontological wager, one that rejects the claim that reality is fundamentally power.

At this point let me briefly sketch a possible theological resistance to Milbank's suggestion that Christian theology offers a distinctly

92. Ibid., 272.
93. Ibid., 273–74.
94. Ibid., 274.
95. Ibid., 272.
96. Ibid.

meta-critical thought in virtue of its rhetorical appeal to a culture of more "desirable habits." For Søren Kierkegaard and René Girard, both of whom shall figure prominently later in this book, the essentially Christian requires a kind of "conscious" resistance to *all* human cultures, not in the sense of the Frankfurt school's privileging of autonomous human action, but in the sense of faith's refusal to be made into a cultural object and not a self. This is to be distinguished from Kantian autonomy, and so from its implication in fortifying the boundary of the secular, because faith is opposed, not simply to culture as routinized, but rather *to the self's own desire to be one with the established order*. In other words, Kierkegaard and Girard may force us to say, against Milbank, that *any* cultural habituation must be resisted, not because the subject is "essentially" atemporal and autonomous, but because a human being can only be a "synthesis" of the temporal and the eternal by taking a reflective distance from her reification as a cultural object. The problem here is not that the secular is founded upon an unavoidable ontology of violence, but that sin implies willing *not to be oneself as spirit*, which means that a habitual comportment even to the most "Christian" of cultural orders would only imply despair. Thus Milbank's appeal to a non-foundational but rhetorically persuasive way of being "routinized" might not in itself offer the human being anything more edifying than what Christendom offered to Kierkegaard. To approach true subjective edification, one must be far more willing than Milbank is to engage in an "existential" questioning of *any* narrative inscription. With this in mind, let us proceed now to consider Milbank's most explicit defenses of rhetoric in what are the most rhetorically charged sections of his book.

Milbank on Heidegger

As we have seen, for Milbank the task of postmodern theology is to show that "differential ontology is but one more *mythos*."[97] Theology can do this first of all by pointing out that an *a priori* maintenance of difference as violence and will-to-power is not adequately historicist; and secondly it can do so by narrating a "different genealogy, one which sees in history not just arbitrary transitions, but . . . *a true concrete representation of the analogical blending of difference*."[98] The first part of the strategy

---

97. Ibid., 279.
98. Ibid. Emphasis added.

consists in demonstrating, in various ways, that the genealogy of postmodernism is overly confident in the "structure" of its narrative. In other words, Milbank suggests that while postmodern historicism allows that "cultures exist as interpretations," it claims or at least proceeds as if "the *arbitrary* displacement of one interpretation by another can be objectively narrated."[99] Milbank counters by asking, "why should the natural, active, creative will not be understood . . . as essentially the charitable will, the will whose exercise of power is not a will to dominate . . . but rather to endorse . . . increase the capacity of, the human other?"[100] One need not assume, in other words, as Nietzsche and the neo-Nietzscheans seem to do, that all differences are "negatively related," as if "warfare" were the *a priori* truth of our existence. To concede that this conclusion is *not* necessary, and that the Christian suggestion of an "analogical" relation among differences is at least equally possible, is to be truer to postmodern historicism. As such, this concession offers the possibility of what Milbank calls "a *purer* 'positivism,' a purer philosophy of difference still less contaminated by dialectics."[101] This putative "purity" is unique to theology (if not to Christianity in particular) because religious thought is premised on a permeability of the boundary between finite and infinite. It is this permeability that precludes any view of the immanent that would only *see* it with reference to an *a priori* logic, which means theology alone can support genuinely historicist, *a posteriori* commitments.

The critical relationship of theological historicism to secular reason in its postmodern guise becomes especially clear in Milbank's discussion of Heidegger. Milbank says that "according to Heidegger, an 'authentic' human existence takes account of the existential circumstances of the life of *dasein*," which means that it "takes responsibility for its own mortal life and exhibits a 'care' for the distinctive possibilities handed down to it."[102] The problem is that we do not live authentically, that we "lapse into an 'everydayness' which is absorbed . . . in the merely instrumental and manipulative arrangements that pertain between things and people."[103]

---

99. Ibid., 281. Emphasis added.

100. Ibid., 288.

101. Ibid., 289. This is also the core of Milbank's critique of Slavoj Žižek in *The Monstrosity of Christ*.

102. Milbank, *Theology and Social Theory*, 297.

103. Ibid.

In our finite living, we presume to relate to other beings, and also to ourselves, as "things" that we can understand and whose destinies we can command. But this "forgets" the opening of Being itself in beings, and thus ignores the "irreducible questionableness of the relation of beings to Being."[104] For Heidegger, as Milbank notes, authenticity requires that we "remain with this questionableness, and not seek in any way to reduce the mystery of the ontological difference."[105] In other words, because of the tendency of *Dasein* to live "inauthentically," with an instrumental relation to things, Heidegger's recommendation is to remain radically *disinterested* in adjudicating between the directness/indirectness of particular finite constellations' relationships to the opening of Being in time. For to be "interested" in this mystery will always reduce authentic living to mere using.

Milbank rejects this recommendation to "remain with questionableness" for a couple of reasons. First, he doubts whether this sort of living is really possible, given the "necessity for commitment to some historical tradition, to some mode of linguistic ordering," which suggests to Milbank that "we must always see our preferred finite stance . . . as a particularly privileged key to Being itself."[106] But this is not a significant objection on its own, for this necessity of commitment to a privileged relation to the mystery of Being's opening in time might simply confirm Heidegger's similar suggestion that we always live in forgetfulness of that mystery. Heidegger and Milbank seem to agree, in other words, that all human living is characterized by a kind of interested resolution of existential "questionableness." But inasmuch as Heidegger suggests that any such interest is inevitably a "lapse," he seems to Milbank to be claiming that sin as inauthenticity is not simply one human possibility among others, but that sin is in the nature of "ontical" life as such, written into the order of creation. Thus Milbank will highlight those places where "ontical presence is, for Heidegger, *constituted* through its concealment of Being as such."[107] In other words, Being's opening in time is, for Heidegger, its concealment, which means that just "to be" is already and unavoidably to be "fallen," to have committed "treason" against Being. Milbank seeks by highlighting this "inescapable ontological 'fall'" to

104. Ibid., 298.
105. Ibid.
106. Ibid.
107. Ibid., 300.

show that precisely where Heidegger wants to remain, unlike the forgetful history of Western philosophy, an existential thinker of authenticity, he actually betrays that inclination by virtue of his fidelity to a certain inescapable "structure" of Being's temporalization. Heidegger's "radical" stance on existential authenticity means that inauthenticity ceases to be an existential qualification at all, and becomes a sort of "objective" state—not a way of living that can be opposed by another way, but the very "structure" of our life:

> Heidegger's phenomenology of *dasein* . . . is supposed to show that there is a "guilt" more fundamental than moral guilt . . . Hence in the structure of thrownness, as in that of projection, there lies essentially a nullity, and it is impossible to cancel guilt by doing the right thing, impossible to make an adequate response to the sublime in "ethical" terms, as Kant supposed. Instead, we must simply "be guilty authentically" (an idea which the Lutheran tradition had unfortunately paved the way for).[108]

When Milbank says it is "impossible to cancel guilt by doing the right thing," he especially means to indicate that for Heidegger, guilt, despite its existential connotations, is an "objective" quality, and therefore that the human being is finally defined not as a way of living but as an objective "inhabitant" of an *a priori* structure.[109]

Milbank agrees with Heidegger about the necessity of historicism for any retrieval of what the history of philosophy has forgotten—i.e., the "mystery" of temporalization—but he suggests that, just as Nietzsche and the Nietzscheans are finally faithful to an account of difference as

---

108. Ibid., 301.

109. And on this score, I must emphasize that Milbank's reading of Heidegger on fallenness is at best ungenerous and at worst simply mistaken. In *Being and Time*, the "falling" of *Dasein* is never an objective category and is instead always defined existentially, a description of a particular comportment of the human will to itself and to the world. He says explicitly, for example, that "an *existential mode* of Being-in-the-world is documented with the phenomenon of falling," in *Being and Time*, 221. And correspondingly, "*authentic* existence is not something which floats above falling everydayness; existentially, it is only a modified way in which such everydayness is seized upon" (224). In other words, for Heidegger, the questions of falling, everydayness, and authenticity are questions not of "structures" that do not pertain to the subject, but instead are precisely and always questions of *Dasein's* existentiality. In this sense, what Milbank calls "being guilty authentically" is not for Heidegger some sort of resignation to an objectified and therefore corrupted world, but is precisely the possibility of a *transformation*, via a new existential mode, of the whole of *Dasein's* Being-in-the-world.

inevitable violence, so too does Heidegger violate his own historicist principles by resolving the "mystery" of ontological difference beforehand into an ontological fall, an inevitable concealment. For Milbank, by contrast, a genuine fidelity to the "mystery" of ontological difference cannot foreclose the possibility of a "hierarchization" of particular commitments and traditions, because any "flattening out" is, as a critical posture, fully dependent upon the sustainability of a structural proposition about the inevitable ontic "concealment" of Being. To be more precise, the Heideggerian critique of "interestedness" stands or falls with his claim about the "fall" of Being in its temporalization, which is, according to Milbank, only one possible wager, a *mythos* that Heidegger only pretends has a "metaphysical" authority.

Milbank opposes Heidegger's characterization of the relationship between Being and beings with a characterization of this relationship as "analogy," not from the perspective of a more "fundamental" philosophy, but from that of one who is already situated within a tradition of acting. He writes: "when I talk about 'the analogizing process,' I am trying to give a Christian theological equivalent to Heidegger's temporalizing of Being."[110] This opposition runs parallel to Milbank's attempt to give a theological equivalent, by reference to the Trinity, of Derrida's account of finite existence as a "supplementation" that is inevitably "treacherous."[111] From Milbank's Christian perspective, and from *any* genuinely historicist viewpoint, neither "temporalization" nor "dissemination" is unavoidably "concealment" or "treachery," for metaphysical justifications aside, they might instead be the opening in the finite of particular possibilities of "participation in divine Being."[112] If we are really historicists, in other words, purveyors of the "purer positivism" of meta-critique, then we should be ready to recognize that if the deployment of Being in time is really questionable, then it cannot be *necessarily* arbitrary. It is possible to grant instead that "a series of discriminations are irreversibly made within this process," and that "*without these preferences* it would collapse back into nihilism and univocity."[113] Even if we are not talking about specifically Christian preferences here, it is the *possibility of preferring* that saves thought from the nihilism of a secular wager, because one can only

110. Milbank, *Theology and Social Theory*, 305.
111. See ibid., 306–13.
112. Ibid., 305.
113. Ibid. Emphasis added.

loose the chains of *a priori* necessities by conceding the possibility that the relation between finite and infinite is a meaningful, if mysterious, "exchange of predicates."[114] Without the possibility of preference, the opening of Being in time would remain the (metaphysically) inevitable concealment that it is for Heidegger, a mystery before which the existing human being constitutes an objective violation, without even being given the chance to become an existential one.

Of course, one can maintain, as I would prefer to do, that Heidegger's assertion of the radical "questionableness" of our lives, and by extension his refusal to connect the possibility of authenticity with preferred commitments, is the result of an existential rather than a structural rigor. That is, one can argue that Heidegger is working with an understanding of human desire that refuses to see it liberated from its possessive inclinations simply by virtue of an attachment to a particular tradition or series. This putatively (for Milbank) nihilistic indifference to "attachments" could have the consequence of making possible a liberation of desire even in relation to "unchosen" or non-preferred attachments; that is, one could claim that with Heidegger's proposed indifference, "everything is possible," which is what Milbank refuses to consider. Milbank will suggest instead that to rule out the possibility of an authentic, "interested" living only "excludes, and does not refute, the possibility of a non-possessive desire."[115] But, as I am suggesting, this particular reading of the Heideggerian reception of Kierkegaard's refusal to "objectify" the religious unnecessarily rules out Heidegger's option to reply that the "possibility of a non-possessive desire" means nothing if not the possibility of living "disinterestedly." It is Milbank, in other words, who would need to justify the strange pairing of serious objective "preference" with a "non-possessive" desire. Milbank thinks he can do this by reference to "a real social practice, a transmission of desire that is (despite the overlays of power) still faintly traceable as a *pure persuasion without violence*."[116] The difficulty Milbank faces, therefore, is that of tracing a real social practice that calls human beings to self-*denial*, but which appeals to them nonetheless "persuasively."

---

114. Ibid.
115. Ibid., 320.
116. Ibid., 321. Emphasis added.

Milbank's Rejection of the "Dialectical"

Milbank addresses the possibility of a "dialectical" form of communication in relation to Alasdair MacIntyre's philosophical appeal to antique virtue in the face of modern secularity. However, as we shall see, this tack allows Milbank to remain unsatisfyingly evasive of the possibility of a dialectical *theology*, which generally speaking takes *sin* (not simply the passions or the body, as for ancient philosophy) to be the fundamental difficulty for any direct communication of authentic religiousness. Thus, we shall need to determine later the amenability of the theological possibility to the more technical, philosophical dialectics that Milbank criticizes.

That Alasdair MacIntyre advocates a return to antique and not specifically Christian virtue is evident to Milbank in his attachment of virtue to "Socratic dialectics." This connection of virtue with dialectics implies that for MacIntyre the practice of virtue is at least to some extent communicated or taught by rational argumentation. And this, to Milbank, is MacIntyre's not-quite-thoroughgoing relativism, which Milbank himself intends to overcome via the complete "detachment of virtue from dialectics."[117] Milbank suggests that just this sort of relativism is required of theology; or in other words, he suggests that the Christian account, in contrast to antique reason, "pushes the practice of virtue much closer to a rhetorical than a dialectical habit of mind."[118] The problem with MacIntyre's putative theology is finally that he thinks too much of its rational appeal, or that he is too willing to allow that Christian faith "gives better answers to problems always found dialectically problematic."[119] For Milbank, this importation of a "new foundationalism" into the Christian ethic makes it all too incapable, like ancient and modern secular reason, of advocating a genuine *Sittlichkeit*. In Milbank's view, the recourse to dialectics is finally what prevents Plato from finding "a way of simultaneously pointing to the universally valid and objective and to the customary particulars which instantiate it."[120] And just as the city is

117. Ibid., 327.
118. Ibid., 328.
119. Ibid.
120. Ibid., 329. One must say that Milbank has become much more sympathetic to Plato in this regard, most likely due to the influence of his own student, Catherine Pickstock. See Pickstock, *After Writing*, esp. chapter 1, for an account of Plato as a forerunner to Christianity, precisely in virtue of his account of beauty as mediating the

for Plato ruled by reason and thus closed off from unruly strangers, so too does the dialectical communication of virtue appeal to the subject's possibility of a "heroic," rational overcoming of the unruliness of her own passions. This might not be a problem if the rational could really achieve a transformation of the passions, the universal of the particular, through a *peaceful* practice of dialectics. But as Milbank tries to show, the relation between the two is always one of "war." Therefore, he writes,

> A solution is only really possible in terms of a tradition like Christianity, which starkly links particular to universal by conceiving its relationship to transcendence in a *rhetorical* fashion. In this respect, Christianity offers a social alternative to *either* the civic mode of sophistry and democratic politics on the one hand, *or* dialectics and "aristocratic" politics on the other.[121]

Here we can see that "rhetorical" is meant to indicate a direct relationship between the universal and the customary, and so too between the appeal of the practice of virtue and the whole, passionate human person. Whether and to what extent *sin* might hamper this directness, admittedly in a manner different from the ancient conception of a juxtaposition between reason and what is "unruly" in the human being, never becomes clear in Milbank's book, which to me indicates the evasiveness of dealing with dialectical communication in this fashion.

Milbank tries to identify the "indirectness" of dialectical communication with the assumption of a fundamental violence in both Plato and Aristotle. In Aristotle, whose ethics are generally thought to be more "embodied" than Plato's, Milbank suggests that *phronesis* does not really activate a practice that can integrate the whole person into the life of virtue. This is because *phronesis* "*interrupts* the spontaneous flow of the appetites with a reflection which seeks to ensure that they are exercised with the right measure."[122] In other words, the most important thing for Aristotelian virtue is the intellectual discernment and residually "heroic" application of the right measure onto the passions. The relation between the measure and its application, then, is not "direct," which implies that those emotions to which the measure is applied have no access in and of themselves to the criterion of their virtue. The same is true

---

"plenitude" of the Good.

121. Milbank, *Theology and Social Theory*, 329. Emphasis added on "rhetorical."
122. Ibid., 349. Emphasis added.

for Plato, who like Aristotle could not imagine a "full exercise of virtue ... within the domestic sphere."[123] Thus for Plato the *polis* was at least "partly constituted as a machine for minimizing the *oikos*,"[124] especially in relation to the possibility of true—i.e., political and rational—virtue. This delimitation of the domestic, and by extension, the bodily, is one of the ways in which antique reason manifests its conception of virtue as "at war" with the passions, and thus of the universal as at war with, or at least "bounded off" from, the particular. As Milbank puts it, for antique dialectics more generally, "while reason aims to rule through reason not force, it finds that it must, after all, supplement itself with a rule of force over force."[125] And this is why, finally, "the thought of a domestic, tribal rule that would be peaceful without civic law did not occur to [the Greeks]."[126]

This "thought," however, upon which the possibility of a genuine *Sittlichkeit* and therefore a genuine overcoming of secular reason hinges, *does occur* to the Christian account of virtue, which is contained

> in the Bible, in the ideas of the protection of guilty ones (like Cain), the periodic reversions of property distribution to relatively equal portions among family units, expulsion from the community of the non-cooperating offender (instead of confinement), and of forgiveness and canceling out of debts.[127]

It is not as if this thought *cannot* occur to antique reason, or as if dialectical reason genuinely discovers a rational foundation for the separation of *polis* and *oikos*, reason and passion; rather, it *does not occur* simply by virtue of antique reason's *a priori* belief in a primordial violence between the two spheres. That is, antique reason's incapacity to provide a genuine meta-critique of the secular "arises from *an entirely mythical belief* that both in 'the soul' and in 'the city' (themselves mythical entities) there reside permanent powers 'outside reason' escaping the full reach of intelligibility."[128] The "thought" of a genuinely peaceful communion of the corporeal and the intellectual occurs to Christianity because it does

---

123. Ibid., 364.
124. Ibid.
125. Ibid., 370.
126. Ibid., 368.
127. Ibid.
128. Ibid., 370. Emphasis added.

not *believe* in the permanent reality of all "conflictual elements." Instead, and chiefly for Augustine, Milbank suggests, "evil, or untruth, is not a *simulacrum*, not a bad copy of a real thing, nor even a 'mistaken' combination, but rather a 'pure negation' . . . simply a *lack*, and therefore [is] defined in relation to *desire*, not to logic."[129] For Christianity, therefore, evil does not have to be "logically reconciled" with the good, for it is *naught*—which means, in turn, that the "fact" of its ostensible irreconcilability has no weight outside the myth of evil's permanent reality. This implies that a virtuous way of living is possible in *every* situation, via participation in "charitable" relations, not via an objective reconfiguring of the "logical" situation with recourse to the walls of the *polis*. And this is why, in response to secular reason and in distinction from MacIntyre, Milbank does not "bring forward dialectics, *nor even* virtue in general, but rather Christian virtue in particular."[130] We can now see more precisely why this "bringing forward" is a specifically *rhetorical* communication; for only rhetoric names an appeal to the whole human being, to all of his reasons and passions. Thus only rhetorical communication is adequate to a wager of the ontological primacy of peace that refuses the myth of violence to which all secular reason subscribes. Let us now move, finally, to consider the particular rhetorical appeal that Milbank seeks to make.

Persuasion/Inscription: Christianity as Social Mechanism

Despite the intellectual acumen of the book, Milbank's rhetorical offer of a Christian narrative, a Christian "social science" whose suspicion overwhelms that of secular sociology, must be, on his own account, the offer of a practice and not simply a set of ideas. As he puts it, "if Jesus really is the word of God, then it is not the mere 'extrinsic' knowledge of this which will save us, but rather a precise attention to his many words and deeds *and all their historical results*."[131] This means more precisely that a Christian social science as the offer of a narrative in which one can be inscribed is an appeal not just to the one-time event of Jesus, but also to "the continuing story of the Church."[132] Thus, when theology, and in an

---

129. Ibid., 375.
130. Ibid., 331.
131. Ibid., 385. Emphasis added.
132. Ibid., 387.

exemplary way, Augustine, advocates the principle of "the ontological priority of peace over conflict" as a way of criticizing other "organizing logics," it must be "firmly anchored in a narrative, a practice, and a dogmatic faith, not in universal reason."[133] For if this principle was not so anchored, if it was only accessible to a purely noetic faith and not to the living of the whole person in the world, then it would be nothing but a confirmation of the thesis of secular reason that "the religious" is utterly "sublime," and so must remain without organizing impact on a "routinized" world. The wager of ontological peace, in other words, is different in *content* from the nihilist courage of secular reason, but this difference in content is one and the same with its *formal* inextricability from a real, embodied social order. If it is to be truly meta-critical, the appeal of Augustine's claim that "the peace within the city walls opposing the 'chaos' without, is, in fact, no peace at all compared with a peace coterminous with all Being whatsoever,"[134] must be rooted in a genuinely possible practice of spiritual but embodied living—a true *Sittlichkeit*. Only thus does theology fully confront and evade sociological suspicion, for only by this "universal" appeal to a particular positive *praxis* does it demonstrate its indifference to sociology's mythical cordoning off of the religious from the social.

Unsurprisingly, then, Milbank takes issue with any theology that fails to offer "a positive, alternative practice"[135] to the violence of secular reason, and especially with the thought of René Girard, to whom we shall have occasion to return later. Milbank suggests that while Girard is correct to emphasize the Gospels' refusal of violence on the basis of "another" ontology, he nevertheless gives too much credit to the mechanisms of human violence, such that the "alternative" to violence can be seen only momentarily in Jesus, but cannot be given "a collective, political form."[136] For Milbank, however, the gospel is truly "redeeming" only "in the form of a new *social mechanism* in which we can be situated."[137] When he makes this claim, Milbank means to emphasize our inevitable narrative inscription—that we only really "exist," as he says elsewhere,

133. Ibid., 390.
134. Ibid., 392.
135. Ibid., 395.
136. Ibid.
137. Ibid., 397.

"in the framework of an emplotment."[138] Theology thus cannot offer just a negating interruption of our inscriptions in cultures of violence, but an alternative narrative framework in which one can become a "character." Therefore theology should try to "*persuade* people—for reasons of 'literary taste'—that Christianity offers a much better story" than those of either modern or antique reason.[139] The chief reason the Christian story is better or more tasteful, for Milbank, is that it makes human beings "fuller" characters—i.e., it does not appeal only to a subject "purified" of the passions, nor offer only a noetic ascertainment of a one-time-only interruption of peace, as for Girard. Instead, it appeals directly to a positive and actualizable social practice such that the whole person may be included in the emplotment.

On Milbank's reading, the wager of secular reason offers total "self-control," albeit control of a self whose immanence is "bounded off" from any transcendent influences. Milbank's theology tries to demonstrate that secular reason's offer of human transparency-to-self is really based on a mythical belief in the ontological primacy of conflict, and therefore that it offers only a "peace" that is primarily a violent victor over the chaos of nature. This "peace" takes shape as the battle of human dialectical reason against lower-order human desires, and of a politics of abstract equality over the "offenses" of particulars who are unwilling to be assimilated to its measure. Here one might think, for example, of the relentless liberal persecution of religious "fundamentalists," who refuse to derive their self-understandings from liberalism itself, or of the inability of any liberal government to deal with the problem of urban homelessness without resorting to tactics like the removal of homeless persons from the places where their ugliness is most obvious. This, just like the *polis* refusing to accommodate the *oikos* in ancient Greece, is liberalism's unwillingness to broker a real peace with those who are too ridden with the "unequal" to be accommodated by liberal rhetoric. These will feel the brunt of liberalism's regulative power only, which also makes plain the true nature of its rhetoric. The rhetoric of Christian theology, by contrast, is for Milbank a persuasion of "pure peace," because instead of going to "war" with the offender, theology's ontological wager does not allow the "offense" any purchase in reality which would warrant a

---

138. Ibid., 265.
139. Ibid., 330.

counter-offense, which means that the name of truly Christian action is not "victory," but "forgiveness of sins."[140]

Milbank acknowledges that there are some who do not believe Christianity has or needs such a perceptible "idiom" of social behavior,[141] or an "ethics" that broadens its perceptible impact beyond the soul of the individual believer. These claim that "the protestant view of the Church, which understands it as an association of individual believers who possess, outside the social context, their own direct relationship to God, articulates more fully what was always latent within the Christian self-understanding."[142] On Milbank's account, as we should recognize by now, any such notion of the self as extricated from the "social" with respect to the self's "religious" life is all too indebted to secular reason's boundary between the personal and the social. Augustine, Milbank says, does not in any way anticipate this Protestant development, for he "does not endorse, indeed utterly condemns, every tendency towards a view of personhood as 'selfownership.'"[143] For Milbank, in other words, there is a direct correlation between a properly theological acknowledgement of the inextricably inscribed nature of selfhood—and the corresponding impossibility of extracting one's religiosity from the narrative in which one finds oneself—and a sort of self-dispossession. To commit oneself to a "preferred" narrative, then, is to give up the possibility of owning oneself at some sublime remove from one's actual, historical living.

We can understand the logic of this arrival at self-dispossession by virtue of narrative inscription, but we might also say that at no point does Milbank deal adequately with the existential difficulties posed by "commitment," difficulties that might make Heidegger's indifference to particular traditions by virtue of the "questionableness" of Being's opening in time equally if not more appropriate. In other words, there is no obvious reason to believe that the simple act of commitment to the Christian "tradition"—i.e., to the "Church"—somehow exceeds, apparently by virtue of the unique *object* of this commitment, what Heidegger

---

140. Ibid., 411. See also ibid., 417, where Milbank says that Christianity's distinctiveness, its "point of contrast with both antiquity and modernity, lies in its 'reconciliation of virtue with difference,' or of *Sittlichkeit* with freedom. Only because it allows difference does it truly realize *Sittlichkeit*, whereas the antique closure against difference meant that it really promoted a heroic freedom which was only for the few."

141. Ibid., 398.

142. Ibid., 399.

143. Ibid., 401.

would call the lapse into "everydayness" that characterizes an objective-possessive relation to what must properly remain the utterly mysterious opening of infinite Being in time. Thus, for Milbank to be really persuasive about the opposition of a "narrative" existence to "Protestant" self-ownership, he would need to describe an interestedness in tradition that is, shall we say, disinterested in its interestedness, at the very least, and perhaps more accurately, disinterested in being interested at all. For one's narrative inscription may provide, precisely through the medium of "commitment," a way of comprehending oneself as objective and in an object-relation to other emplotted "characters." In other words, an "idiomatic" existence may offer possession of oneself as a "character," and Milbank does not deal adequately with the capacity of sinful human desire to "own itself" precisely through an objective, "plot-relation" to the past and future. Given this possibility, the Heideggerian "remaining with questionableness" might more fully evade the problem of "self-ownership" that Milbank is trying to overcome.

At this point Milbank can reasonably object to the charge we are pursuing, by emphasizing that the kind of "persuasion" he is talking about makes an object-relation to one's narrative inscription impossible, because this persuasion is always also "enacted," a sort of existential rather than exclusively noetic appeal. (But even here, as we shall see, it remains a question whether or not the impossibility of objectivity is really *rhetorically* appealing to human desire.) Milbank says, for example, that the nature of the Christian narrative, its fully *sittlich* appeal to the whole human, itself precludes any tendency toward objectification. This is because according to the Christian story, with its affirmation of the participation in transcendence of all created difference,

> the created world of time participates in the God who differentiates; indeed, it *is* this differentiation insofar as it is finitely "explicated," rather than infinitely "complicated." Just as God is not a "substance" . . . so also there are no substances in creation, no underlying matter, and no discrete and inviolable "things."[144]

---

144. Ibid., 424. Interestingly, Milbank modifies this statement in the second edition of *Theology and Social Theory* (2006), where he writes, "Just as God is not a 'substance,' because he is nothing fundamental underlying anything else, so also there are no absolute self-standing substances in creation, no underlying matters not existent through form and no discrete and inviolable 'things'" (431).

For the Christian narrative, creation itself is not a thing, but the "process" of divine differentiation, which means that to be a Christian, to be inscribed in this narrative, is to become an "agent" of this process, one who enacts a creative willing of further, peaceful differentiation. Interestingly, this suggestion implies an irrevocably "existential" Christianity, an account of authentic existence to which Heidegger, following Kierkegaard, might also subscribe. Milbank continues by describing Christian peace not as an "objective" unity, a community that is a "thing," but rather as *an activity of being related to harmony*:

> Unity, in this Christian outlook, ceases to be anything hypostatically real in contrast to difference, and becomes instead only the "subjective" apprehension of a harmony displayed in the order of the differences, a desire at work in their midst, although "proceeding" beyond them (as the Holy Spirit).[145]

Christian unity is not, therefore, an objective state, but a subjective "apprehension," which is always an active work-in-desiring. And thus the rhetorical appeal of the Christian narrative, the Christian way of living, is an appeal to a sort of "existential" human desire, a desire not unlike Kierkegaard's "passionate inwardness," as we shall see in greater detail below, especially in chapters 3 and 5. For Milbank this particular appeal is coupled with an account of sin that is akin to existential despair, a willing *not* to be a self in the movement of spiritual love, but to be a "thing-in-itself": "Christianity, uniquely, does not allow violence any real ontological purchase, but relates it instead to a free subject who asserts a will that is truly independent of God and of others, and thereby a will to the inhibition and distortion of reality"[146]—reality being, for Milbank, not a "substance" but the *process* of harmonious differentiation.

It is my contention, however, that such an "existential" Christianity cannot be communicated directly, rhetorically, or in any form that actually intends to communicate something. For the desire of human beings to "be something" in despair rather than to become no-thing in faith means that the Christian possibility of salvation, or Christian truth, can only be communicated in an indirect form, which is to say, a form that is indifferent to its very communication and therefore is something like an "anti-rhetoric." Milbank would balk at this and say that an indirect form

---

145. Milbank, *Theology and Social Theory*, 428.
146. Ibid., 432.

fails because, just as the *polis* excludes the *oikos*, and just as Heidegger tells us to be utterly disinterested in our commitments, so a dialectical form of communication does not offer truth as something comprehensibly related to all of our known "ways of living," but only as a sublime noetic object. But we might push back, as I will suggest in chapters below, and maintain that only an anti-rhetoric is attentive enough to the subject's desire for objective reification so as to remain capable of animating what cannot be directly appealing to such desire—a way of living "as if not."[147]

Conclusion: Rhetorical Narrative, *Sittlichkeit*, and Desire

In this chapter I have attempted to do several things; primary among them was to give a detailed account of Milbank's critique of secular reason as nihilism, a critique upon which the recent "Radical Orthodox" assertion of theology's proper position as a "metadiscourse" is based. Also significant was my attempt to elucidate the connection in *Theology and Social Theory* between the uniquely Christian possibility of *Sittlichkeit* and the necessarily antidialectical, narrative/rhetorical form of its communication. Third, I tried to draw out and emphasize those places where Milbank's narrative approaches a sort of "existential" communication, in the sense of appealing not to a desire for objective self-possession but to the desire of the whole unified person, a desire attuned not to substance but to the *movement* of Being's emanation as such. Finally, in all of the above I have attempted also to inject some critical comments that hint at the direction of this book as a whole. In particular on this score, I raised the possibility that a rhetorical form of communication is not sufficiently attentive to the challenges posed by fallen human desire, especially in its proneness to temptation—what Heidegger calls "the '*falling*' of Dasein."[148] I have suggested that an indirect form might be more appropriate to the communication of a truth that demands an "existential mode" of living, which implies a dying to the desire to be a "thing" or a "self-standing substance." Let me now by way of conclusion return briefly to each of these major elements in the chapter.

Milbank's book anticipates the theological agenda of Radical Orthodoxy inasmuch as it seeks to reunite theology with social theory,

---

147. See 1 Corinthians 7.
148. Heidegger, *Being and Time*, 219.

and even to defend theology as the last bastion of authentic social theory, by construing theological discourse as a compelling refusal of the secular "boundary" between religion and the social. Milbank is therefore especially concerned by the tendency of modern and particularly Protestant theology to entertain the sociological "reduction" of religion to mere "social factors," and even, in the case of neo-orthodoxy, to *accept* this reduction, ostensibly in the name of preserving the utterly otherwise character of "true religion." What any such reduction of religion to the social assumes is precisely *the existence of the social*, as a realm that is fully transparent to human reason and therefore totally explicable even in the absence of a spiritual or transcendent referent. This transparency is made to sound obvious or inescapable by virtue of an account of immanent causality which pretends to be exhaustive, capable of registering even "charismatic" deviations from an all-pervasive and rationally measurable "routinization" of immanent causality. Milbank suggests, in opposition to this paradigmatically modern, "explanatory" approach to history, that the sphere of the secular is not an undeniable reality, but the mythical invention of a subjective *belief* in the transparency of the immanent to human reason. Milbank offers the counter-example, the counter-wager, of Maurice Blondel, whose "emanative *poesis*" calls Weberian immanence into question. For Blondel, every human action, in unity with its thought or "conception," seeks and requires a transcendent completion, which means that "reality," as historical movement, is a theory/praxis that always already bears an undeniable relation to the "supernatural," albeit a relation that is inaccessible to totalizing reason.

Next we saw how the postmodern challenge to theology goes beyond that of modern secular reason insofar as it purports to give up on an inviolably rational account of immanent causality. Postmodern thought is able to claim, for example, that Weberian sociology or Hegelian philosophies of history are all equally narrative "conjectures," and not somehow rationally inescapable. Therefore it can also relativize the conjecture of Christian theology as just "another mythos." Milbank seizes critically upon this utter relativization of conjectures and demonstrates compellingly how it signifies postmodernism's willingness to smuggle in what is still a modern, metaphysically "necessary" philosophy of history—in its presupposition of *inevitable incommensurability*. Milbank then suggests, in particular against the Heideggerian reading of the "questionableness" of our relationship to Being, that a truly thoroughgoing historicism needs to advocate particular preferences in order to avoid a very un-historicist, metaphysical commitment to an *a priori* "ontology of violence." So Milbank must, in order to overcome postmodernism's complicity in the "boundary" of the secular (by virtue of its having rendered "the social" utterly transparent, if not to reason then to genealogy), offer a narrative that is indeed to be *preferred*.

In order to persuade us to be interested in the particularly Christian narrative, then, Milbank cannot go "beyond" historicism and return to antique "dialectical" communication, as Alasdair MacIntyre advocates. For such communication, based as it is upon the ancient Greek division between reason and the passions, the *polis* and the *oikos*, can only reinforce the boundary between, for example, the truly "ethical" and the familial or embodied (i.e., between "religion" and the "social" as the predictable realm of necessity). The dialectical form of communication therefore tries in effect to persuade the subject that he is inevitably divided from himself, just as the truly ethical or political sphere is inevitably divided from the domestic. The dialectical in this sense appeals to and tempts one "part" of the human (the rational), at both the intra-psychic and the social levels, to assert its power and its ownership over itself and its subjects. Milbank's explicitly *rhetorical* form of communication, by contrast, appeals to the whole person, in the sense that it offers the possibility of living a wager that the human being is not inextricably divided from himself, and nor is the universally "ethical" unquestionably divided from embodied, customary living. In short, then, the rhetorical form of communication is true to the thoroughgoing historicism which calls secular reason radically into question, *and*, in its particular wager of the ontological primacy of peace, the rhetoric of a genuine Christian theology is uniquely appealing to the whole human being, as the possibility, via "inscription" into the church's particular story, of being at peace with oneself and others.

Given that Christianity on this account is not a noun but a particular *way* of living in history, Milbank will not say that to be offered a role in this story is to be offered a substantive "identity." For unlike the dialectical form of communication, which offers the possibility of self-control at least to the rational part of the soul, the rhetorical bids the whole person to be given over to a living inscription and thus to be given up as a "thing" to be possessed at all. So there *are*, as Milbank says, "no substances," but only shifting relations and subjective apprehensions.

This means, as I have suggested above, that Milbank's rhetorical offer of the Christian narrative is not the offer of a thing but of a way of being, an offer to the self of a possible existentiality, not an objective community but the chance to participate in a particular process of commun*ing*.

Finally, I tried to suggest in a preliminary way how it is strange for an appeal to a non-objective, existential way of living to be paired with a rhetorical form of communication that (by its very nature) intends to persuade—and thus *to communicate a preference* for a particular tradition and narrative.[149] I argued that at the very least this invites a reintroduction of an objectivism of desire, which evidences a lack of attention to human sin as the desire to possess oneself *as objective*. The direct appeal of any narrative, the offer of any directly persuasive "plot," ultimately does very little to address human sin so understood. In the next chapter I shall try to demonstrate why the rhetorical offer of a narrated or inscribed existence becomes ever more objectifying, for example in Catherine Pickstock's localization of the essentially Christian in the Roman Rite, and in David Bentley Hart's identification of Christian truth with beauty. From that chapter, in combination with the present one, I think it will become clear that Radical Orthodoxy remains too satisfied with its own "structural" or intellectual differences from the structures of secular "conjectures," and that it thereby fails to address the really critical element in any communication of the essentially Christian—the effectuation of a subjective shift from a despairing self-reification to a faithful willing to enact the eternal in time. This shift, I would like to suggest in the book as a whole, cannot be the result of a direct persuasion in relation to a particularly compelling "history," but occurs only "dialectically" (in the Kierkegaardian rather than the Hegelian sense), in relation to the offer of nothing and no-place. For it is only when nothing, no identity, no substance, no tradition, is offered *as the possibility of true life* that a subject can relate himself to the "offer" while at the same time dying to his erotic attachment to identity, substance, tradition, etc., and thereby become not a reified thing but a participant in the life of the Spirit. Radical Orthodox rhetoric is not quite willing to take *this* distance from its form, which means, finally, that its rhetorical "appeal"

---

149. So recall that Milbank wants to read history as "a true concrete representation of the analogical blending of difference," *Theology and Social Theory*, 279.

is all too similar to what Heidegger calls the "tranquilizer" offered in all "idle talk."[150]

150. See Heidegger, *Being and Time*, esp. 221ff.

2

Language and the Fear of Death

Introduction

IN THE PREVIOUS CHAPTER we explored the critique of secular reason that undergirds Radical Orthodoxy's new "theological imperative." Specifically, we came to see that for Milbank the problem with secular reason consists in its hypostasization and separation of the immanent from the transcendent. According to his genealogy, moreover, this crucial trait is not only modern; indeed, it turns out to be as characteristic of antique philosophy's denigration of the passions and postmodernism's false historicism as it is of modern sociology's overt immanentism. The inability of any of these ways of thinking to attain to a genuine *Sittlichkeit*—a construal of the transcendent or the universal as possibly "occurring" in the particular situation—negatively indicates the singular achievement of Christian theology: only for Christian thought is being not a finite or infinite "substance," but rather *a charitable way of being related* in one's living—to the world, to others, and to God.[1]

To rehearse all of this briefly, for Milbank and Radical Orthodoxy, secular reason assumes a logically inviolable boundary between finite and infinite being, and so naturally propounds a "dialectical" form of truth. Its inability to countenance any traversal of the finite/infinite distinction means that it will limit the meaning of an ontological

---

1. Thus does Milbank say that for Christianity, "there are no substances in creation" (*Theology and Social Theory*, 424).

"inscription" in truth to a being's possession of certain objective qualities; and since some of these qualities will lie on opposing sides of the "boundary," the very (dialectical) truth of our being is likely to be one of irreconcilable division. Our "immanent" attributes will render us inexorably opposed to "transcendence"; and, in virtue of our interior, rational subjectivity, we shall at the same time find ourselves negatively related to our own passionate, material nature. With all objective difference hereby cast in terms of negation, secular reason's "nihilism" is laid bare. By contrast, for Radical Orthodoxy, Christianity's gospel espouses a decidedly rhetorical form of truth, a form that asserts no inviolable boundaries, but appeals to and persuades the whole, passionate person into a truthful way of life, whose movement is at once transcendent and immanent. Such a life takes the incarnation of God in Christ not as a paradoxically mysterious objectivity, an effective non-presence, but as a concrete provocation to live in proximity with the spiritual or universal at every particular moral moment. Therefore Christian theology's rhetoric invites and makes possible an "emplotment" that enlivens and reconciles the subject with himself and the world by virtue of the irreducible movement of creation itself, which only "is" as the excessive gift of the God who is *caritas*.

To understand Radical Orthodoxy's dialogue with secular reason's nihilism in this way, as the wager of another form of communication, more in keeping with a reconciling form of truth, helps us to recognize the putative urgency of its theological imperative. That is, in our present context, in which the "linguistic turn" has rescued the historicist from philosophy's derision, theology finds itself ably poised to *consummate* philosophy. To explain: where philosophy would like to point out the impossibility of dialectical mediation among competing narratives, it is only theology, with its wager of ontological peace, which can be fully committed to the mystery of ontological difference, without reverting to the metaphysics of necessary violence. In the present chapter we shall try to weigh more precisely the importance of this moment for theology. I will argue that what Radical Orthodoxy helpfully indicates, by unmasking all of secular reason's "metaphysical" justifications, is the existential urgency of Christianity's spiritual calling. That is, Radical Orthodoxy's critique of secular metaphysics effectively suggests that you cannot escape the earnestness of the religious imperative to "be reconciled" by appealing to an objective definition of yourself that would get you out of so living.

But we shall also examine particular cases in which Radical Orthodoxy seems to want to "go further" than this. First, through a reading of Catherine Pickstock's *After Writing: On the Liturgical Consummation of Philosophy*, we will come to see how the Radical Orthodox critique of all secular "gestures of security" against the possibility of true life, precisely in its effort to elevate the merits of a particular theological grammar, in fact reduces the existentiality of secular gestures to their "bad syntax." In consequence, I argue, Radical Orthodoxy risks being able to point only to a syntactical/structural, and not an existential, alternative to nihilism. Second, we shall explore David Bentley Hart's provocative suggestion that even the most apparently reasonable "offense" at Christian truth is more "aesthetically" than "metaphysically" justified. But here again we shall witness a sort of "going further," in that Hart is not content to expose the dubious claim to being "metaphysically" exempt from Christianity's call to live, but presumes also to mitigate the ostensible tastelessness of the essentially Christian, and thus to *overcome*, via theology, the very possibility of offense—in this case, especially the Nietzschean offense.

In these discussions of Pickstock and Hart, moreover, we shall have occasion to consider and respond to characteristic Radical Orthodox dismissals of dialectical communicators—in Pickstock's case this will require an exploration of Heidegger on death, and in response to Hart we shall offer a reconsideration of Emmanuel Levinas' ostensibly "gnostic" ethics. In the chapter as a whole, then, I hope to demonstrate that Radical Orthodoxy's emphasis upon theology's rhetorical form threatens to reduce the existential urgency of Christianity to an academic one, which inevitably forgets what Radical Orthodoxy was about in the first place—the possibility of spiritual life, which only a human being, not a "culture," or a "grammar," or a "rhetoric," can approach. In regard to this most authentic of Radical Orthodox concerns, it will turn out that the "dialectics" of Heidegger and Levinas come much nearer to the mark than our rhetoricians will allow, precisely insofar as these thinkers refuse to make the offer of spiritual life a direct one.

In interrogating the supposed "urgency" of theology's adoption of rhetoric in these ways, I shall not be able to make an equally urgent appeal to some other form of theology. Rather, I shall advocate a form of communication that seeks no adherents to any "theology," but investigates and pursues Biblical truth in a way that allows it to remain paradoxical, standing in an indirect relation to the despairing/believing human subject. This will put me in the perhaps awkward position of writing a book that is most adamant that it not be taken with any urgency. My peculiar emphasis in this regard will become more comprehensible (but I hope not less pronounced) as we proceed. But for now let us turn to Catherine Pickstock, whose book, *After Writing*, will provide much of the material for discussion in this chapter.

The Sophistic "Gesture of Security Against the Void"

In the first chapter of *After Writing*, Catherine Pickstock undertakes to show that "postmodern" philosophy is still very much indebted to its ostensible dialectical opponent, metaphysics.[2] She argues that Jacques Derrida's critique of Plato is particularly revealing in this regard, in that Plato can in fact be used to uncover *Derrida's* fidelity to the metaphysical dichotomy of presence/absence. This argument takes shape in Pickstock's re-reading of Plato's negotiation of the differences between "writing" and "speech" in the *Phaedrus*.[3] In Pickstock's rendering, the Derridean suggestion is that Plato's preference for orality signifies a metaphysician's nostalgia for the pure, self-present "origin" of being, of which the written record is a mere "supplement." On this reading, Plato's privileged orality effects a suppression of temporality, difference, or more broadly of the ambiguous and unmasterable articulation or "supplementation" of being in time. To counter such "nostalgia," Derrida insists upon "the transcendental *writtenness* of language,"[4] the inexorably "supplemental" character of all temporal "signs." Pickstock's own reading of the *Phaedrus* is meant to assert the opposite—that an insistence upon language as written is, "after all, a rationalistic gesture which suppresses embodiment and temporality."[5]

---

2. Pickstock, *After Writing*.
3. Plato, *Phaedrus*, in *Plato: The Collected Dialogues*, 475–525.
4. Pickstock, *After Writing*, 4.
5. Ibid. I should emphasize that Pickstock's argument on this score is more convincing as an inventive reading of Plato than it is as a revelation of Derrida's "rationalism." See David Bentley Hart's "Review Essay" of Pickstock's book, in *Pro Ecclesia*, where Hart suggests Pickstock makes Derrida out to be a "simpleton," and argues that in fact Derrida "is not a champion of inscription over against speech (except ironically), but a critic of a certain metaphysical mystique of the spoken—or, rather, of the unspoken and unwritten—and of any philosophy that envisages a retreat from that very force of 'dissemination' that permits thought to move" (370).

Pickstock's argument vis-à-vis Derrida hinges on her interpretation of Phaedrus' enthusiasm about the transcription of Lysias' speech on *eros* which he has in his possession. Derrida privileges Phaedrus here by reading his enthusiasm as signaling a belief that truth is unavoidably supplemental and thus "written." Disdaining any fantasies about making the "original" present, Phaedrus hereby becomes the consummate anti-metaphysician. Pickstock, however, believes that Phaedrus' satisfaction with the written speech reveals his belief that truth may be accumulated and held at a timeless remove from its performance in time.[6] On her account, therefore, the Socratic, oral practice of "dialectic" indicates no quest for disembodied, un-supplemented being, but represents instead the practice of truth in time, the *enactment* of being's temporal differentiation.[7] Pickstock writes that Phaedrus "fetishizes" the real as a text because it permits a mobility of truth that allows for a direct and "pure" relation to it at any moment, since the written text is immune from the variations inherent in any temporal *performance* of language. Thus Pickstock calls Phaedrus' repetition of Lysias' speech a "*simulated* orality," which "would engage a fully metaphysical obsession with a lost original."[8] By contrast, a "true" orality would eschew the attempt to repeat truth as a present possession, and constitute instead "a new and different performance in itself."[9] By virtue of Phaedrus' possessive relationship to the written, in other words, Platonic orality can be read as juxtaposed not to temporality, facticity, and supplementarity, but to all attempts to transpose a truth that must be *lived*, in the inexorable differentiation of temporality, to a secure "space" where it can be *owned*.

A more typical reading of Plato, such as Pickstock suggests is found in Derrida, is unable to imagine this alternative to a metaphysics of presence—i.e., to imagine "that instead of being at once radical absence *and* original presence, the good might be an inaccessible and inexhaustible plenitude."[10] Such a Platonic alternative suggests primarily that the transcendent "good" is not irrevocably bounded off from the immanent, "since the sun which shines light onto beings is present in

---

6. See Plato's *Phaedrus*, 228a-e.
7. Pickstock, *After Writing*, 6.
8. Ibid., 8.
9. Ibid.
10. Ibid., 11.

the gift of insight, truth, and beauty."[11] The suspicion of the postmodern anti-metaphysician is that "recollection" of this good, pursued through the oral practice of dialectic, disparages the written and factual in order to return to a "purer" self-presence than that which can be mediated in writing, or indeed, lived in time. For Pickstock, however, Platonic recollection is not "a mere identical re-attainment of something rooted in 'the past,' which cancels out all that has happened since. Rather, the eternal transcendence of the good which causes a kind of overflowing into physicality *keeps us within the movement of time.*"[12] This argument would have us believe that the "writing" which Socrates opposes is precisely a means by which to achieve a falsely "originary" relation to being. Against writing's afforded epistemological security in this regard, "Socrates proposes the partial nature of all knowledge, and suggests that our only access to it is via *specific physical performance*,"[13] which is to say, dialectic. The performance of dialectic is therefore an interpretive pursuit of the good, mediated by an erotic attraction between the philosopher and the transcendent's irruption or emanation in its "supplement." Through a discerning *eros*, the philosopher "recollects" the truth of the good inasmuch as it shines forth, partially, in things that are present. Thus does the philosopher also, by virtue of the good's "contagion" and consequent production of a philosophic "madness," recollect himself in light of the good and participate in its temporally differentiating emanation.[14]

For Pickstock's Derrida, by contrast, the Platonic preference for orality is evidence of nostalgia for a good defined objectively as primordial unity and identity, inexorably violated by "the different," or the supplement. Derrida therefore privileges writing, or in Pickstock's words, effects a "colonization of supplementation by writing,"[15] whose emphasis is not on the absent and fetishized original (represented by speech) but on the "disseminated" sign. This manner of emphasis on the supplement is meant to preclude access to the origin, by making the "measure" of temporal differentiation irreducibly aporetic. Only thus can the temporal supplement have its due, since hereby one is prevented from "reading" the supplement only in terms of how it "presents" its

11. Ibid., 12.
12. Ibid., 13. Emphasis added.
13. Ibid., 19.
14. Ibid., 21.
15. Ibid., 20.

origin—it *cannot* present its origin, so the supplement at last becomes its "own thing." But for Pickstock, to posit such an arbitrary measure obtaining between the origin and its sign least of all moves us beyond an objectivism of presence/absence. That is, for Derrida to say that the presence of the supplement is, in the undecidability of its arrival, the irrevocable absence of the origin, is not exactly to confound the dualistic logic upon which a metaphysics of presence turns (even if it is to "overturn" it).[16] And so it is the more surprising claim of Pickstock's book that the Platonic account of transcendence (later fulfilled by Christianity's arrival at a *constitutively* "supplemental," Trinitarian ontology) already gets us beyond a metaphysics of presence—or metaphysics in the conventional sense. For in the Socratic view, the transcendent origin is not objectively absent from the supplement, which would therefore be derided; but instead the good is plenitudinously present *in* the supplement, mediated temporally and erotically: "On account of the excessiveness of transcendence, the good is always overflowing into that subject which, via *eros*, strives to participate in it."[17] Therefore Socrates does not fear the supplement, the temporal, or the different, precisely because *the good supplements*, or makes itself ever again partially available to the mediation of eros.[18]

Pickstock's reading of Socrates' preference for orality—as a preference for a temporal way of life in pursuit of the good over a life that is written and thereby possessed apart from its performance—also informs her sense of the Platonic view of representational poetry in the *Republic*.[19] The common tendency would be to read Plato's critique of dramatic imitation as but another denigration of the temporal supplement as mere fakery. Thus his advocacy for religious liturgical performance alone would amount to the moralizing corollary of a nostalgia for the "pure origin." But instead, for Pickstock, Socrates advocates liturgy alone because, as representation, it allows of no "unmoved" spectatorship

---

16. This line of argument is similar to Milbank's suggestion that Heidegger's is a false historicism because its insistence upon the "questionableness" of Being's temporalization really capitulates to the metaphysical presupposition of secular reason.

17. Ibid., 22.

18. Hart's "Review Essay" is especially critical of Pickstock's sympathy for the Platonic here, arguing that she ignores how "Platonic *eros* is contaminated entirely by a tragic abhorrence of change" (371), and that this only dilutes the force of her ultimate appeal to Christianity's uniqueness.

19. See *The Republic of Plato*, esp. Book X.

or recitation (think of Lysias' speech), but implies a necessary participation. Socratic liturgy is not, then, "a constative representation now and then of what is praise-worthy, but constitutes a whole way of life."[20] The Platonic injunction concerning imitation, therefore, is not to avoid all secondary accounts as such, all temporal supplements. Instead it is to be related to supplements as possible occasions of one's own enacted formation by the good, instead of as discrete "representations." To put it another way, the difference between the poetry that Socrates problematizes and his alternative of liturgy is not the difference between mere imitation and pure objective presence, but between a supplementation-as-representation, to which one can relate objectively, and a representation-as-participation. Therefore the Socratic goal is that "the city itself becomes the true drama, *inhabited* rather than represented, and the life of the philosopher-lover *enacts* the true poetry, for that which he utters is harmonious with his whole mode of living."[21] Pickstock concludes that while Phaedrus treats himself and others (and the real as such) as fundamentally written and thus definable, for Socrates "there is a suggestion that a person's identity is defined and performed not only by his position in a particular place, but also by a kind of journeying, an 'identity' which is always *in media res*."[22]

Therefore, while the linguistic turn[23] has enabled both theology and postmodern philosophy to affirm that we exist only in the supplement, only by virtue of a linguistic inscription or emplotment, Pickstock's reading of Plato allows her to qualify this affirmation by suggesting that an emphasis on language as constitutively *written* severely limits the possibilities of language/selfhood. Whereas Derrida sides with Phaedrus against the putative Platonic/metaphysical abstraction of existence from its supplemental inscriptions, Pickstock identifies in the sophistic emphasis on the text a construal of language which ultimately threatens supplementarity and difference, insofar as it reifies the subject and the real in a "static *schema*." Thus she claims that the characteristics

20. Pickstock, *After Writing*, 39.
21. Ibid., 40. Emphasis added.
22. Ibid., 45.

23. The importance of the linguistic turn to Radical Orthodoxy is evident in Graham Ward's comment that "in the contemporary linguistic turn . . . Christianity is again given the opportunity for continuing, for mapping out for today, for making intelligible for today, a theology of signification so fundamental to scripture and in the traditional teaching of the Church," in Ward, *Cities of God*, 9.

of sophistry finally "constitute an anticipation of the characteristics of immanentist modernity . . . not because of their reliance on language as such, but rather on account of their separation of language *from itself*, or from its ultimate character as an expression of liturgy."[24] For Pickstock, that is, the linguistic turn only accomplishes an overcoming of metaphysics if language is construed as fundamentally "praise of the divine," oral and enacted rather than written and objectifying. Construals of language as fundamentally written are objectifying because they keep the presence/absence distinction in play, refusing to countenance its traversal via what Pickstock calls a "specific performance." Within a "transcendentally written" language, therefore, there is no possibility of imagining a *way* of living in the face of death; there are only various opportunities for self-objectification, various "gestures of security" against the void of time's passing.

In tracing the influence of this antique gesture of despair upon the construction of modern language as such, and in conjunction with the assumption (shared with Milbank) that we only live by virtue of and within our linguistic emplotments, Pickstock also implicitly claims that we moderns *live* the sophistic gesture of security against the void simply by virtue of our wholly spatialized and thus "nominal" language. And here arises the total—because "redemptive"—urgency of theology's new, rhetorical form of communication, its recasting of language as fundamentally movement and practice. Here is where we begin to see, in other words, that Pickstock's construal of the dilemmas posed by modern language implies that one may be barred from participation in true life simply because one is situated within a "bad construal" of language. This implication, I suggest, is tantamount to a definition of the human being *as the syntax in which he or she exists*, which is a somewhat ironic implication on the part of one so opposed to the objectification of the person in writing. It will be helpful to remain mindful of this dubious possibility as we consider Pickstock's construal of the development of modern language.

---

24. Pickstock, *After Writing*, 46.

Modern Spatialization

The Gesture of Modern Epistemology

In her chapter on the influence of sophistic "spatialization" upon modern thought and language, Pickstock begins with that now ubiquitous fruit of abstraction—technology. She admits that technology as we know it is a persuasive force in entrenching the notion that reality can be schematized and written, since modern technology presents us with what she calls "an all too seductive *facility*" in our manipulations of objects, which seem therefore to derive unproblematically from truth-as-writing.[25] Yet Pickstock does not want to suggest that technology is the *cause* of this "spatial illusion," for as she goes on to say, "the illusions which it can encourage are only *legitimized* by an increasing denial of genuine transcendence, understood as doxological reliance upon a donating source which one cannot command."[26] She concludes that this fundamental denial is generated not by technology as such, but by human beings' *fear* of participating in a "transcendence" that is deployed in something as uncontrollable as the passing of time.[27] Thus Pickstock acknowledges, on the one hand, the existential attraction that an atemporal reification of reality in writing exercises upon human beings—in all times and places, we might say—but at the same time she would like to locate the turn to this reification historically, to give the seductiveness of the illusion varying degrees of intensity on the basis of objective, not existential, criteria. This is precisely the conflict and perhaps contradiction that works its way through most of Pickstock's book: on the one hand she makes the claim that human beings who are fearful of their own passing away turn to a written and thus spatialized identity—while an "authentic" relation to transcendence remains possible at every moment—and on the other hand, the claim that such a temporally-mediated participation becomes less possible as the result of changing objective/historical circumstances. So she writes that our technological facility indicates that "the structures of sophistry are now so boldly inscribed into our linguistic and social practices that *a liturgical attitude toward reality becomes increasingly*

---

25. Ibid., 48.
26. Ibid. 49.
27. See ibid., 52–53.

remote of access," and she aims in her chapter to "trace the expansion of the unliturgical world."[28]

Pickstock begins her endeavor by considering the predominant suggestion in modern thought that the material of any discipline can be made available, and even simple, via the application of a properly universal "method." Here she refers in particular to Peter Ramus' reduction of language to diagrammatic definitions—divisions of subjects into their most simple, graspable, and *therefore* "real," elements. For Ramus, "true definition, as opposed to description, was to be as brief as possible, so as to allow the essence of the thing being examined to be made superlatively clear."[29] Of course, this meant that language and definitions ought to be superlatively abstract, or that the possibility of a comprehensive understanding hinged upon the capacity to pull the subject of inquiry out of its complex temporality and to give it an "elemental" representation. The proponent of the "divide and simplify" method (e.g., Ramus) will claim that this new approach does not "distort" but rather "distills" the real into its native simplicity, where it is unburdened by the superfluous additions of scholastic language and the accidental complications of temporal mutability. Yet as Pickstock will argue, the "convenience" of modern epistemological methods "has a sinister aspect, for by adopting the stance of methodizer, the pedagogue obfuscates the confusions of reality, *generating an apparently objective ontology, from a secretly subjective method.*"[30] The "confusions of reality" are obfuscated by deferring to the mind's capacity for schematic clarity, which effectively requires us to say, "the appearance of disorder is *merely* real whilst the method and the mind which deploys it are *supra-real.*"[31] The subjective comforts of a certain epistemological method hereby come to determine ontology.

The identification of language as schematic with the "supra-real" accomplishes for Pickstock the denigration of language as such, which she says is constitutively "praise." Language can be understood as praise in the sense that our linguistically inscribed existence is most fully realized when we are engaged in a *performance* of language that refers to, and so participates in, transcendent being. On the Ramist understanding, by contrast, language is constitutively diagrammatic, which evacuates

28. Ibid., 49. Emphasis added.
29. Ibid., 51.
30. Ibid., 52. Emphasis added.
31. Ibid., 53.

all performative or rhetorical dimensions from the essence of language, recasting these elements as superfluous "ornamentation."[32] This development is ironic, Pickstock notes, for Ramus begins with the intention to move beyond the putative "obscurantism" of Scholasticism "by seeking to assimilate 'common parlance,'" and yet this ultimately results "in a voiceless style."[33] Pickstock suggests that this style is now reflected in the structure of modern language as such, which has become increasingly insulated from the necessity of a living enactment, increasingly comprehensible in its pristine, "textual" form:

> For example, whereas formerly, syntax had been time-bound and aggregative in structure, and punctuation such as colons and commas had functioned to indicate pauses or emphases relating to oral delivery, with the progressive introduction of spatial models, syntax and punctuation now became more abstract and logic-bound.[34]

In such a language, structured to preserve schematic clarity rather than to provoke new performances and non-identical repetitions, we have reached the fulfillment of Phaedrus' sophistic impulse to be *so close* to the factual that one can take it everywhere in an atemporal (and thus, counter-factual) form. This is all to say, in other words, that modern linguistic inscriptions no longer afford human beings the opportunity for a Socratic-type participation in transcendence, because they inscribe all "persons" into an ideal objectivity which is only diminished by its temporal deployment or practice.

If Pickstock's reference to Ramus is meant to capture a historical turn in the direction of a non-liturgical world, Descartes comes to represent for her a significant acceleration in this direction. Pickstock, like many Radical Orthodox thinkers, first singles out Duns Scotus as the key originator of a "univocal ontology" according to which the complexity of being becomes "available and immanent."[35] But she claims that Descartes cements the Scotist move when, in the *Regulae*, he defines being "as that which is clear and distinct, available to absolute and certain intuitions."[36] Descartes' privileging of absolute certainty adds to Ramist

32. Ibid., 55.
33. Ibid.
34. Ibid., 56.
35. Ibid., 63. See also Pickstock, "Duns Scotus."
36. Pickstock, *After Writing*, 63.

thought a more explicit attempt "to demolish" material reality as the different, which is why for Descartes, "the ideal method is produced in solitude."[37] Hereby we enter upon the era of the "object,"[38] as that which can be known because it is *only* written. The Cartesian object is known with the certainty and simplicity of a diagrammatic logical conclusion, worked out in the purity of solitude, and, known as such, this object supremely *is*. Thus we can say that while the Cartesian object purports to be a simplification or reduction of the material to its fundamental elements, by virtue of the criteria of epistemological certainty (utter self-identity and immutability), Cartesian objectivity ultimately abides "within an interior which has no exterior."[39] In other words, despite the best intentions of the Cartesian method (to secure the "reality" of the factual and material against the terrors of time and mutation), for Pickstock Cartesian objects are in fact "arbitrarily related in advance by a conventional system of order and hierarchy, *in such a way that they instantiate a break with the natural order.*"[40]

Obscuring the Subject

An immanentist ontology therefore has the outcome of making the existence of the real dependent upon the subject's capacity for this kind of spatialized objective knowledge, her capacity for imposing a static schema onto a world that is otherwise too temporally/materially complex to be known fully. But this situation, in which the subject "confers existence"[41] in an active gesture of imposition, does not provide the subject with the requisite security against the incipient nihilism of her living. In other words, the subject who is conscious of her gesture in this regard must also dwell in the anxiety provoked by the discovery that the real as objective is but an invention, an inside without a real outside. To know this about one's gesture of security is not really to be "secured" by it, but to come face-to-face with the "void" against which one sought protection. The subject herself, in her very subjective capacity, must therefore be obscured from her own view. Pickstock believes

---

37. Ibid., 60.
38. Ibid., 63.
39. Ibid., 67.
40. Ibid. Emphasis added.
41. Ibid., 70.

that Descartes accomplishes precisely this obfuscation, by "substituting method for memory."[42] That is, Descartes abolishes memory as the material and temporal means of subjective participation in knowledge and elevates a methodical "intuition," which effects the "textualization of the subject" as such.[43] As Pickstock puts it, "memory is crucial for self-continuity whilst allowing for variation, and so its replacement by formal, isomorphic structures transposes the subject's continuity-with-difference into self-identity and permanence, the prime criteria, that is, for the Cartesian object."[44]

The question is, of course, how can the subject ever be convinced of not being herself as a material-temporal person? Pickstock argues that several developments in the trajectory of modern thought and culture serve to enforce and maintain the subject's experience of the real as objective, and eventually make it *impossible* for the person to be anything but an object. She begins with experimental science's extension of the sophistic gesture by providing identically repeatable demonstrations designed to make the *mathesis* historically apparent and so to "confirm" it as the real. Successful experimentation can assuage the subject's anxiety about imposing objectivity upon reality by producing temporal "events" that make reality as schematic actually present to the witness. This is not to say, of course, that experimental science restores the subject as a person capable of "recollecting" and so participating in truth within the flux of time, but rather that experimental science makes it possible to "read" even visible, temporal reality, at least in certain controlled situations, as immediate to a formalistic, schematic "intuition." Successful experimentation thus persuades the subject that there is no distance, no "gap" between reality as apparent, material, and temporal, and reality as timeless and objective, which the subject would need to traverse by some perverse act of self-imposing will. Not just anyone, of course, could serve as a witness to this production of evidence of the transcendental writtenness of the real, but only those "qualified" to read reality as fundamentally objective. In the scientific age, therefore, a select group of "virtuosi" comes to confirm and perpetuate a construal of reality as objective, which serves to obfuscate the fact that such a construal is an expression of a human power defiant of its own anxious situation within

42. Ibid.
43. Ibid.
44. Ibid., 71.

temporality. As Pickstock explains, experimental science's virtuosic city "involved a disguised projection of human power which operated not according to a consensus about its values and implications but according to an unquestioned advancement of knowledge in the service of the promotion of hidden sovereignty."[45]

According to Pickstock, however, the parties to this gesture of human power eventually required another and stronger distraction from their anxiety that objective reality remained a subjective imposition—an anxiety provoked by the fact that a reflective, temporally existing person can never achieve the monadic presence-to-self that an atemporal object can. Therefore a self-forgetting more secure than that offered by experimental science was in order. Pickstock suggests that this further requirement was fulfilled by the theatricality of baroque society. This is a surprising claim at first, since the ornate excesses of baroque culture would seem "to occlude the calm units of Ramist or Cartesian cartographies."[46] But in spite of this ostensibly differentiating excess, "it was the *universality* of the apparent disorder, its systematic diffusion, which betray its chaos as strategic, studied, and fully contained."[47] In other words, the theatricality of baroque cultural operations, like the rhetorical flourish of its architecture, are betrayed in their pretensions to universality as clumsy mythological justifications of human power deployed as the relentless objectification of reality. That is, because the entirety of the baroque polis was encompassed within the king's sphere of influence, no subjective action could fall outside the purview of his power; his presence could be fabricated everywhere as a "bedazzling" force, a theatrical display into which subjects were incorporated, not as actors but as dumbfounded objects. Pickstock argues that this turn of baroque pageantry back to a more ornate style of writing—albeit now empty of "rhetoric" in the true sense of referring beyond itself—was inevitable; for "the more one surrenders the localism and traditionalism of substantive content for the universality of a formalist method, the more this method is inevitably lacking and requires supplementation by mythology."[48] In other words, the more one adheres to a notion of

---

45. Ibid., 81.
46. Ibid., 83.
47. Ibid.
48. Ibid., 88.

reality as the written, the more one comes up against the human subject's resilience in the face of such reductions to self-identity and immediacy."[49]

Modern Language as Final Solution

Up to this point, the rhetorical efforts of the sophistic preference for writing and the consequent turn to spatialization are still engaged in battle with the subject understood as a *way* of living, a mode of temporal enactment, and not an object. In other words, such efforts of spatializing reason are negative acknowledgements of the subject's reflective capacity, and of the possibility that the subject might be related to the "real" by virtue of a mediation that is erotic and temporal rather than epistemological and spatial. The former relation engenders a living that derives from the constant repetition of its recollecting pursuit of the good in time, rather than from an epistemologically derived "certainty" about the subject's location within the space delineated by a schematic method. But the development of modern language brings us to another, more sinister situation, in which this rhetorical battle is finally won by sophistic reason. Pickstock makes this claim via an exposure of the noun-centric nature of modern language. She argues that the modern prioritization of the noun is a linguistic equivalent to the development in the nineteenth century of arts like photography, which "seemed to actualize a summoning of reality distilled from the flux of time, as a spatial given."[50] Just as photography makes "being" available to a gaze that seeks an atemporally static and epistemologically certain reality, so too does modern language render reality as a series of nouns devoid of persons as temporal actors. Pickstock offers a particular example of this process of "nominalization," which renders a real, enacted situation or event as a given, timeless "thing": "the nominalization 'allegation' is a condensed transformational equivalent of the clausal 'X has alleged against Y that Y has done A,' and so . . . is ideally suited to discourse which places a premium on the transference of information in as economical a way as possible."[51] The key aspect of nominalization is therefore that it "elides

---

49. We might note that this suggested re-mythologization of a spatialized reality is in keeping with John Milbank's suggestion in *Theology and Social Theory* that secular reason is *more* in need of a dubious metaphysical justification than are forms of religious reason. See Milbank, *Theology and Social Theory*, 136.

50. Pickstock, *After Writing*, 89.

51. Ibid., 93.

Language and the Fear of Death   73

grammatical voice."[52] Whereas previously language (as fundamentally oral, for Socrates) made the life of the human actor possible, in the modern period it has become something by which we "name" reality as a thing. Our language thus removes "the personal *from itself*,"[53] precluding language from being the medium of true living.

It seems important to note, however, that the practice of photography does not achieve the inexorable objectification of reality, which is only really accomplished through a particular relationship of the photographer or the viewer to the "objects" of this art. That is to say, the objectification of reality that occurs in conjunction with the practice of photography is not really a possibility of the "thing" called photography (this would be a wholly nominalizing description), but of the subject who is related to photography and to photographs in a particular way. Various "ways" of being related are possible in relation to the photograph, such that "salvation" from the spatialization that photography seems to produce does not require the elimination of the art of photography so much as a turn in the subject—a turn that makes a genuinely erotic "seeing" possible in relation to photography, beyond the merely auto-erotic gaze of objective possession. And surely the same thing might be said about modern language—that the objectification of reality it seems to indicate is only really significant, in a theological sense, in reference to the individual human subject's comportment to that reality, which language alone, as a "thing," cannot determine. But this, strangely, is what Pickstock will not allow. Her fidelity to the tenet of post-linguistic-turn philosophy that "there is after all nothing outside language"[54] leads her to suggest that the possibilities for subjectivity are inextricable from the determinations of the particular linguistic "construal" of reality in which the subject finds himself. Modern nominalization's rendering of a reality devoid of living persons effects "asyndeton," or the peculiar voice of modern language, by which the subject is determined as "superficially active and fundamentally passive."[55] When we exist in a language characterized by "asyndeton," in other words, the result is that "when we *think* we speak or act with all the contingency of an open and temporal

52. Ibid.
53. Ibid., 95.
54. Ibid., 90.
55. Ibid., 100.

event, *that contingency is choreographed in advance*,"[56] which implies that our very subjective living is inexorably inscribed as a "thing" within a spatial, pre-given order.

The "Linguistic Turn"

The central implication of this claim, to which I have alluded already, is that as a result of his objective situation, the modern subject is excluded from the possibility of a truly spiritual life, enacted in time. Sin becomes a "necessity," not by virtue of existential but of historical/philosophical determinations. Whereas a more existential account of sin would suggest that one's exclusion from spiritual living is always *one's own*, and that life in the Spirit is not easier or more difficult in any particular era—for it is never *either* straightforward *or* impossible to live the truth, as Jesus seems to indicate in the Gospels—Pickstock's suggestion is that such life is indeed impossible within "modern syntax," and by extension that it becomes more straightforward, less "remote of access," once the possibility of persuasion into a theological syntax becomes apparent. Thus Pickstock's manner of fidelity to the claim that "there is nothing outside language" leads her to identify each human subject with his contextual syntax, as if there were an utterly direct relationship between the subject and language. By extension, the subject's redemption from a "bad" context coincides with a new construal of that subject. The "truth" of the linguistic turn which theology hereby seizes upon is that rhetoric is not to be eschewed for its directness in bringing about any transition between competing "grammars." And hence theological rhetoric, in its unique capacity to effect the persuasion of subjects into a "liturgical" grammar, is elevated to a quasi-redemptive status.

It must be true, of course, that Christian theology, which understands everything to have been created in and through God's "Word," finds the linguistic turn accommodating in certain respects. And it seems to me that Pickstock is fundamentally correct to suggest that the Christian *logos* is not offered as an atemporally discernible script, and instead that creation is *spoken* into being by God's very breathing or "spiriting" of his Word. The real is "in" this Word as the spoken, the lived, and the breathed. And thus I agree with Pickstock that the sophistic preference for the written, traceable up to the modern emphasis on

---

56. Ibid. Emphasis added.

method, is representative not of the possibility of life in the Word, but of a human "gesture of security" against the dangers to self-possession posed by a genuine life-in-truth. We know this life poses dangers for us because Christianity can only refer to it by pointing to Jesus, who truly *lives* because he would rather die than become reified as something written. For example, one might consider the situation described in Matt 16:21–23, in which Peter would like to protect Jesus from the danger of this living, would like to cling to him perhaps in the manner in which Phaedrus clings to Lysias' written speech, and Jesus rebukes him forcefully. This Word apparently cannot be had directly, because the preference for directness is the expression of a subjective decision to deal with the anxiety provoked by life's passing via an appeal to the security of objective self-possession. To say that this existential danger looms largest in the modern context is to suggest that our identities in modernity have become inexorably written. By extension, such a claim objectifies sin *as* a particular language, which leaves theology able to offer only an alternative writing, not really a life "after writing." If life is after writing, in a Word that moves in the way of the Spirit, then no particular written context, no particularly bad or objectifying syntax, can make the prospect of true life more "remote of access," as is Pickstock's suggestion. Rather, in every situation, there must remain the possibility of being "spoken" into being, of being brought to life by the breathed Word of God. And this ultimately implies that "theology," as a particular construal of the real, can never bring us closer to this possibility in and of itself.

No situation is then an urgent one "for theology," if urgency pertains to living, as Christian urgency does. No theological construal of reality or of language can bridge for me the gap between death and resurrection, between the objective dispossession implied in a surrender to life as a *way* and not a *thing*, and the power of that same life, as life *in the Spirit*. Only faith can bridge it, which is to say, only a way of living that continually wrestles with doubt and overcomes it, not by addressing and "resolving" it, but by banishing it.[57] Thus I suggest that the best insights of Radical Orthodoxy imply that theology must *not* pretend to be a direct form of communication. Instead it must remain a living response to a Word whose urgency intends precisely to make the sinful and fearful human being into a living person, which means to strip him of every

57. See Kierkegaard, *Philosophical Fragments/Johannes Climacus*, 83ff.

possible self-identification, and of the security of every grammar, such that he might be born of love, not theology. We shall have occasion to return to these suggestions in chapters below, but for now let us move to consider how Radical Orthodoxy's rejection of "postmodern necrophilia" is related to its rejection of any "dialectical" or indirect form of theological communication.

Necrophilia

The Postmodern Rejection of Capital

In her chapter entitled "Signs of Death," Pickstock begins by making reference to the continuation of the sophistic preference for writing in the modern prioritization of epistemology as a history of "necrophobia." This description accords well with her claim that the impulse to spatialize the real is a way of dealing with the uncertainties intrinsic to temporal existence. We can see how the possibility of having a direct relation to a truth secure from the contingencies of temporal life would appeal especially to a subject whose greatest fear is his own passing. It is fear of death, in other words, that most obviously translates to a love of truth that does not die because it does not live in time. But Pickstock wants to see this necrophobia through to its self-consistent and finally rhetorically repulsive end in postmodernism; and for her this means demonstrating that "lurking beneath the surface of necrophobia, is a much more fundamental *necrophilia*."[58] While Pickstock maintains her critical focus on Derrida here, we shall see that ultimately Heidegger is for her the real instigator of postmodernism's more explicit captivation by death.

Pickstock begins by drawing a connection between the modern sophistic gesture and the rise of capitalism. Recall that the modern turn to a wholly nominal language affords the subject an "existence" only via its inscription in a series of nouns. The person becomes a noun among nouns, secured—and precluded—from the dangers of a genuine, enacted personhood. The subject's anxiety about his death is therefore resolved insofar as he comes to be a possessing and self-possessed thing. But of course, real material "things" do not last in the way that a spatialized, atemporal rendering of reality suggests they do, which explains the modern turn to capitalism's production of novel objects always

---

58. Pickstock, *After Writing*, 103.

ready to be consumed as the old ones pass away.⁵⁹ The capitalist desire for accumulation of goods and property, Pickstock explains, is "driven by an anxiety to cancel lack and to retain presence through identical repetition."⁶⁰ For Pickstock this desire to possess life as a timeless "thing" is based on a confusion about life itself, for it "mistakes the passing away *which is life* for sheer deletion, so effecting a pseudo-eternity of mere spatial permanence."⁶¹ In that such a confusion accomplishes its own exclusion from such genuine passing, Pickstock argues that the modern, "phobic" determination of ontology by epistemology is in fact "secretly doomed to necrophilia, love of what has to die, can only die."⁶² Capitalism trades on this unconscious love of death by offering ever more (though less permanent) objects of "life" to subjects who so believe they love life that they will consume every objective appearance of it.⁶³ The fundamental problem that modern thought runs up against, in other words, and which culminates in capitalism, is the futility of its wager of "death as opposite and unnatural to life."⁶⁴ The result of this wager is that we are incited to give up on the possibility of any "living-with-death," and encouraged instead to love the destruction of that living.⁶⁵

Postmodern thought accomplishes for Pickstock the unmasking of this necrophobia, insofar as it rejects consumerist anxiety about mutability in the name of a more consistent, and we might say, "post-phobic" *love* of the passing. While this seems to make postmodernism more amenable to genuine temporal living as Pickstock describes it, she seeks to demonstrate that postmodernism's love is still for the destruction of true life, or that in postmodern thought there are "unacknowledged

---

59. William Cavanaugh has recently explored the existential function of capitalism in his *Being Consumed*, esp. 33–58.

60. Pickstock, *After Writing*, 104.

61. Ibid.

62. Ibid.

63. Ibid., 105.

64. Ibid. We might note again that this entrenched opposition between death and life is very much in line with Milbank's characterization of the "boundary" between transcendence and immanence on which all secular reason rests. Just as for Milbank this metaphysically presupposed boundary is what precludes a true *Sittlichkeit*, so too for Pickstock the opposition death/life renders impossible any temporal living that might at the same time share in the transcendent good.

65. See also Rowan Williams' short but profound book, *Writing in the Dust*.

lapses into identical repetition."⁶⁶ Pickstock begins with Derrida, who she claims makes the following argument: "(1) life is presence-to-self; (2) there is no presence-to-self; (3) there is only exteriority which is the opposite of presence-to-self; (4) therefore there 'is' only death."⁶⁷ This figures as a critique of the modern pretension to objectification because it suggests that the "signs" that are meant to represent a spatialized real are in effect empty, even at the very moment when they presume to "signify." The *actual presence* of the self-identical and atemporal "being" determined by the criteria of modern epistemology is always and inevitably *postponed* in the very instant of its "presentation" by the sign. All signs are thus signs "of death." With reference to the modern mobilization of capitalism, then, the Derridean argument would effectively say that one should not credit produced commodities with the "presence" they promise in the first place, such that one will no longer be inclined to replace them the moment they prove inadequate to that presence—i.e., the moment they begin to pass away. For Pickstock's Derrida, that is, there "is" only death because there "are" only *signs*.

On the one hand, and to repeat what I already implied, this suggests a greater fidelity to the temporal "life" Pickstock is concerned about. That is, Derrida's fidelity to writing embraces the "emptiness" of the sign in a way that suggests its inescapable surrender of identity to the flux of temporality. For Pickstock, however, Derrida's refusal to equivocate on the "deathliness" of the sign indicates that for him the opposition between life and death remains intact, which must finally exclude him from theology's sympathy. The precise problem here is that Derrida "does not *question* whether life is to be correlated with monadic presence-to-self . . . nor even whether death really *is* a stage which one can never exceed."⁶⁸ For Derrida, in other words, there remains an "abyssal" distance between self-present "life" and the temporal passing of the sign. The sign *as such* is made to be inadequate to true life, irrespective of the varying qualities, the actual "differences," of particular signs. So Derrida's exposure of the deathliness of the modern/capitalist pursuit of self-presence in "objects" of consumption goes too far, in that it will not allow that the inescapable passing of temporality might still provide occasions of transcendence; it will not allow "that dying in time might lead

66. Pickstock, *After Writing*, 106.
67. Ibid., 107.
68. Ibid.. Emphasis added.

not to the abyss but to a greater living towards eternity."[69] For Pickstock, therefore, the abyssal distance between being's presence-to-self and the emptiness of the temporal sign, the distance articulated by what Derrida calls *différance*, results from a "structural" incompatibility of presence with temporality, rather than from a particularly abysmal way of living. Thus there are for Pickstock's Derrida no comportments to signs which may be better attuned to life than others, because all signs are "abyssally" equidistant from life; and this for Pickstock indicates Derrida's ultimate complicity in the modern, sophistic gesture of security against true living.

Recall that for the modern prioritization of epistemology, what was "real" was whatever could be known apart from its temporalization—whatever could be spatialized in writing. The confirmation of such objects of knowledge would occur temporally via the experimental production of "events" that were identically repeatable, and thus not subject to time *as flux*. A more genuine living, which might reconcile life with the apparent death of time's passing, occurs for Pickstock in the practice of, and surrender to, *non-identical* repetition. Derrida's critical capitulation to the necrophobia/philia of modernity is therefore his inability to conceive of a temporality that does not reduce every momentary instantiation to the same measure. In other words, if every sign is *equally* "deathly," and every relation to being as articulated in time is in the same measure removed from being as life, then temporality is not genuine flux, but "univocal" repetition, the incessant arrival of the same "formal-because-empty-identity."[70]

It may be helpful to point out again that this reading is closely related to Milbank's suggestion that postmodern historicism is not adequately "historicist." Just as Milbank will say that Heidegger's advocacy of "indifference" to all particular historical forms (in virtue of their equally "concealing" relationships to being) really expresses his fidelity

---

69. Ibid.

70. Ibid. What Pickstock herself does not "question" here is whether the abyss between life and its temporal signification is due to the difficulty of achieving a direct knowledge-relation to being in virtue of any "sign." In other words, she will only allow *différance*, Derrida's term for the undecidable process of ontological differentiation, to be read as a feature of an ontology in which being is schematically or structurally separated from the temporal sign—that is, in which *différance* indicates a distance that is established *a priori*, without any regard for different *ways of being*. I think it would be misleading to say that hers is a necessary reading in this regard.

to the metaphysical *a priori* of arbitrary ontological difference, so too Pickstock suggests that Derrida's discovery of the sign's inexorable emptiness finally precludes him from advancing beyond modernity's spatialized ontology. For in the end, "the claim that there can be only death is identical with the claim that there can be only identical repetition."[71] This is finally how Derrida's love of the different, of the putative "flux" of that which is instituted by *différance*, is for Pickstock brought back around to Phaedrus' and modernity's sophistic love of the written as atemporal and spatialized—a love of the death of life as genuine *differing*, or as non-identical temporal articulation. And thus here most explicitly modernity's fear of death is exposed as a more fundamental "necrophilia."

Heidegger on Death

As it turns out, for Pickstock as for Milbank, Heidegger ultimately has much to do with postmodern thought's theological bankruptcy. This becomes clear as Pickstock pursues the "morbid ethics" of Derrida's predecessors—Levinas and Heidegger—ethics which suggest that to be with the other, to give oneself to the other, is to give "death." As she writes of Levinas, "in establishing ethical responsibility for the other even to the point of *one's own* death... Levinas must assume that one's death is *one's own*, in order for it to be so offered."[72] This is because what is available to the "postmodern" thinking of identity is not, as it is for Pickstock, the possibility of achieving temporal consistency via the enactment of "non-identical repetition." Instead, given the abyssal distance between temporal flux and self-present being—which for Derrida implies the inexorable "deathliness" of my very temporal self, and for Levinas the scarcely traversable distance between my "political" and my "ethical" identities—my true "self" can only name the utter death of the possibility of any temporal selfhood. In the view of such an ethic, I *am* the death of myself, which to Pickstock implies a blatant refusal to *live* a selfhood that is given to me in time, and which I cannot own. Postmodernism would rather have us own ourselves as the death of our true living, than allow for a surrender to a continuously donated selfhood. And this, Pickstock suggests, is rather explicit in Heidegger:

---

71. Ibid., 108.
72. Ibid., 111.

Heidegger wrote that by facing up to one's own death, "one is liberated from one's lostness in those possibilities which may accidentally thrust themselves upon me," thus seeming to prioritize an *essence* of ourselves, according to a metaphysical distinction between substance and accident. It would also seem, from this quotation, that being resolute in the face of death is not a *disinterested* stance, as Heidegger claims, but rather a defiant strategy of security against the arrival of the unknown.[73]

In other words, on Pickstock's reading of Heidegger, that my death is distinctly *my own* implies that I am "essentially" my death, that the death of myself is "the known" par excellence, the paradoxically self-present tranquility by which I can secure myself against the flux of time's passing. On this understanding, life for Heidegger becomes identical with the *death of living*, which is to imply that Heidegger's "necrophiliac urge" is no advance, but "just a cover for an all too modern necrophobic desire to get to death before it gets to you."[74]

Here I propose to offer a brief response to this reading,[75] which will parallel and perhaps further clarify my misgivings about Milbank's take on Heidegger above. In fact, for Heidegger an authentic "facing up" to one's death never implies an objectifying essentialism of the human subject, as Pickstock claims. Rather it indicates the possibility of a *way of living* that is antithetical to any "gesture of security." Death is "essential" to Dasein not because it frees Dasein from the "accidents" thrust upon it by the temporal, but because a relation to what Heidegger calls the "existential conception" of death actually makes Dasein possible as what it "is." And on this score, Dasein is *not* fundamentally a non-existing object in an atemporal, spatialized schema (i.e., "death"), but is precisely "the entity which *exists*."[76] Heidegger expands on what he means by an authentic Being-towards-death by suggesting that death as Dasein's "ownmost" possibility effects "a freedom which has been released from the illusions of the 'they,'"[77] by which he means a freedom from an untruthful way of living, a freedom "essential" to Dasein as the possibility of existing *in truth*. This is not the freedom of tranquil possession of unchanging "at-

---

73. Ibid., 111.
74. Ibid.
75. See also my essay, "Heidegger's Paul and Radical Orthodoxy."
76. Heidegger, *Being and Time*, 286.
77. Ibid., 311.

tributes," but a freedom from all objectifying identifications with timeless attributes. Facing up to death therefore does not mean becoming an atemporal "essence," but becoming *essentially* Dasein, essentially *existing* and therefore "anxious"[78] rather than tranquil.

According to *Being and Time*, in the everyday, public language of the "they," death is made into an event that happens, but is prevented from becoming a possibility that actually belongs *to me* as an entity that exists: "in Dasein's public way of interpreting, it is said that 'one dies,' because everyone else and oneself can talk himself into saying that 'in no case is it I myself,' for this 'one' is the '*nobody*.'"[79] This way of alienating myself from the possibility of *my own death*, for which "no one can be my representative,"[80] is the "consoling solicitude" intrinsic to the everyday understanding of existence. If only you buy into this, says the "they," you shall have security against the morbid notion that dying is somehow definitive of your "ownmost potentiality-for-Being," or that true living could mean existing in the anxiety provoked by the "non-relational" character of death's impendence, existentially understood. No, in the language of the "they," all genuine "life" is utterly free from the challenge of non-relational possibilities; to live the public life is to live only toward possibilities that are utterly relatable, "actualizable" in the sense of coming under my control. To live in this everyday manner is to be "tranquilized" in one's potentiality-for-Being, to be related only to possibilities of spatialized security, insulated from the demand upon Dasein to live. And thus it is "a matter of public acceptance that 'thinking about death' is a cowardly fear, a sign of insecurity on the part of Dasein, and a somber way of fleeing from the world. *The 'they' does not permit us the courage for anxiety in the face of death*."[81] What Heidegger opposes, therefore, is just what Pickstock calls the sophistic "gesture of security" against the void, a gesture fundamentally opposed to the anxiety that is "essential" to Dasein insofar as Dasein is not essentially an atemporally secure "thing," but the "non-relational potentiality-for-Being."[82] "The 'they' concerns itself with transforming this anxiety into fear in

78. Ibid.
79. Ibid., 297.
80. Ibid.
81. Ibid., 298. Heidegger's emphasis.
82. Ibid.

the face of an oncoming event,"[83] which means that to be "freed" from the illusions of the "they" is to be released from the "falling" tendency to insulate life from all anxious non-relational possibilities, or from all uncertainty. This falling seeks to protect life from the intrusion of that non-relationality which is intrinsic to Dasein's existence in the temporal.

Clearly then, Pickstock's suggestion that Heidegger's advocacy of facing up to death as *one's own* essentializes the subject in an atemporal tranquility is easily refuted by a more careful reading of *Being and Time*. But Pickstock might respond, as Milbank does, that if the "falling" that characterizes everydayness is somehow *structurally* necessary, in virtue of the utter questionability of Being's temporal deployment, then we might still say that for Heidegger Dasein's "ownmost" potentiality is somehow "spatially" precluded from effecting a reconciliation of life and death. In other words, if Heidegger is suggesting that the structure of temporality as such necessitates an ontological "fall" from Being's purity, then freedom from inauthenticity must require a structural and ultimately death-denying resolution, rather than an existential, living one. But in response to Milbank's suggestion to this effect, we have seen that for Heidegger, the "phenomenon of falling" is not in fact the inevitable correlate of a metaphysical *a priori*, but the documentation of "an *existential mode* of Being-in-the-world."[84] It should not be surprising, then, that in Heidegger's analysis of death we find the same thing—namely, that the question of "authenticity" is always a question about ways of living, which may be mutually exclusive, but in terms of "existential" rather than "metaphysical" structures. Thus it is not because of the putative deathliness of the temporal, but because of the temptation of the public "gesture," that inauthenticity is opposed to Dasein's *essential* possibility: "When Dasein, tranquilized, and 'understanding' everything, thus compares itself with everything, it drifts along towards an alienation in which its ownmost potentiality-for-Being is hidden from it."[85]

Facing up to one's death therefore does not mark salvation from temporality as the sphere of the empty sign, but a breaking open of the sort of spatialized "understanding" that prevents genuine living. Anxiety is provoked by facing up to one's death because here it is seen that what is essential to Dasein is its potentiality-for-Being, or the call to live without

83. Ibid.
84. Ibid., 221. Heidegger's emphasis.
85. Ibid., 222.

any definite security in regard to its possibilities, without an identity defined in any written schema. To face up to one's death for Heidegger means to be dispossessed of oneself as "written" in the public language of the "they." And therefore it does *not* mean, as Radical Orthodoxy is wont to claim, that only the tranquility of "death" is life, because temporal living is inevitably empty. Rather, as Heidegger claims in a sentence that for some reason does not warrant either Pickstock's or Milbank's attention, "inauthenticity characterizes a kind of Being into which Dasein can divert itself and has for the most part always diverted itself; *but Dasein does not necessarily and constantly have to divert itself into this kind of Being.*"[86] Facing up to one's death does not mean coming to possess yourself such that temporal passing cannot rob you of identity; rather it means facing up to your potentiality for living without controlling how your possibilities will be actualized, your capacity to live all of your relations "non-relationally." This is precisely how, in facing up to death, one comes face-to-face with one's "essence" and "totality"—not as an object, but *as the possibility of living*. This "essence" of Dasein must be lived (like Socrates) and not owned (like Phaedrus) because Dasein is the entity that *exists*, the entity that lives its relations by "anticipating" rather than "actualizing" them in idle talk. Thus, "anticipation turns out to be the possibility of understanding one's *ownmost* and uttermost potentiality-for-Being—that is to say, the possibility of *authentic existence*,"[87] not of tranquil security.

Pickstock's difficulty with the postmodern—and with Heidegger and Derrida in particular—indicates Radical Orthodoxy's rejection of dialectical communication more tellingly than does Milbank's critique of MacIntyre, because the "postmodern" construal of authenticity is *more* indirect than is MacIntyre's appeal to "rational adjudication." To put this differently, the "dialectical" in Heidegger and Derrida approaches something much closer to the life-as-enactment that Radical Orthodoxy feels is available through one's inscription in a "theological narrative" than does MacIntyre's "antique" dialectics. Postmodernism's resistance to truth as objective, and consequently not *lived*, ought to resonate with a theology that claims that the true "form of life" is not an objective form, but a *practice* of *Sittlichkeit*. That Radical Orthodoxy characteristically rejects this sort of dialectical thinking as a capitulation to the

---

86. Ibid., 303. Emphasis added.
87. Ibid., 307.

"structural" presupposition of secular reason is problematic in the sense I have already mentioned, namely in the sense that it may leave room only for a structural, and not an existential, alternative—a possibility we shall need to pursue further below. For now let us turn our attention to David Bentley Hart's clarification of rhetorical theology's opposition to the dialectical.

Hart and Levinas on Time and Infinity

Pagans and Gnostics

Radical Orthodox theology's characteristic dismissal of dialectics is perhaps nowhere more clearly articulated than in David Bentley Hart's book, *The Beauty of the Infinite*, and particularly in his polemical reading of Emmanuel Levinas. In *The Beauty of the Infinite*, Hart develops a critique of modern and postmodern thought much along the lines of Milbank's exposure of secular reason's "nihilism," and uses that critique to emphasize theology's rhetorical task in its present context. And like Pickstock, Hart believes that modernity is characterized by its insistence upon the ontological priority of abstract, epistemologically certain and pristine "presence." This primal being is thus dialectically opposed to the conditions of change, passing, and difference in which we "actually live." As a proponent of a theological aesthetics, Hart cannot tolerate such an abstract conception of being, for it effectively sunders "that radiant unity wherein the good, the true, and the beautiful coincided," and wherein God's transcendence could be understood as a ubiquitous immanent irruption, rather than an irrevocable "absence."[88] Also like Pickstock, Hart believes that postmodernity effects a mere reversal of this prioritization, whereby no reunion of the good with the beautiful, of the eternally true with the passing and differing, can be brought into view: "If metaphysics is the regime of immutability, presence, and interiority, the [postmodern] discourse of the unrepresentable 'corrects' this by insisting upon the 'priority' of change, absence, and exteriority."[89] The effect of this reversal, initiated for Hart by Nietzsche, is postmodernism's emphasis upon becoming rather than being. But in order to ensure that its emphasis does not remain a Hegelian subjugation of genuine flux to a metaphysically prior "logic" of being, postmodernism is buttressed, especially for those

---

88. Hart, *Beauty of the Infinite*, 44.
89. Ibid., 52.

like Gilles Deleuze, with a "myth of affirmation whose only practical expression is a war against representation,"[90] which is to say, a war against the possibility of a "resurrected" sign.[91] Thus, speaking again in terms of language, we can say that the postmodern reversal effectively liberates the temporal for an utterly "rhetorical" existence, freed of its representational slavery to any schematized and pristine "being."

One might think that here again "the postmodern" comes to coincide with all emphatically post-linguistic-turn theology. But once again for Hart, its supposed advance remains nihilistic and takes on a particular hostility to the Christian rhetoric he holds dear. For on the Nietzschean account, "every rhetoric is free to unfold itself, but it must also somehow acknowledge that it is *necessarily violent* by virtue of its rhetoricity; and if it is a rhetoric of peace, it is doubly violent for dissembling its warlike intentions."[92] This is so because a "rhetoric of peace," as both Hart and Radical Orthodoxy would construe Christian rhetoric, aims to effect *Sittlichkeit* as the genuine reconciliation of the finite and the infinite, or in other words to "persuade" human beings (though not "experimentally," as is modernity's bent) of the possible unity of the eternal and the temporal. Indeed, its aim is to "resurrect the sign" by figuring that beauty which, while appearing immanently, nonetheless becomes the site of what Hans Urs von Balthasar calls "the unity of the transcendentals."[93] Thus theology's rhetoric, we might say, offers both a critique of the modern pristination of being as abstract presence, and at the same time a counter to the postmodern assumption that the temporal and the changing "figure" nothing (but death). Hart suggests that Christian rhetoric exceeds the problematic signification of a monadic presence in virtue of its uniquely Trinitarian referent, whose "essence" is never, even at the "origin," one of static self-presence, but rather of infinite, "ex-ousiac" self-deployment in love.[94] The persuasion of this rhetoric therefore does not depend upon the production of stable representatives of abstract, spatialized "being" (recall Pickstock's characterization of capitalism), but upon its capacity to deploy difference

---

90. Ibid., 64. See Deleuze, *Difference and Repetition*.

91. See Pickstock, *After Writing*, 253ff.

92. Hart, *Beauty of the Infinite*, 64. Emphasis added.

93. See Balthasar, *The Glory of the Lord: A Theological Aesthetics*, vol. 1, *Seeing the Form*, 17ff.

94. See Hart, *Beauty of the Infinite*, esp. 155ff.

according to the measure of divine movement, a movement of love and aesthetic delight. This difference of delight is the movement by which the sign's emptiness-in-itself is made, not merely "adequate," but exceedingly full; and thus Christian rhetoric becomes the language in which a true *Sittlichkeit* is possible.

When, instead, liberation of the temporal from its slavery to identical representation means that no difference can any longer be "reconciled," even by the measure of *caritas*, then a peculiarly anti-Christian ethos is "shaped and sustained," an ethos Hart calls "pagan exuberance tempered by gnostic detachment."[95] It should not be surprising that Hart too names Heidegger as the one who ensures the inexorably violent, anti-ethical nature of postmodern rhetorical "exuberance": "one must credit Heidegger," Hart suggests, with having recovered "from the buried ruins of antique philosophy . . . a truly sacrificial ontology."[96] In other words, what is for Heidegger the utter questionability of being's temporalization is interpreted by Hart to imply that "for being to be in beings, for it to be manifest, it must be forced (or 'nihilated,' or 'destroyed') into the limits of the ontic, its power must be wrested into the juncture as definite and limited forms of wavering perdurance."[97] We have seen above, however, that for Heidegger "death" is Dasein's ownmost possibility precisely insofar as the existential conception of death utterly unhinges the "thingness" of Dasein, shattering Dasein's reification in "idle talk." In Heidegger, that is, the existential question of Dasein's relationship to "life"—as either "tranquilization" or "anxiety" in relation to possibility— is always at the center of any discussion of the "destruction" of being. But for Hart, quite like Pickstock, the "limited forms" of thingness are a structural necessity of temporalization rather than the result of a tranquilizing existential comportment, which means that for him "death" in Heidegger represents Dasein's ownmost *impossibility*, the impossibility of becoming an entity that exists, *in time* and among "things."

It is in this fashion that Hart argues that postmodernism's "exuberant" refusal of a reconciling rhetoric is based on its accurate derivation of a sacrificial ontology from Heidegger. The "ethical" corollary of any such ontology can only generate a kind of "gnostic detachment," which Hart believes is most debased in its Levinasian form. In Levinas's work,

95. Ibid., 91.
96. Ibid., 225.
97. Ibid., 225-26.

precisely at the point of its "commendable" effort to secure the Other, the infinite subject of the moral command, from the totalizing machinations of philosophical categories, Hart suggests that this Other is actually prohibited from being anything at all: "such is the severity of [Levinas's] logic that the other—to remain truly other—cannot in any way actually *appear*."[98] To put it differently, Levinas so wants to save the Other from being present to a gaze that can only "represent" its objects upon the horizon of being that he goes beyond a critique of ontology to a rejection of being itself "as simple elemental strife."[99] For Hart, as we have seen, any "ethics" that divorces the good from all that appears effectively enjoins us to forgo the finite, visible[100] site of infinite being, which is why for him Levinas's suggestion that "'relation' with the Other is impossible within the economy of representation or according to the dynamism of *natural* desire or delight" is explicitly indicative of nihilism.[101] Moreover, any "God" that could be allied with an ethical "good" that is so beyond the realm of our living must be utterly beyond *us*, too, in what Hart takes to be the heterodox culmination of postmodern ethics: "Like the god of the Gnostics . . . Levinas's God never meets us within the scope afforded by our own being or nature."[102]

But again, as with Heidegger, in whose work we saw that death is not the "sacrifice" of existence, but instead shatters what we thought about existing previously and calls us to authentic living, we must ask whether Levinas is possibly provoking us to a radical re-thinking of what we presume to be "our own being or nature." Hart refuses to allow the possibility of such a reading—I think we can say, because of his own "structural" fidelities:

> Admittedly, Levinas's ethics is, in part, an attempt to escape the sacrificial delirium of natural or "pagan" sacrality, but, in that he can imagine no (sacramental) way of return to the world, his own

---

98. Ibid., 77.
99. Ibid., 83.
100. Here one thinks of a connection with the position of Frederick Christian Bauerschmidt, who eschews Karl Rahner's ostensible "ironic stance toward the contingent particularities of Christian story and practice" in favor of Hans Urs von Balthasar's aesthetic, in which Balthasar "seeks the unrepresentable mystery of God not through abstraction from particular categorically apprehended forms, but precisely *in* those forms." See Bauerschmidt, "Theological Sublime," 208.
101. Hart, *Beauty of the Infinite*, 78. Emphasis added.
102. Ibid., 79.

sacrifice (of being, of nature) is no less awful . . . [I]n denying this continuity and indeed replacing it with an opposition, he can offer merely his ghastly world-renunciation.[103]

At this point we should start to wonder whether the construal of Levinas that is offered here, in which he comes across as a relentless proponent of what Hart calls the "gnostic detachment" side of postmodernism's ethos, is not itself unnecessarily shrill. That is, if Hart has so structural a reading of the "sacrificial delirium" of the postmodernism ostensibly derived from Heidegger, can we expect that his rejection of postmodern ethics would be based on anything more than a caricature?

Ethics as an "Optics"

On a more careful reading of Levinas's ethics, especially in *Totality and Infinity*, one discovers that his justification of an unconditionally moral human posture does not in fact depend upon a rejection of being itself, but rather on a way of seeing and living that does not capitulate to the "evidence" of any totalizing vision. Indeed, from the very beginning, Levinas is emphatically concerned with questioning the ontological priority of violence, in a manner that resonates with Hart's concerns about postmodernism. Thus the fundamental question for Levinas is whether or not "the true" is best described as "the permanent possibility of war."[104] Morality's presumptuously "unconditional" demands would have no place in a world conditioned as war, a world that would demand instead the art of calculating one's way to victory. Levinas does not say that being *is* war, but suggests that it appears so to philosophical vision because philosophy characteristically casts the world as "an objective order from which there is no escape."[105] All individuals, all persons supposedly independent in their identities, appear to philosophical thought as mere objects in relation to others, "bearers of forces unbeknown to themselves."[106] If morality concerns the unconditional demands of really independent—that is, *transcendent*—persons, then its very meaning requires that it be possible to restore to persons objectified by philosophy

---

103. Ibid., 83.
104. Levinas, *Totality and Infinity*, 21.
105. Ibid.
106. Ibid.

"their lost identity."[107] In other words, if morality is not to be derisory (mere "gnostic detachment"), then there must be a real, true peace that does not issue from war[108]—this Levinas calls "eschatological" peace. As he puts it, "eschatology institutes a relation with being *beyond the totality or beyond history*."[109] What is at issue here, I want to emphasize, is the question of different "relations with being," not the question of the need to reject being itself.

It is true that Levinas calls the eschatological relation with being "metaphysical," explaining that an "otherwise" relation with being is concretized in me as a peculiar sort of "desire"—not a desire for "the bread I eat, the land in which I dwell, the landscape that I contemplate," but a desire that "tends toward *something else entirely*, toward the *absolutely other*."[110] Does not this insistence that another being's true, "ethical" identity is beyond the scope of my mundane desires only confirm Levinasian thought as a gnostic renunciation of the apparent world, as Hart avers? No indeed, for Levinas argues that it is really neediness that fails to relate to the other as such; instead it already *comprehends* her according to the shape of its own lack. It is precisely "natural," economic desire, in other words, that renounces the "real" other and invents a "gnostic" one in its stead. For even as I would express my neediness to the other and try to make her "fit" my need, I betray my prior, social relation to her—which means that, primordially, *nothing* relates us or "explains" our relation: "the metaphysician and the other can not be *totalized*."[111] By this Levinas means to suggest that a "mundane" relationship with alterity is not simply the requirement of phenomenal life as such (which Hart assumes), but rather is already a particular *way* of living and seeing. In Levinas's words: "The *way* of the I against the 'other' of the world consists in *sojourning*, in *identifying oneself* by existing here

---

107. Ibid., 22.

108. Note here the resonance with Kant's *Perpetual Peace*, and the differences he draws there between a "political moralism" and a "moral politics." In particular, Kant claims that political moralism, which moralizes the pragmatic violation of right, is in fact *less* "realistic" and so less practical than truly moral politics, which is willing to "bend the knee" before right, or in other words, to act in accordance with eschatological peace. In *Kant: Political Writings*, 93–130.

109. Levinas, *Totality and Infinity*, 22.

110. Ibid., 33.

111. Ibid., 35.

at home with oneself."[112] If the metaphysical relation demands a breach of this "sphere of the same," it does not imply a breach of the "real world," but a *breach of oneself.*

Of course, an absolute "breach" is only really justified if "the absolutely other, whose alterity is overcome in the philosophy of immanence on the allegedly common plane of history, maintains his transcendence in the midst of history."[113] And therefore we must move to the question of how exactly the "transcendence" of an ethical being is indeed maintained, precisely *in the midst of* (not "otherwise than" in Hart's caricatured sense) history's chronicle of the inexorable deaths of such beings. For Levinas, history marks one way of "seeing" the temporalization of being, whose verdict is determined on the basis of the visible: "Historical events are the visible par excellence; their truth is produced in evidence. The visible forms, or tends to form, a totality. It excludes the apology," which Levinas will also call the "plane of the inner life."[114] Therefore, if history "is to lose its right to the last word," we must appeal to a judgment of "the invisible," which can manifest "the offense that inevitably results from the judgment of visible history."[115] But how can a judgment of the invisible be "concretely brought about"?[116] From what perspective can "interiority," in which the thinking subject maintains a "minimal distance" from her historical definition, be judged "true" and even "fundamental"? How can we know that reality itself might unfold as a time of wills and not a history of dead works (or "deathly" signs)?

Historiography's time would have us believe we only "live" temporally by virtue of a continuous abdication of interiority's possibilities,

112. Ibid., 37.

113. Ibid., 40.

114. Ibid., 243.

115. Ibid., 243. Note the interesting resonance here of Levinas's search for the "invisible offense" of historiography with Walter Benjamin's "historical materialist" enterprise in the sixth of his "Theses on the Philosophy of History": "Historical materialism wishes to retain that image of the past which unexpectedly appears to man singled out by history at a moment of danger. The danger affects both the content of the tradition and its receivers. The same threat hangs over both: that of becoming a tool of the ruling classes. In every era the attempt must be made to wrest tradition away from a conformism that is about to overpower it." In the next thesis, Benjamin continues by saying that because every document of "civilization" is a "document of barbarism" in that it tells a story of death and even kills in the very telling, the historical materialist "regards it as his task to brush history against the grain." Benjamin, *Illuminations*, 255–57.

116. Levinas, *Totality and Infinity*, 244.

making us into fated "things" at every successive present moment. This time therefore makes interiority finally "irrelevant" to our "real" identities. Without becoming actual, interiority's possibilities never achieve objective status; and nor, for that reason, do they achieve a claim upon the historiographer's or the philosopher's attention. Levinas's phenomenology of erotic love is meant to offer an alternative interpretation of temporal existence. His choice in this regard does not mean that ethics is founded on sex and childbirth, but only that "paternity," which he describes as the "primordial effectuation of time," *may* "be borne by the biological life, but be lived beyond that life."[117] Erotic love can offer an example of "paternity" because its progression, from desire to consummation to the child, can be read as an allegory of the movement of a "non-historical" time, and can thereby suggest the possibility of a non-historical living. In erotic love, Levinas writes, the lover seeks contact with the beloved in the "caress," which consists "in soliciting what ceaselessly escapes its form toward a future never future enough, in soliciting what slips away as though it *were not yet*."[118] Erotic love as such seeks this "not yet," the child, and thus we can venture that it indicates the possibility of living a time that proceeds always toward the not yet—not inevitably toward a particular objective present, but madly toward a non-objective future. Here we would be correct to recall Heidegger's characterization of death as Dasein's "ownmost" possibility, for in relation to death, the subject is maintained in her anticipatory comportment, instead of "falling" into a conception of the future as boring actualizable possibility. The present as such, to this way of living, does not kill (as an utterly sacrificial ontology would claim), but affords the possibility of a seeking that wills even to be "breached." The very concrete experience of erotic love exemplifies the possibility of living in this way, of living a time that is not controllably "causal": "The relation with the child—that is, the relation with the other that is not a power, but fecundity—establishes relationship with the absolute future, or infinite time."[119]

In this manner Levinas concludes that *eros* is "reflective" of that eschatological sociality in which we may live even now, insofar as we allow it to bring about a relationship with time as "the non-definitiveness of the definitive," a time that adds "*something new to being, something*

---

117. Ibid., 247.
118. Ibid., 257–58.
119. Ibid., 268.

absolutely new."[120] The "reality" of our temporal existence is therefore not necessarily political, for in virtue of our possible comportment to the future as mysterious newness, it is possibly moral. Thus will Levinas ultimately say that in spite of our deadening philosophical vision, the essence of time is the infinitude of being.[121] Morality is not derisory, then, and does not "dupe" us into gnosticism, precisely because "resurrection" rather than abdication "constitutes the principal event of time."[122] The finally critical point here is that it is possible to live, in the present, the truth of an eschatological peace, or that there is no "reason" not to. And for this living, the "sublimity" of the Other is in fact most present, facing us in our minimal, interior distance from *every* present, and evoking that desire which arises only when our same-making egoism, one and the same with our philosophical vision, is broken.

The possibility of such an existential reading of Levinas, in which his ethics come across as *more* concrete than Hart's directly assumed "dynamism of natural desire," is totally obscured by Hart's polemic, in which he concludes that Levinas "so scrupulously purges the ethical of the fruits of being . . . that [being] becomes an almost demonic category."[123] Hart continues, in a statement whose baldness is helpful in revealing the implications of Radical Orthodox sympathies in this regard, that "it is the fate of every purely 'dialectical' theology or discourse of transcendence to fail to reconcile worldly being with the highest good, and so to reduce the former to something malign and irredeemable."[124] We have seen that this is not at all what "dialectical" discourse does, at least in its Heideggerian and Levinasian guises; indeed we might now say that to "save" theology from the putative dangers of Heidegger and Levinas is to refuse to wrestle with the existential problematic raised by any direct relationship to a "discourse" of reconciliation—to wrestle, that is, with the potential similarities between such a directness and what Heidegger

---

120. Ibid., 283.

121. Ibid., 284.

122. Ibid. Interestingly, this "good news" bears comparison with Pickstock's articulation of "the final phrases of the *Pater Noster*," in which the congregants pray for deliverance from an evil identified "as time construed as spatial and linear, for immanentist time is perforce a sequence of evils . . . We ask, therefore, to be released from the enduring and violent closure of secular time, which regrets the past and despairs of the future." See *After Writing*, 236ff.

123. Hart, *Beauty of the Infinite*, 85–86.

124. Ibid., 86

would call a "falling" inscription in "idle talk." In short, it is possible that Radical Orthodoxy's characteristic rejection of a caricature of "the dialectical" enshrines its own intended status as a "metadiscourse" in a manner entirely complicit in the logic of "spatialization." Let me conclude this chapter's discussion by attempting to flesh out this potential problem more clearly, with specific reference to Hart and Pickstock's claims about theology's presently urgent task.

What Is Christian Urgency?

The Need for a Tasteful Theology

Since the dismantling of modern epistemology and its consequent understandings of truth, there are many "attacks" which theology can abide quite easily. For instance, it can stomach the modern charge that as a discourse it remains too historicist, that it cares too little about demonstrating its claim of the incarnational incursion of true life in time by reference to stable, "monadic" representatives of that life. In other words, it can abide the charge that it does not succeed where capitalism and modern experimental science ostensibly fail, in the production of life and truth as demonstrable "substances." Theology has indeed always been too post-modern for that charge to prove damning, for its referent has always been the archetype not of substance but of movement, interval, and relation. It can also abide the charge, in this case leveled by postmodernism, that it is not historicist enough. This is the charge located by Milbank in Heidegger, and by Hart in Nietzscheanism, which says that to side with the changing and the temporal above monadic self-presence is to be barred from "preferring" some intervals over others, from measuring them with reference to a fanciful *caritas*. As we have seen, theology can respond to such an accusation by pointing out that the prohibition of preference only manifests the residue of a metaphysically justified measure of *indifference*, the fruit of an *a priori* conclusion that temporal flux is arbitrary, and that only "death" is life.

In light of its freedom from both modern and postmodern suspicion, does there remain any challenge that theology *cannot abide*? According to Hart, the most significant remaining danger to theology, and to the church itself, resides in the derision of the one who *agrees* with theology's anti-metaphysical advocacy of "preference," but who finds Christian "taste" especially despicable. For Hart this means that theology especially cannot abide the scorn of Nietzsche and his followers, whose anti-metaphysical critique is most poignant when it derides Christian taste as the foulest and most disorienting. Nietzsche deploys this critique in two ways in *The Antichrist*, both of which Hart identifies as crucial, when he writes, "the church should not be able to abide . . . a rhetorical assault on the form of Christ, nor can it very well suffer any insinuation that it enjoys no true historical continuity with or access to the life and teachings of Jesus of Nazareth."[125] Nietzsche's attack on the "form of Christ" makes reference to the fact that "Christ desired no power and suffered from no resentment toward his persecutors—indeed, he loved them. For Nietzsche this means Christ was a dreamer."[126] For Nietzsche, that is, the form of Christ can appeal only to a "childish" taste, whose ultimate expression is the life-denying path of the cross—which is to say, nihilism. And of course, this aesthetic critique of Christ's form cannot really be separated from the second critique, since there can be no living, "historical connection" with a form that disavows the striving for power intrinsic to "living connections" as such. In Nietzsche's view, to really have a taste for Christ is to be sick of life, which implies that to have a taste for Paul's church is to be doubly sick, for it is on the one hand to "affirm" the death of life, but at the same time to fail to live it as Christ does, by "dropping off."[127] According to Nietzsche, that is, to be a Pauline Christian is to cultivate a taste for the blandness of unseasoned bread and wine in meager portions, but without allowing it to become what it was for Jesus—his *last supper*.[128] The "historical continuity" of the church with the dying Christ is only possible as a Christian *failure*, a mechanism of priestly life-support that makes it impossible either to leave the hospital or to "pull the plug." Historical Christianity is therefore the supreme lie, because it takes weakness and "makes it blessed,"

---

125. Ibid., 117–18.

126. Ibid., 122. See Nietzsche, *Antichrist*, 568–656.

127. And on this score, Nietzsche is clear that what Christ "really means," what he really offers, is not a faith, but a way of living—a way of dying: "only Christian *practice*, a life such as he *lived* who died on the cross, is Christian . . . To reduce being a Christian, Christianism, to a matter of considering something true, to a mere phenomenon of consciousness, is to negate Christianism . . . 'Faith' was, at all times . . . a *screen* behind which the instincts played their game . . . one always *spoke* of faith, but one always *acted* from instinct alone" (*Antichrist*, 612–13).

128. See *Antichrist*, section 30, where Nietzsche suggests that really to be like Christ is to understand "love" as "the only, as the *last* possible, way of life."

instead of crucifying it, and because it never actually *wounds*, as Christ himself was wounded.[129]

First of all it seems wise to concede that Nietzsche's offense at the form of Christ, and at the Christian claim that this form can be *lived*, is awakening, at the very least, in the sense that any would-be defense of Christianity must henceforth wrestle with the possibility of such an aversion. Or perhaps we might say that Nietzsche's offense awakens us to the possibility that we too are offended in these ways, the possibility that we will find ourselves "wounded" precisely here, by the Christianity that Kierkegaard says is always an "attacker."[130] In any case, Nietzsche's aversion raises the question of what it could possibly mean to go through such an offense, or others that are akin to it. Hart's contention, which brings out the central point of contention in this book, is that the possibility of the Nietzschean offense must not remain something that each individual believer must "go through," repeatedly. Instead this offense must be "overcome" aesthetically, such that "going through" it is no longer a matter of existential anxiety, but of direct rhetorical accomplishment. Thus comes to light a critical difference—between a theology that would say the despairing offense of Nietzsche is something that only the believer's movement of faith can "banish," and one that says "theology" can overcome Nietzsche's polemic by articulating the essentially Christian narrative "more tastefully." This difference is that between a theological communication that *communicates nothing essential*, except that faith is confirmed *when you* have faith (and theology cannot help you with that),[131] and a theology that becomes prolific and heavy with "offers" of help.

For Kierkegaard, the difficulty of confirming 1 Tim 3:16, that "he was believed in the world," the precise claim that Nietzsche seeks to discredit, is the challenge that the believer must go through, *by having faith*, whereas Hart and Radical Orthodoxy presume to "go further" than this, in order to make the Christian tradition itself persuasively

---

129. Nietzsche, *Antichrist*, 631–32.

130. See Kierkegaard, *Christian Discourses*, 162ff.

131. One can think here of Kierkegaard's interpretation of 1 Tim 3:16, "God was revealed in the flesh, was justified in the Spirit, seen by angels, preached among the pagans, believed in the world, taken up in glory," of which he says, "But this 'He was believed in the world'! This does pertain to you, does it not; it pertains to you alone, or it is for you as if it pertained only to you, you alone in the whole world!" From *Christian Discourses*, 234ff.

"Christian." Accordingly, Hart counters Nietzsche's suggestion that Christ is a dreamer, and that his form is not possibly *lived* except in a gnostic "Kingdom," by claiming that

> Christ showed that the world was a text that could be read differently: according to the grammar not of power, but of agape. The Christian contention, then, would be that this "dreamer" could also, in reenvisaging the world, initiate a real historical sequence, a positive if oft-imperiled "new creation."[132]

Such is the urgency of theology's attention to its rhetoric, for Hart: if the church *can* narrate a "history" of agape, the modern and postmodern inability to think incarnation, *Sittlichkeit*, transcendence-in-immanence, etc., can be decisively removed as an obstacle to Christian faith and life. In our situation especially, where the persuasiveness of what Hart calls "narratives of the sublime" looms large, "theology cannot avoid considering the aesthetics of its rhetoric, and *whether its rhetoric can truly reflect the being of the world.*"[133] That is to say, theology can and must, in the form of its communication, become the "verification" of 1 Tim 3:16, "he was believed in the world," such that its hearers will be persuaded that Christianity has a true "presence" in the world, and *thereby* become willing to participate in the life that animates it. By contrast, "dialectical" theology does not, as Radical Orthodoxy is wont to suggest, propound the impossibility of the Christian life; but it does, as a form of communication, *refuse to become or even "demonstrate" the possibility of faith for the single individual.* Dialectical theology thus does not persuade—not because it cannot admit the possibility of a reconciled life in the Spirit, but because it will not "go further" than reflecting on the existential requirements facing the individual human being who would live in this way. It will not admit that the worldly presence of the "essentially Christian" is verified by anything else but this living, which means precisely by the living of the individual reader who finds herself addressed by those requirements. Opposing himself to such an indirect verification, Hart is convinced, by contrast, that Christian rhetoric can of itself "give the lie" to despair:

> To allow [as theology does] that the symbolist of the Gospels could be also creative, forceful, imperious, and capable of dis-

---

132. Hart, *Beauty of the Infinite*, 122.
133. Ibid., 127–28. Emphasis added.

crimination and judgment—to allow, that is, that the "idiot" whose rejection of power was final and still free of resentment could genuinely enter into history, or constitute an apprehensible aesthetic form among the many forms cast up by time, or pose against all philosophies of will and power the historical example of a community able to live, however imperfectly and infrequently, by charity rather than force—would give the lie to Nietzsche's own narrative of cosmos and history, his own metaphysics and (more importantly) aesthetics.[134]

And it is true, of course, that Hart and Christian theology generally can give narrative accounts of creation and history which "rival" that of Nietzsche, in the sense that they are no less (or more) metaphysically justified than his account. But to use that narrative in any way to mitigate the gap that inheres between the "account" and how one relates oneself to it is to forget the locus of the question so central to Radical Orthodoxy itself—the question of whether or not the divisions of "secular reason" can be reconciled by virtue of a temporal enactment of spiritual life. This question is indeed a matter of Christian urgency; but I suggest that it does not need, and nor can it abide, any theological resolution, for only a human being, as opposed to an idea or "language" as such, can have faith.[135]

Pickstock's Theologically Reconciled Caesura

We have also seen how Catherine Pickstock, though she writes of a spiritual existence that cannot be "written," nonetheless finds the possibility or impossibility of a "liturgical attitude towards reality" to be legible in the "syntax" of particular cultural situations. Thus she ironically finds the modern context to be utterly deficient, religiously speaking, because it seems to offer the subject no character whose role is "written"

---

134. Ibid., 123.

135. Laurence Paul Hemming puts this nicely in his recent article on contemporary theological uses of "analogy." See Hemming, "*Analogia non Entis sed Entitatis*," where Hemming suggests that theologians engaging in rhetorical battle with postmodernity want to say that an analogical world-view (which suggests that the "intervals" of a rhetorical theology, for example, are related analogically to the supplemented "being" which is reflected therein) does an "ontological kind" of work; they want to say that "analogy" persuades us that "theology and being are one" (121). Hemming wants "to interject and say that only the believer can know this—only he or she can act upon, and so enact, *live* this. It cannot be claimed as a general truth of being . . . there is *no* analogy of being *as such* and apart from Christian believing" (121).

adequately. This contradicts Pickstock's own best insights about the differences between a liturgical and a spatialized existence; and moreover it confounds what seems to be the thrust of Paul's "as if not" ethic in 1 Corinthians 7, which seems (at least to me) to assert, "However it is you are 'written' (and I grant that there are many ways), *no matter how apparently spiritually deficient is the text, or indeed, how spiritually excellent*, you can and must *live as if your inscription does not define you.*" Thus I suggest it is both Pickstock's "theological" anti-modernism *and* her nostalgia for the inscription offered by the Roman Rite and by the "syntax" of early medieval Christendom generally, which threaten her fidelity to extra textual "life." Let us try for a moment to get a sense for the latter.

In a characteristically romanticized reference to "the Middle Ages," Pickstock suggests that, in contradistinction to our own modern, asyndetic syntax, "lay fraternities and craft guilds . . . incorporated the individual within a ritualized social collective whose principal end was the attainment of a state of charity."[136] To be born into this society was to be inscribed in a "reciprocal framework," in which "the liturgical cycle of feasts and festivals . . . freed charitable donation from the anxiety of private choice."[137] The dubious impression given here, that the liturgical cycle did your living *for* you, is strengthened by the fact that in Pickstock's Middle Ages, there was apparently no possibility of despair, no possibility of a *subjective misrelation* to the liturgical, and thus no sense in which the essentially Christian had to be *appropriated* by the subject at all. As she writes,

> It might seem that the specifically *ritual* performance of peace and alliance in some sense belied its genuine attainment, but this would be to presuppose a duality of ritual and non-ritual modes of practice, and thence mistakenly to correlate ritualized with artificial actions and to segregate such forms of action from the "real" or "everyday." But mediaeval social practice was definitively ritual or liturgical in character. *There simply was no duality of the liturgical and the mundane.*[138]

Yet such a "ritual" resolution of the dualism of abstract, written, atemporal being and embodied, changing temporality can only inhere, I would

---

136. Pickstock, *After Writing*, 143.
137. Ibid., 144.
138. Ibid., 146. Emphasis added.

argue, on the basis of a fantastic portrayal of an unreflective and at the same time "spiritual" human life. Because only *a human being* can live "liturgically" in relation to reality, for Pickstock to favor a syntax that makes it impossible *not* to live in this way is to capitulate to the very sophistic gesture of security that she disparages in Phaedrus. Pickstock makes no effort to mitigate this problematic suggestion, and even exacerbates it, when she says, "at this stage, virtue, including peaceableness and the exercise of charity, was regarded as something visible and apparent in outward and public signs which could not dissemble: there was as yet no 'ironic' space."[139] This suggestion is strange especially because the Jesus of the Gospels certainly seems to have realized that though a rich man may participate, externally, in the ritualized cycle of wealth-distribution, and may give to the benevolence fund and build the temple all by himself, still a widow with two coins to her name could, by no external measure, be more readily held up as an example of charity.[140] In his injunction to give in secret,[141] moreover, Jesus seems to have understood that publicly visible signs of charity could indeed dissemble—and even that they might always dissemble.

Pickstock decries the inward "piety" that I seem to be defending as the harbinger of the modern slide to secular reason.[142] For her, Protestantism's "novel" insistence upon the dissemblance of the externally measured act is entirely complicit in the modern sundering of (now abstract) love from temporal, worldly power, so as to produce "a loveless power and an impotent love, which no longer had any primary role in the sacral economy."[143] We can certainly agree that the "syntax" of medieval ritualism went some distance toward preventing this division of infinite, spiritual love from the economic demands of temporal life. But again we must say that infinite urgency and temporal economy can only be brought together by the faith of an individual human being. As a syntactical construction, this reconciliation resides at a distance from its living actualization; and moreover, as such a construction it will offend anyone with even a mild sense for temporal economy. A *direct* inscription into such a syntax can therefore only be self-forgetful. Pickstock will

139. Ibid.
140. See Luke 21.
141. See Matthew 5–7.
142. See Pickstock, *After Writing*, 147ff.
143. Ibid., 157.

of course say (albeit parenthetically) that "none of this account is supposed to imply that a liturgical order was perfectly realized in the middle ages . . . rather that certain social and intellectual conditions of possibility for such an order were present."[144] But even this claim is strange, for it implies that the true living which is "after writing" has written conditions of possibility. Hence the ultimate urgency for Pickstock, as for Hart, of theology's reconciling rhetoric. Any form of communication that refuses to offer, of itself, a persuasive reconciliation is for her too faithful to the modern refusal to believe that the sign can be resurrected, and therefore that death and life can be reconciled.

Pickstock's own explicit dismissal of the dialectical accordingly comes next, this time in relation to characteristically Protestant understandings of the relationships between the historical, sacramental, and ecclesial bodies of Christ. She claims that "these three foci, which had traditionally been ordered in relation to one another in such a way as to place an implicit *caesura* between the first and second foci, later came to be organized with the *caesura* placed between the second and the third."[145] Originally then, the mystical or sacramental body of the church was "not simply a moral designation, but physical and natural,"[146] which is to say that the natural, "ecclesial" body was always inexorably "mystical." This construal must be revived, Pickstock argues, for it figures as a real living protest against the more typically modern *caesura* between the temporal and the spiritual. As she puts it, "the 'mystery' of the ecclesial body is precisely its 'real' synaxis."[147] In distinction from modern and postmodern tendencies to despair of any "life" present in the sign, the direct communication of the unity of these foci poses the "condition of possibility," we might say, for the sign's resurrection.

The shift to an insistence upon a *caesura* between the second and third foci is I think correctly identified by Pickstock as characteristic of a "dialectical" form of theological communication. For Pickstock, this latter insistence is tantamount to a denial of transubstantiation as a lived unity of sacrament and ecclesia, which reduces the relation between the mystical and ecclesial bodies to a mere "inert fact, in the manner of a

144. Ibid.
145. Ibid., 158.
146. Ibid., 160.
147. Ibid.

discontinuous miraculous 'arrangement' of reality."[148] In other words, and ironically from Pickstock's point of view, the working of the Spirit's power in the world is objectified by the Protestant or dialectical *caesura*, which means genuinely existential Christianity is precluded by the dialectical. My argument in this book, as should be clear by now, is quite the opposite—that the "dialectical" relationship of the latter two foci is precisely the result of an existential rigor, not an "epistemological" one. The problem with any rhetorical advocacy of an "existential" ontology, which is what Pickstock's book amounts to, is that it tends to become too confident in its alternative "written" arrangement; it must, for rhetorical purposes, locate Christianity's proper urgency in an anti-modern "construal" of the mysterious and natural bodies of Christ as inexorably united. But what this misses is that the construal is not urgent. *The living of that unity is urgent*; and therefore the dialectical form of theological communication—which refuses to "go further" than articulating the difficulty of enacting this unity, and so refuses to "resolve" the terms in a description instead of a *life*—remains more faithful to the essential urgency of Christianity. None of this is to say that Pickstock never acknowledges the existential demands of "the liturgy."[149] But it is to suggest that the urgency which she gives to reviving the "writing" of the Roman Rite, and the role she gives to such writing, as a "condition of possibility" for the "performance in liturgical time of eternity,"[150] perpetually obscure the fact that such a performance never inheres except in the human being who enacts faith, and that this faith cannot be entirely ritualized if Pickstock's theology is not to capitulate to the tenets of a fully "spatialized" linguistic turn.

Moving On, Without Going Further

It is with this critical sympathy for the concerns of Radical Orthodoxy in mind that I suggest we turn our attention to the characteristics of

---

148. Ibid., 163.

149. See ibid., 198, where she claims that speaking the liturgical language, which employs a self-dispossessive "impersonation," is a "ceaseless struggle for the worshipper, for whom the secular assumptions of empirical priority and instrumentality, as well as the immanentist import of spatialized structures, inimical to voice, gift, and redemptive sacrifice, perpetually threaten to suspend the ontologically necessary dispossession of the 'I.'"

150. Ibid., 219.

indirect or dialectical communication, which will inevitably mean disabusing theology, as a discourse, of any salvific urgency. In this second "half" of the present volume we shall come to see how the Kierkegaardian claim that "Christianity must not be defended" implies that Christian truth cannot be *written*. We shall try to explore, with particular reference to Kierkegaard's *Concluding Unscientific Postscript* and *Practice in Christianity*, how indirect communication does not safeguard the essentially Christian from those who would be offended by it, but from the human desire to obfuscate the possibility of offense. It will be shown, in other words, that the dialectical does not better "defend" Christianity by making it plausible, even in the face of Nietzsche's objections, but rather safeguards it *from being protected* and thus domesticated, and therefore safeguards *you* from being "persuaded" by it—so that it remains possible for you to become a Christian! After dealing with these implications of indirect communication, we shall have occasion to discuss the "individualism" it ostensibly implies; and in connection with the work of René Girard, we shall advance the dialectical suggestion by which Radical Orthodoxy is quite provoked—that to become a Christian is to be held "devoutly apart" from any objectifying cultural situatedness. Finally, through a reading of Kierkegaard's *Works of Love*, which will help us to understand Girard's refusal to offer what Milbank calls the "idiom" of peaceable behavior,[151] we shall be able to see how the individualism of the dialectical nonetheless motivates a true sociality, albeit a sociality *ex nihilo*. In all of this I hope to show that the Radical Orthodox concern to place the urgency of Christianity's promised reconciliation into confrontation with the "dialectic" of secular reason is aided rather than stymied by the indirect communication of Christian truth, precisely insofar as the latter does not allow the human being's possibility of spiritual life to slip from view, even if it does not, as a form of communication, guarantee or confirm that possibility.

---

151. See Milbank, *Theology and Social Theory*, 392–98.

3

Consummation or Complication?

Introduction: Immediate Oppositions

IN THIS CHAPTER WE shall move from Radical Orthodoxy's rhetoric to a consideration of the dialectical form of theological communication in the work of Søren Kierkegaard. At first glance, this would appear to be more of a break than a transition, given that Catherine Pickstock and David Bentley Hart go to great lengths to exclude the possibility of having any productive conversation with Kierkegaard.[1] Rather than evading the difficulties raised by these treatments, I will begin the present chapter by giving brief consideration to each of them.

Pickstock's rejection of Kierkegaard comes at the end of *After Writing*.[2] Here she tells the reader that she has tried to provide "the articulations of a model of a liturgical attitude which alone offers a genuine restoration of both the subject and of language as such," the origins of which "are to be found in antiquity," but are fully realized only by "*a specifically Christian construal of liturgy*."[3] In her conclusion she tries especially to clarify the necessity of the "Christian" addition to the ancient origins of the liturgical attitude she has been describing. At this crucial

---

1. As we will see later in this chapter, Milbank's own treatment of Kierkegaard is much more sympathetic, and in his more recent work in dialogue with Slavoj Žižek, Kierkegaard has even become the crucially contested ally. See *Monstrosity of Christ*.
2. See Pickstock, *After Writing*, 267ff.
3. Ibid., 268. Emphasis added.

moment, then, Kierkegaard must come up explicitly, for as Pickstock writes, "the clear contrast between Platonic recollection and Christan repetition drawn by Kierkegaard would seem to render my question [about what Christianity 'adds' to the Platonic] redundant."[4] Without explaining exactly how Kierkegaard articulates the difference between the Platonic and the Christian, Pickstock tells us that her own reading of Plato makes it harder to discern such a contrast:

> Insofar as for Plato recollection does not entail knowing identically the past as it was experienced by the pre-existent soul, but non-identically, through inspiration via *eros*, we can infer an intimation of a gesture towards prospectivity and difference. This would seem to close the gap between recollection and repetition, and thus urge the question: why Christianity?[5]

For Kierkegaard, as we shall discover below, the Incarnation moves Christian religiousness beyond the Socratic notion of the temporal as "in principle" participating in the eternal, and makes a particular incursion of God in time decisive for the existing individual's relationship to the eternal. That God becomes a particular human being means that the human does not discover eternity within itself and in its own living, but *needs to be made eternal*. This is the heightened paradox, to which one cannot relate without a consciousness of sin, a consciousness that one is in fact "polemical against the truth."[6] Recollection is hereby made dubious, and a decidedly forward-moving repetition is substituted. But for Pickstock, ultimately, the shift hinges not upon the newly revealed existential qualification of sin, but rather upon a "speculative" difference, the difference that "in Christianity there is no doctrine of pre-existent souls," which she takes to imply that "our journey 'back' to God perforce cannot reach an unmediated anterior optimum, but is *essentially* mediated by [the Christian] tradition's series, both in its historical retellings, and its present and future narrations."[7] The point here is that Platonic recollection, even when it is mediated by Socratic *performance*, still is not free of a nostalgia for the pure origin in virtue of its "doctrine" of pre-existent souls, whereas Christianity is "doctrinally" safeguarded from taking this

4. Ibid..
5. Ibid., 269.
6. Kierkegaard, *Philosophical Fragments/Johannes Climacus*, 15.
7. Pickstock, *After Writing*, 270.

gnostic route. The object of Christian recollection must always be its own tradition, the historical series in which individual Christians are inscribed. Thus the Christian's performative hope is never the attainment of an abstract anteriority, but always that of another performance. What finally keeps even this from being tragic, which it might remain for Plato, is yet another speculative guarantor, that of the doctrine of the Trinity:

> The Trinitarian God is an *eternally* supplemented reality, always both "before" and "beyond" its *logos*. And this alone secures a divine self-sufficiency, without reduction to presence, whereas Plato could only think the "supplementation" of the Forms by their manifestation in time, in a manner which compromised the self-sufficiency of the divine, and therefore compromised in turn the pure, non-necessitated "gift" character of time and finitude.[8]

If time itself is the "gift" of this "eternally supplemented" reality, then participation in the eternal can never be abstracted from its temporal situatedness. For the Christian account alone, therefore, "participation in eternity still remains . . . a journey *through* time, within a community of people."[9]

At this point we can anticipate Pickstock's explicit rejection of Kierkegaard, since for Kierkegaard, to "exist" on the basis of the community is a "temptation" that sin as despair is all too willing to entertain. By contrast, Pickstock believes keeping the "historical series" essentially in the picture is what safeguards Christianity's fundamental difference from the Platonic. Unsurprisingly, then, she zeroes in on what Kierkegaard calls faith's "contemporaneity" with Christ, which suggests that faith faces, in the same measure in all ages, the paradoxical requirement of holding together a particular man with the "God conception." That is, no matter how loudly the historical "series" may shout of Christ's divinity, a true faith must always wrestle with, and become contemporary with, the contradiction that God became historical as a particular human being. This requirement functions as a warning against the tradition's pretension to make it *easier* to stand there, beside this Jesus of Nazareth, and conclude that he is "very God." Just as Christ's being God was not immediately evident to the disciples, the best of whom denied him no less vigorously than the worst of the spectators, so too "the tradition"

8. Ibid.
9. Ibid.

cannot make it any more immediate to us. This is the meaning of the contemporaneity faith requires—it fundamentally denies immediacy, thus preserving faith *as faith*.

I think we can say that this point is wholly lost on Pickstock, who concludes that because of its relativization of "the tradition" as directly communicative of the object of faith, contemporaneity in Kierkegaard ultimately means "the immediacy of truth itself,"[10] which brings Kierkegaard back within the sphere of the "bad" Platonic. Pickstock writes that for Kierkegaard, ultimately, "apostolic testimony, like that of the Socratic pedagogue, dissolves before the glory seen with the eyes of faith, with which it is unsurpassably contemporary."[11] Thus she adds that the requirement of contemporaneity also reveals Kierkegaard's "covert[!] individualism," which "seems to omit the fact that Christ is always repeated, even in his Eucharistic 'immediacy,' by which there is perforce a continuation of the incarnation in the sacraments, and the church."[12] But of course, Kierkegaard has no reason to deny such a claim, that there is a continuation of the Incarnation in every sign. The critical point is that he will not allow "continuation" as a speculative hypothesis to mitigate the difficulty of faith, whose passion is provoked by the objective uncertainty of such a hypothesis. Nevertheless, Pickstock uses his emphasis on objective uncertainty to make him into a covert Platonist, which for her can be overcome only by a new "account": "Kierkegaard's stress on the prospectivity of repetition is only *sustainable* as such in combination with an account of the Church and sociality."[13] So once again we can see that for Pickstock, the essential Christian distinction from other forms of religiousness, or at least from the Platonic, is in the peculiarity of Christianity's "account"—in its reference to an inherently differentiating Trinitarian God, and to an inexorably historically situated recollection. Never does she mention Christianity's qualification of the religious life with the consciousness of sin, which for Kierkegaard brings religiousness to the decisive and absolute-paradoxical level.[14]

10. Ibid., 271.
11. Ibid.
12. Ibid., 272.
13. Ibid.
14. See Kierkegaard, *Concluding Unscientific Postscript*, 573, where he has Climacus write that with "Religiousness B," crucially, "there is no immanental underlying kinship between the temporal and the eternal, because the eternal itself has entered into time

David Bentley Hart offers his own explicit rejection of Kierkegaard in a short piece published in *First Things*.[15] The article in question, entitled "The Laughter of the Philosophers," is a review essay on Thomas C. Oden's recent anthology, *The Humor of Kierkegaard*.[16] Oden introduces his volume with a putatively Kierkegaardian account of humor, which Hart paraphrases as follows: "Humor is able to receive finitude as a gift, conscious of the suffering intrinsic to human existence, but capable of transcending despair through jest."[17] In his essay Hart attempts to show that even on this account of comedy, Kierkegaard should not be held up as a better humorist than J. G. Hamann. This argument is closely connected, as we shall see, to Hart's claim that Kierkegaard's understanding of Christianity is, in the end, "in many significant respects, disastrously false."[18]

Hart suggests that Kierkegaard is nowhere more humorless than in a selection included by Oden from the *Attack Upon Christendom*, in which Kierkegaard says there is no difference between a "pagan" whorehouse and a whorehouse in Christendom. This Hart takes as evidence of Kierkegaard's inability to rise above a despairing assessment of the "contradictions" of our temporal situation, an assessment that cannot transcend such contradictions via "jest." This resonates with Pickstock's refusal to countenance Kierkegaard's indifference to the historical mediations of Christianity, which she takes to be a quasi-gnostic (or at least problematically Platonist) refusal to admit the "resurrection of the sign." Hart counters that,

> Yes, in fact there *are* "Christian" whorehouses, and whoremongers, and whores, and they are nothing like their pagan predecessors, because the formation of conscience within even a defectively Christian culture is something altogether novel; the whorehouse is now full of sinners, whose memories necessarily

and wants to establish kinship there." The difference here is that the person does not recognize his immemorial spiritual qualification, but rather, "the individual, who was not eternal, now becomes eternal, and therefore does not reflect on what he is but becomes what he was not, and, please note, becomes something that has the dialectic that as soon as it is it must have been, because this is the dialectic of the eternal.—What is inaccessible to all thinking is: that one can become eternal although one was not eternal."

15. Hart, "Laughter of the Philosophers," 31–38.
16. Oden, *Humor of Kierkegaard*.
17. Hart, "Laughter of the Philosophers."
18. Ibid.

bear the impress of moral grammars and spiritual promises that the pagan order never knew, and who in consequence may yet awaken to their sin, and who may even find themselves at unexpected moments haunted by charity or tormented by grace.[19]

We must concede, first off, that Kierkegaard does not always practice the same reticence to judge that Climacus displays when he asks, in the *Postscript*, "is it possible that every other person is such a knight of hidden inwardness? Well, why not? Whom can it harm?"[20] In Hart's view, such generosity certainly is nowhere to be found in Kierkegaard's *Attack Upon Christendom*, where the author seems smugly certain about the corruption of those around him. Despite the regrettable difference in tone between these two works, however, one might still reply to Hart that even in the *Attack*, Kierkegaard does not presume to judge the inner religiousness of whorehouse patrons, but only to suggest that the shift between paganism and Christendom, as a "cultural" shift, is not significant in an "essentially Christian" sense. In other words, Kierkegaard could not conceivably disagree with Hart's claim that it is possible for patrons in a Christendom whorehouse to be "tormented by grace." Indeed, his own claim is not directed there; instead he suggests that being able to *name* a whorehouse "Christian" does not mitigate the existential (and comic) difficulty of holding together the God-conception with everything else.

But for Hart, it is precisely Kierkegaard's unwillingness to admit that Christianity's cultural differences have an *essentially* Christian significance that ultimately violates Kierkegaard's own theory of humor, which more properly suggests

> that the *Christian* philosopher—having surmounted the "aesthetic," "ethical," and even in a sense "religious" stages of human existence—is uniquely able to enact a return, back to the things of earth, back to finitude, back to the aesthetic; having found the highest rationality of being in God's *kenosis*—His self-outpouring—in the Incarnation, the Christian philosopher is reconciled to the particularity of flesh and form, recognizes all of creation as a purely gratuitous gift of a God of infinite love, and is able to

---

19. Ibid.
20. Kierkegaard, *Concluding Unscientific Postscript*, 508.

rejoice in the levity of a world created and redeemed purely out of God's "pleasure."[21]

In this regard, Hart finds the work of Hamann superior to Kierkegaard's, in that for Hamann, "the return to finitude was unreserved and utterly charitable; everything he wrote or did was touched with a spirit of festivity; his humor contained no lingering residue of fatalism, irony, or rancor."[22] For Kierkegaard, by contrast, "the Incarnation remains a 'paradox' rather than a delightful 'surprise,' an invasion of worldly time that time cannot comprehend, and that thus forbids any real reconciliation with the world."[23] Hart concludes that for Hamann, uniquely, the idea of a "Christian whorehouse" "would probably have moved him more to reflect upon the prodigality of divine love than to indulge in caustic complaint."[24] Such is Kierkegaard's ultimate lack of faith and humor relative to Hamann, for whom "the kenosis of God illuminates and transfigures everything, *grace transfuses all of nature, culture, and cult.*"[25]

For both Pickstock and Hart, therefore, Kierkegaard's emphasis upon the indirectness of the essentially Christian—evident in his indifference to turning the history of the church into a compelling narrative, and to the cultural differences of "Christendom" as such—is effectively his refusal of any genuine Christian *Sittlichkeit*. For these authors, Kierkegaard's dialectic is thus entirely amenable to secular reason's refusal of a spiritually reconciled way of living. Why then bring such as Kierkegaard into conversation with Radical Orthodoxy at all?

Lingering Resonances: Milbank's Persuasive Absurdity

Kierkegaard as Forerunner of Radical Orthodoxy

Despite the direct opposition to Kierkegaard and dialectical communication that we find at certain moments in Radical Orthodoxy, what is ultimately common to Milbank's and Pickstock's critiques of secular or sophistic reason is their exposure of such reason as a despairing refusal to believe that the religious life can be *lived* in time, or that life

---

21. Hart, "Laughter of the Philosophers."
22. Ibid. For a more comprehensive attempt to restore the importance of Hamann for contemporary theology, see Betz, *After Enlightenment*.
23. Hart, "Laughter of the Philosophers."
24. Ibid.
25. Ibid. Emphasis added.

itself can be lived *religiously*. This concern is, I think, the root of Radical Orthodoxy's urgent appeal to the possibility of a genuine *Sittlichkeit*; and herein we can discern also a significant resonance with Kierkegaard's insistence upon the existential urgency of the religious life, or what he will also call the subjectivity of Christian truth. This resonance is felt especially in relation to the manner in which Kierkegaard disparages speculative thought as an evasion of this urgency.[26] A point of connection between Radical Orthodoxy and Kierkegaard, therefore, can be seen in their common exposure of metaphysical justifications of the objectivity of truth as subjective gestures of despair.

The remaining difference, of course, is that Kierkegaard will disparage rhetorical appeals to Christianity, or persuasions based on the history of the church, just as forcefully as he does speculative thought. So consider, for example, that Milbank's appeal to the "reconciliation" accomplished in the incarnation is meant to suggest that Christianity alone is capable of elevating human passions to their proper participation in spiritual truth, a participation formerly reserved for those free enough of domestic necessity to practice contemplation. The Christian appeal is thus supremely direct, in that the "concrete social practices" to which it appeals will include the fulfillment of desires formerly considered to be outside the purview of the highest truth. Hereby the Christian address does not fundamentally repel any aspect of the human being, but draws the whole self with its promise to "hold together" the spheres that had been inexorably separated—a promise that the passionate and capricious ways the self feels drawn to diverse instantiations of beauty, for example, are not finally irrelevant to the religious life as the possibility of living infinite truth.

And of course it would be petty to deny the basic appeal of Christianity as a construal, to deny the inviting force of the claim that God, in exalting Jesus as Messiah, demonstrates his election of all creation, down to its most apparently irreconcilable, "enfleshed" aspects, insofar as that creation does not renounce its true form. That is, for Christianity creation is elected precisely in the measure that Jesus, in the form of a creature, does not claim authority to justify himself, even before false accusations. In this literal willingness to die to his own

---

26. See Kierkegaard, *Postscript*, esp. 50–57: "Since a human being is a synthesis of the temporal and the eternal, the speculative happiness that a speculator can enjoy will be an illusion, because he wants to be exclusively eternal within time" (56).

self-possession, Jesus' life suggests that God's creation suffers more of an affront from a creature's denial of its *ex nihilo* form than it does from the violence that "tests" God's advocacy for creation. God's election of this man, in other words, for whom creaturely form means a refusal of self-justification, exposes violence as despairing self-protection, and by raising and exalting Christ, God refutes the necessity of that violence as a response to creaturely anxiety. To be in "the way" that is Jesus Christ therefore means *both* to be crucified to the world, *and* to have everything "given back," insofar as one thereby lives the true, elected-*ex-nihilo* form of God's good creation. Such is the glorious promise and power of the resurrection. Yet the question remains: is the appeal that is undeniably present in this construal also effective in the moment of decision, or in other words, at all moments of our living?

Milbank forays into this difficult territory in his essay, "The Sublime in Kierkegaard,"[27] which offers a much more sympathetic treatment of Kierkegaard than either Pickstock or Hart can muster. In particular Milbank aims to be attentive to the ways in which Kierkegaard might be a kind of forerunner of "post-secular" theology, an effort that aligns with his attempt elsewhere to make Hamann and Jacobi into forerunners of Radical Orthodoxy.[28] His sympathy for Kierkegaard's concerns can be productive for our conversation, then, because it suggests that Kierkegaard might not be one of those "dialectical" communicators who must fall prey to Radical Orthodoxy's theological meta-suspicion. At the same time, however, Milbank's essay also raises the question of whether a "marriage" between Kierkegaard and the theological spirit of our age is a good or an ill fit. This is the question, in effect, that I shall try to answer when we turn to the *Postscript* and to *Practice in Christianity*.

Milbank begins his essay with the claim that "writing in the wake of Nietzsche and Heidegger" is "a discourse 'about' the indeterminable," and that as such it is indebted to Kierkegaard's inauguration "of the second phase of critique."[29] By this he means to indicate that Kierkegaard initiated a new way of doing philosophy that implied new "quasi-ontological" categories, enumerated by Milbank as "Repetition,"

---

27. In Blond, *Post-Secular Philosophy*, 131–56.

28. See Milbank, "Theological Critique of Philosophy in Hamann and Jacobi," 21–37.

29. Milbank, "Sublime in Kierkegaard," 131.

Consummation or Complication? 113

"The Moment," and "Anxiety."[30] Repetition on Milbank's reading does not indicate a secondary instance of some original occurrence, but "indicates rather an 'originary repetition,' or the constitution of an identity *only* through its reoccurrence."[31] Repetition as identity-through-reoccurrence is connected to the Kierkegaardian notion of "the moment," which Milbank says "is not really an 'instance,' a 'standing in' a larger category, such that it 'exemplifies' it; rather every moment introduces something new that has itself the weight of categorical uniqueness."[32] Because of the moment's uniqueness, to say that identity is constituted through repetition across successive moments is to assert an irrevocable skepticism about identity. For Kierkegaard, however, "this sceptical implication is certainly gestured towards, but not regarded as an inevitably engulfing abyss. The abyss can be traversed by a 'decision'—to affirm absurdly and without grounds such-and-such a repeated continuity."[33] Here Milbank means to distance Kierkegaardian repetition from, for example, Heidegger's notion of the utter "questionableness" of Being's articulation in time. Milbank says he "agrees" with Kierkegaard that repetition as a mode of engagement in history can affirm the possibility of identity through inscription in a particular series of repeated decisions. Of course, Milbank also claims to agree with the "absurdity" of this affirmation for Kierkegaard, insofar as the absurd in Kierkegaard aligns with his own claim, against MacIntyre, for example, that historical transitions are aesthetically rather than rationally mediated. The postulate that threatens to make any commitment to continuity nonsensical, that Nietzschean-Heideggerian postulate of the *arbitrariness* of historical transitions and of ontological difference as such, effectively seeks to "prise apart Kierkegaard's usage of repetition from his theological interest; indeed to prise it apart from 'interest,' which assumes a subject, altogether."[34] Thus, in all poststructuralist, non-theological readings of Kierkegaard, a "rupture is posed between his *scepticism* on the one hand and his *fideism* on the other."[35] Milbank's main intention in this essay (as

30. Ibid. 132.

31. Ibid.

32. Ibid. This resonates with Levinas' formulation of the "present" as it is seen from the perspective of interiority rather than history. See *Totality and Infinity*, 283.

33. Milbank, "Sublime in Kierkegaard," 132.

34. Ibid. 133.

35. Ibid. 134.

it is, in some ways, in *Theology and Social Theory*), is "to problematize this rupture," by suggesting that one can point "to a subjective 'decision' for atheism and anti-humanism, and so an ineradicable 'subjectivity' that poststructuralism is not owning up to."[36]

Unlike Pickstock or Hart, Milbank argues that the postmodern suggestion of an "abyssal" distance between particular historical moments objectifies reality in a way that Kierkegaard himself was never prone to do. Thus, for Milbank's Kierkegaard, the subject is not inexorably divided by virtue of the putative aporia between the "interiority" of decision and the objective reification of the historical "present." Rather, according to Milbank, Kierkegaard contends

> that the real exhibits infinitely many transitions from rest to motion, and from possibility to act, and that these transitions, despite the regional operation of habitual causal patterns, have the character of positive "leaps" which display no logic outside that of their own occurrence. This kind of transition, which, not being a "state," is an invisible vanishing point for thought (doomed to the effort of representation) he names "the moment," and claims that the moment is the site of specifically human, spiritual existence—"spirit" being that which binds the soul (thinking possibility) and body (living actuality) together. To grasp the moment and ourselves as *out of* the moment, we can only repeat, and never represent it.[37]

What this means, Milbank argues, is that for Kierkegaard, "the subject itself is not the locus of interiority, but is rather 'within' a perpetual transition that it can never survey in a theoretical manner from without."[38] By extension this implies that to conclude that repetition is but the aporetic recurrence "of surface masks and disguises that present entirely assumed and conventional faces of 'identity,'"[39] only betrays an impossible pretension to some theoretical vantage point. By contrast, to hope, in anxiety, for the (absurd) possibility of ethical consistency, "is to make a kind of wager on the reality of an invisible 'proportion' pertaining between our particular series of finite positions, and that entire indeterminate reality which impinges upon, and seemingly undoes, our most meager

---

36. Ibid.
37. Ibid. 136.
38. Ibid.
39. Ibid. 133–34.

theoretical reckonings."[40] In other words, to hope is to make a wager that the movement of our particular historical series might be analogous to the mysterious dynamism of being as such. To deny that such hope is at least possible is, well, impossible for a subject who can never truly attain to a view from "outside" his own temporal situation.

Kierkegaard as Existential Theologian

But now a different question arises: Doesn't the suggestion that faith's wager is unable to engage in theoretical surveys mean precisely that the primary Christian urgency concerns the *living* of this wager, never the accounting for it, or the rhetorizing on behalf of it? Put otherwise, does not going this far with Kierkegaard also rule out or at least radically relativize the "metacritical" significance of theology in overcoming the atheistic wagers of philosophical reason? Milbank does not believe so, which stems from his peculiar interpretation of "absurdity" in Kierkegaard. Believing he can reconcile the absurdity of the Christian wager with the propulsion effected by a rhetorical form of communication, Milbank finds a way to say that Jesus as the revealed form of creation does not "repel" our truest thinking, does not take everything away, but gives it all back. He suggests, in other words, that because theology can show that the dialectical divisions of secular reason are not rationally necessary, but only subjective wagers themselves, the "absurdity" of theology's own wager comes out on top as the *most* rational:

> For here one espouses a *logos* which from the outset embraces the identity of eternity with time (albeit that its mode of repetition is not that of polytheistic proliferation), such that "absurdity" and "paradox" now become names *for* (a higher) reason, and what appeared acutely embarrassing for reason turns out, on the contrary, to disclose the true order and possibility of human thought.[41]

For Kierkegaard, of course, this "espousal" is never merely speculative, but inexorably imposes the task of transforming one's life in accordance with it. The possibility of "identity" between eternity and time faces the one who would so live as the requirement of contemporaneity with the one who identifies these two—i.e., with Christ in the form of abasement.

---

40. Ibid. 137.
41. Ibid. 138.

For Kierkegaard, moreover, this is an *offensive* solution; for Milbank, it is simply the solution: "Since the Christian *logos* persists in the general task of all reason, which is to establish 'identity' by mediating between time and eternity, when Kierkegaard says that he believes 'by virtue of the absurd,' he means 'by virtue of the incarnation,' and so for the best possible *reason*."[42]

Interestingly, Milbank does not herein bypass the necessity of existential enactment for Kierkegaardian "categories" to have real significance. Indeed, he suggests that "'Repetition' (as realizing identity) and 'the Moment' only become fully fledged ontological categories through the practical, existential affirmations of faith."[43] This resonates with the "existential" connotations of Milbank's own notion of linguistic "inscription" in *Theology and Social Theory*—i.e., with Milbank's suggestion that to be inscribed in a viable "plot" or series of transitions is not to be offered an "objective" character, but to be compelled to participate in the *movement* of the series. One has faith, for Milbank, precisely by *living* the manner of temporal transition that is "proportionate" to the way of Trinitarian supplementation. The significance of theology, therefore, is that it can be, in testifying to and so "repeating" the series of transitions inaugurated by Jesus, itself a persuasive enactment of the "measure" of peaceful transition. As *rhetorical*, theology as such for Milbank can be at one with "living." And Milbank believes Kierkegaard is on his side here, when he claims, "Kierkegaard does not suggest that we abandon philosophy (ontology) for religion, rather he 'saves' philosophy by transforming it, *without remainder*, into theology."[44]

Even this claim, which seems to give Kierkegaard an "office" to which he would never have pretended, also hopes to retain the existential dimensions of the practice of "theology." Indeed, for Milbank, Kierkegaard's existentialism is precisely what distinguishes him from poststructuralism, whose true forerunner is not Kierkegaard but German Idealism. For the latter, Milbank suggests, "the sublime had already been substituted for transcendence; Kierkegaard reinscribes transcendence by taking up and subverting the *impasse* of the sublime."[45] Kierkegaard accomplishes this reinscription through his account of the

42. Ibid. 139.
43. Ibid. 140.
44. Ibid.
45. Ibid. 142.

subject's primordial anxiety. For Kierkegaard, anxiety is provoked by the subject's relation to the eternal, which temporal creatures can know only as the dizzying infinity of the future. Kierkegaard suggests that anxiety itself is not sin until it resolves to "fear" that the moment's situatedness at the dizzying edge of the future must finally "destroy 'continuity,' meaning the intense and harmonious realization of human desires."[46] For Milbank, then, the difference in Kierkegaard between sin and faith is the same as that between fear and *eros* in the "in between" of the human spirit. Thus Kierkegaard is no poststructuralist precisely because he "existentializes" the problematic of temporal continuity, which implies that it only becomes reified as a "structural" problematic on the basis of a subjective precondition, not a metaphysical *a priori*. As Milbank puts it, "the alternatives—interruptive terror, or beguiling distance—remain subjective construals, decisive 'leaps' of human disposition."[47] Yet here again the crucial question arises, albeit in a new form: how can we ever be beguiled by the promise of the "intense and harmonious realization of human desires," when it requires the first move of giving up all of those finite projects in which we have already invested our hopes?

Milbank is quick to reply that any over-emphasis on the "first" movement of faith, the movement of renunciation, is at least possibly akin "to the sad passion of aesthetic melancholia," in which "one remains silent about one's desires, forswears their realization and appears to sacrifice *oneself* only because one confines oneself to this private theoretical theatre which snatches one away from the ethical continuum."[48] Milbank admits, of course, that in Kierkegaard there is a "religious rupture" of the ethical continuum, whereby religious love participates, in secret, in the divine economy, giving up the particularities of each and every beloved. This religious will must of course belong to a different economy:

> Not the ethical one which must operate within the constraints of human frailty, of possible death and the inequities of sexual attractiveness, but rather the economy of the love of God, in which even the physically or psychically mis-shapen are loved; where also there is no death, for this love can even love us into existence.[49]

46. Ibid.
47. Ibid.
48. Ibid. 143.
49. Ibid.

Despite this description of the religious as rupture, however, Milbank is only too eager to "go further," and reconcile the divine with the ethical economy—indeed, synthesize them, such that the ordeal of self-sacrifice might be no obstacle, but remain directly tied to the "return" of resurrection. Perhaps unsurprisingly then, Milbank seeks to read the religious rupture of the ethical as no real rupture at all, but as *the explanation* of how the ethical really works.

Getting us Through the "Ordeal"

Milbank here turns to Kierkegaard's *Fear and Trembling*, arguing that the teleological suspension of the ethical, the rupture of the ethical for the sake of the divine economy, "is an anti-sacrifice because it is a completely pointless sacrifice."[50] This pointlessness, the fact that the sacrifice of Isaac can have no ethically "founding" implications because it gives up even that which could be founded on sacrifice (the people itself), demonstrates that the truly religious sacrifice is "the only *possible* salve against the usual sacrificial economy which surrenders the individual to the city."[51] The religious rupture is therefore not so much the interruption as the upholding of the ethical economy, the only way to "get back" the "voluptuous variation" of something like marriage, as truly "ethical." Abraham suspends even the ban on murder, then, not in order to justify the renunciation of the particularity of the beloved in the name of an abstractly universal love, but in order to demonstrate the complicity of all social regulations in the despairing fear of death: "Death is inseparable from the feeding of life by life, so that the absolute upholding of 'life' which demands the ban on murder, will also tend contradictorily to demand sacrifice."[52] Thus Abraham's act of faith is a critique of the sacrificial necessity upon which the ethical, conventionally speaking, is based. Abraham's willingness to sacrifice Isaac—precisely because it has no ethically justifiable end—is "the giving up of the whole—one's own desire, the other, all the others—to God," which "alone makes possible the ethical, which is now 'transvalued' to exclude not murder alone, but also sacrifice."[53] Abraham's devotion is therefore a "rupture" of the ethical

---

50. Ibid. 144.
51. Ibid.
52. Ibid. 145.
53. Ibid. 144, 145. One must say that Milbank's is a clever and highly credible reading at this point, which is capable of wrestling with the offensiveness of Kierkegaard's

only insofar as it indicates a refusal of ethics as necessarily bound to a sacrificial causality. In other words, it *upholds* the ethical as *Sittlichkeit*, in Milbank's Hegelian terms. Ultimately, therefore, on this reading, "for Abraham to make the gesture of sacrificing Isaac is to know that he will not sacrifice him, or that Isaac will return."[54]

Abraham's ordeal of faith is not, for Milbank, the undergoing of an ultimate incompatibility of divine and human economies, but the living of their reconciliation, a reception of the human economy in its proper form, ordained by the creator for whom death is no obstacle. This of course does *not* mean that Abraham does not "give up" Isaac, nor that the Christian life of faith does not have to love the beloved precisely by "giving her up." As Milbank finally explains,

> In the Abraham story one sees how the ultimate vertical rupture of faith is supposed transcendentally to found and guarantee the continuity of ethical life, which is the life of the city. Only when we persist in continuity is salvation realized, but sustaining this achievement requires . . . a faith in the continued possibility of this continuity, despite all disasters. Thus only those forever prepared to surrender their desire and their beloved are ready for the married life, just as for Plato only those concerned with a vision beyond the city are fit to rule it.[55]

Hereby the two economies are reconciled in virtue of the necessity of engaging in the surrender of desire and others at every moment of life, *within* the properly ethical "continuum." And thus does Kierkegaard figure as an important "theological" corrective to poststructuralist

---

text in a way that John D. Caputo, for example, is not. In Caputo's recent book, *How to Read Kierkegaard*, he claims that "in *Fear and Trembling* we see the first signs of a distorted conception of religion that emerges in the last years of [Kierkegaard's] life, where the demands of God above are so overwhelming that they can completely annul the significance of life on earth. Instead of maintaining its tensions, the dialectic collapses. What goes ultimately amiss in Kierkegaard is that he believes temporal existence does not have the stuff, the substance, the wherewithal to withstand eternity if ever eternity makes an unconditional demand upon it, as God here demands the absurd of Abraham" (52). In so reading the religious rupture as a mere intensification of a sacrificial economy, Caputo does not go as far as Milbank in understanding how the divine economy ruptures the ethical as sacrificial, for Milbank claims that Abrahamic faith does not finally surpass but rather *institutes* a true version of the ethical, precisely insofar as Abraham's act can be read as *non-sacrificial*.

54. Milbank, "Sublime in Kierkegaard," 145.
55. Ibid. 146.

discourses about the sublime, in that he reveals, on Milbank's reading, the narcissistic nihilism on which the postulate of any "sublime" distance between the two economies is predicated. As we saw above, the poststructuralist reading of the impossibility of repetition implies that *every* effort of continuity within the ethical economy must traverse a "sublime" distance, which makes that economy necessarily "sacrificial," in that every transition sacrifices the consistency of subject and object to an arbitrary, aporetic measure. Yet Kierkegaard shows, in a metacritical fashion akin to that of Milbank, that this arbitrary measure is but a subjective construal, a decision against the possibility of hope and faith—taken in order to safeguard the self, by means of sacrifice, from the surrender required by any true hope that transitions are mediated according to the measure of "gift."

At this point it will be helpful to sum up the relation of Milbank's reading of Kierkegaard to Pickstock's dismissal, such that we can move ahead with a clearer sense of the relation between Radical Orthodoxy and Kierkegaard. Recall first that Pickstock's concern to construe the Christian religious life as a life "after writing" is opposed, she believes, to Kierkegaard's "covert individualism." For her Kierkegaard's reluctance to credit the historical tradition of Christian communing with any communicative relevance vis-à-vis living truth means he cannot reconcile the religious "rupture" with the promise it bears of "getting everything back." Kierkegaard's account of faith as contemporaneity is finally too gnostic, too despairing of the capacity of historical transition to "measure up" to the movement of Trinitarian supplementation. For Milbank, by contrast, it is precisely Kierkegaard's account of "repetition," or historical transition, that overcomes the postmodern—and indeed, the "bad Platonic"—since the Abrahamic rupture of the social/ethical continuum is in the name of "getting it back," in its fullness without the sacrificial elements. Accordingly, Milbank is much more sympathetic to Kierkegaard's indifference to the particularities of Christian history, or even his "reduction" of Christ's historicity to the "fact" of the Incarnation. Milbank claims, somewhat warily, that this reduction of "the historical"

> constitutes a necessary "destruction of the historical by the historical," since true historicity resides in a suspended "moment" that has already been, but is again, and again ceaselessly repeated and postponed. However one-sided and *possibly* apolitical we may find this Christology, Kierkegaard's main point is that it is

the "how" of the Christian process, the "style" of Christian life that is decisive, and not propositions concerning past facts, which always invite a probabilistic and speculative reduction.[56]

In other words, Milbank's rejoinder to Pickstock would be to suggest that "the point" of Kierkegaard's indifference to tradition is his reluctance to reify it in a manner that would allow history to be written and thus objectified. Hereby the requirement of "contemporaneity" is seen to be reflective of Kierkegaard's emphasis upon the *enactment* of the religious life, a warning against reading past facts as the "text of truth."

At the same time, of course, we cannot miss the fact that Milbank too would like to offer a narrative of the tradition of the church as "a true concrete representation of the analogical blending of difference,"[57] and that he therefore believes the "how" of the Christian process, as he calls it, can be communicated in such a narrative. Even in his sympathetic reading of Kierkegaard, therefore, Milbank is confident about the rhetorical power of his and Kierkegaard's theological historicism, the power it has to expose speculative metaphysics, in all of its ancient, modern, and postmodern variants, as despair, and thus to make the "leap" of the Christian subjective construal of historical transition the most persuasive one. For him, ultimately, Christianity's introduction of the absurd does not radically complicate religiousness, but emphasizes the rhetorical mediation of *all* subjective wagers; and, thereby disabusing the nihilistic ones of their rational justifications, Christianity becomes the most persuasive way of being, even the most difficult to refuse. It is with this suggestion in mind that we must finally turn to Kierkegaard.

"Difficulty" in the *Postscript*

Expectancy as Venturing, not Trading

Certain differences between Kierkegaard's and Milbank's uses of the absurd become immediately apparent in Kierkegaard's *Concluding Unscientific Postscript to* Philosophical Fragments. The question that will attend our discussion of the latter is whether the absurd must be read as Milbank reads it in order to retain theology's existential distinction from postmodern secular reason—that is, whether Kierkegaard's *Postscript*

---

56. Ibid. 147.
57. Milbank, *Theology and Social Theory*, 279.

must be mined, despite its apparent protests, for a rhetorical function of faith's "absurdity."

In the *Postscript*, Kierkegaard has his pseudonymous author, Johannes Climacus, tell us that his intention is "to make it difficult to become a Christian . . . because, viewed essentially, it is equally difficult for every human being to relinquish his understanding and his thinking and to concentrate his soul on the absurd."[58] Since this relinquishment is the qualitative difficulty of the essentially Christian, Climacus refuses, even in a lengthy treatise on what it means to become a Christian, to allow the treatise to serve as a mitigation of the difficulty. He refuses to claim to have written something whose "idiom" mirrors the movement of the Christian life itself, and thus his book contains no final assurances about its capacity to effect that movement in the individual human being, but instead the opposite: "What I write contains the notice that everything is to be understood in such a way that it is revoked, that the book has not only an end but has a revocation to boot."[59] Such a discourse contrasts with that of Radical Orthodoxy in that for Climacus there is no direct relationship between a construal of the "what" of Christianity and living its "how." To believe there might be, to believe that linguistic consonance with a construal is already a first step on the road of enactment, is to obscure the difference between the medium of writing and that of existence. As Climacus puts it, "there is no shortcut to the absolute good," which means "the merit of the religious discourse is in making the way difficult, because the way is the decisive thing—otherwise we have aesthetics."[60]

For an existing human being there is no "certainty" of the eternal absolute good, because in existence such a good can be known only as a relation to the future. For Climacus this means that in an individual's passionate interest in the absolute good, by which he "gives up" at every successive moment his passion for relative goods, he never attains a certainty about the "return" on his venture. The impossibility of this certainty is in the nature of existence as such: "the future and the present do have a little moment between them, which makes it possible to expect the future but impossible *in praesenti* to have any certainty and

---

58. Kierkegaard, *Concluding Unscientific Postscript*, 557.
59. Kierkegaard, *Postscript*, 619.
60. Ibid., 428.

definiteness."[61] Thus the actual living of a religious expectancy of eternal happiness is always to be characterized as *venturing, not trading*. The daringness of the religious venture has the same rigor at every moment, for every moment bears a relation to the future that is "*eo ipso* one of uncertainty."[62] Therefore even the championing of exemplars of this venture (e.g., Abraham) can never be meant to resolve the listener's own relation of expectancy, whose essential uncertainty is the provocateur and proper object of his passionate interestedness in his eternal happiness.

This suggests a distinction from Milbank, who uses Kierkegaard's account of the moment and repetition in conjunction with Abraham's exemplarity in such a way as to be able to say that "for Abraham to make the gesture of sacrificing Isaac is to know that he will not sacrifice him, or that Isaac will return."[63] What Milbank means, of course, is that Isaac is not the typical scapegoat sacrificed *to* the city, because in this case Isaac *stands for* the whole of the city, the promised people as such. In venturing not just Isaac but everything, Abraham therefore demonstrates the truly ethical gesture, which translates ethics out of the realm of sacrifice entirely. Yet Milbank seemingly overlooks the fact that to "know" in this way that Abraham *will not sacrifice Isaac*, to be able to "read" his gesture as an anti-sacrifice, is still not to know *that he will get Isaac back*, in that one can never know, in one's own ethical "ventures" of the whole, that God has in store what he did for Abraham. I can *believe* this, but the "exemplar" of Abraham cannot bridge for me the gap of expectancy to which I must relate in despair or in faith, in my own present moment of living. The religious address must therefore always remain with the difficulty, which keeps my own possibility of faith before me, as a gift whose reception is my interminable task. The task is interminable because it must be repeated at each moment, but it is a gift because it requires a continual renunciation of self-ownership, and therefore implies a striving for which, in and of myself, I have no sustaining resources. But what does it mean, exactly, to say that such a religious discourse, whose

---

61. Ibid. 424. Note the resonance of this account of temporality with Levinas' description of our "minimal distance" from the present, which denotes the expectancy of a future that can never "fuse" with the past and "delineate a fate," but always adds "something new to being" (*Totality and Infinity*, 283).
62. Kierkegaard, *Postscript*, 424.
63. Milbank, "Sublime in Kierkegaard," 145.

intention is to make it difficult to become a Christian, is at the same time directed toward the *possibility* of spiritual life for the human being?

The answer lies in what Climacus claims to have discovered thus far about Christianity—he has not comprehended it entirely, but knows at least this much: "that it wants to make the single individual eternally happy and that precisely within this single individual it presupposes this infinite interest in his own happiness as a *conditio sine qua non*."[64] In other words, Christianity wants to address the greatest of all human passions, the desire to be eternally happy, and it wants to make the single individual happy in this way without making said person into something he is not. Christianity, then, and Christian truth, is fundamentally an *existence-communication*. This implies that precisely in wanting to make the human being eternally happy, in addressing his infinite interestedness in becoming so happy, Christianity is not a truth *to be appropriated, once and for all*, but rather the *"how" of appropriation is the truth*.[65] Hence the folly of what Climacus calls "critical theological scholarship," which pursues the objective truth of Christianity with the immanent vision of a discipline like history, but which also "looks as if something for faith, something pertaining to faith, should suddenly result from this criticism. Therein lies the dubiousness."[66] Such dubiousness comes from the fact that a subjective passion, faith, is extinguished rather than satisfied by the attainment of objective certainty: "in this objectivity one loses that infinite, personal, impassioned interestedness, which is the condition of faith, the *ubique et nusquam* in which faith can come into existence."[67]

So what about appeals, if not to the objective accuracy of scriptural texts, then to something more fluid and so ostensibly closer to truth as appropriation, like the history of the church, the most common appeal of Radical Orthodoxy? Climacus admits that this is a more sensible appeal, and possibly a superior demonstration of the truth of Christianity: "the Church eliminates all the proving and demonstrating that was required

64. Kierkegaard, *Postscript*, 16.

65. Ibid., 313. Climacus says elsewhere that the one who wants Christian truth to be decided objectively "remains naively convinced that if only the object of truth stands firm, the subject will be ready and willing to slip it on. Here we instantly witness the youthfulness that has no inkling of that subtle little Socratic secret: that the relation of the subject is precisely the knotty difficulty" (*Postscript*, 37).

66. Ibid., 25.

67. Ibid., 29.

in connection with the Bible, since that is something past, whereas the Church is something present. To demand from it a demonstration that it exists . . . is nonsense."[68] But this demonstration is not quite all that is required—in addition one would like to know that this church is indeed the same apostolic church of two millennia ago; and in order to show this, we must invoke the uncertainty of historical transition and becoming, which means we are returned to the realm of "approximation," ill-fitted to satisfy an individual's passion for eternal happiness. Here we partake again of the "misunderstanding" that wants "to assure oneself objectively and thereby avoid the *risk* in which passion chooses and in which passion continues upholding its choice."[69] The passion of faith chooses by virtue of the absurd, which is cast here as *risk* rather than persuasion. Instead of reading the history of the church as "a true concrete representation of the analogical blending of difference," then, as Milbank does, Climacus compares the existence of the church and its "relevance" for faith with the hiddenness of love between a married couple, which he says

> is not a historical phenomenon; the phenomenal is the insignificant, has significance to the marriage partners only through their love, but looked at in any other way (that is, objectively), the phenomenal is a deception. So it is with Christianity . . . The invisible Church is not a historical phenomenon; as such it cannot be observed objectively at all, because it is only in subjectivity.[70]

Climacus believes that Christianity's "satisfaction" of the individual's infinite passion for eternal happiness puts said individual, who continues to exist in time, into a perpetual state of forward-moving expectancy, by which he must venture everything relative at every moment for the sake of the eternal good, while still remaining in the relative ends. It follows that the essentially Christian is never *established* in virtue of some particular genealogical arrangement of the relative ends. Rather, the essential task is undertaken in the continual inward movement of giving up the relative ends, a task whose premature "accomplishment" would conflict with the Christian life as expectancy in relation to an end that

---

68. Ibid., 39.
69. Ibid. 42. Emphasis added.
70. Ibid., 54.

is not directly "present" in the relative.⁷¹ The goal of the religious life is therefore not to renounce the relative visibly, but to pursue the relative *as relative*, to pursue it knowing that its attainment is, eternally speaking, a divine "jest": "If, for example, Napoleon had been a genuinely religious individuality, he would have had a rare opportunity for the most divine amusement, because seemingly to be capable of everything and then divinely to understand this as an illusion—indeed, that is jest in earnest!"⁷²

The human being cannot be satisfied with a truth that resolves the "knotty difficulty" of the subject's living relation to it with the salve of persuasion by a construal, for such a solution takes the person in question further away from himself as a "synthesis."⁷³ This implies that the path of religiousness cannot be given to me by another. A theologian can make Christianity present to me as a "what," or can even suggest to me that Christianity is a "how," but she can never refer to an exemplar of this "how" that allows me to bypass the difficulties of enacting it myself. The possibility of the "how" is confirmed for me only in my own living, which means that the "path" of such a life is not waiting for the best construal to make it more widely palatable. On the contrary, the path is blocked by palatability, which tempts the subject to overlook the task of confirming the viability of the religious life through her own enactment of faith. This means that "the course of development of the religious subject has the peculiar quality that the pathway comes into existence for the single individual and closes up behind him."⁷⁴ Thus, when the how of appropriation is the entirety of what the truth means, when the truth is to *exist* in the truth, then "communication is a work of art; it is doubly reflected, and its first form is the subtlety that the subjective individuals must be held devoutly apart from one another and must not run coagulatingly together in objectivity."⁷⁵

---

71. See ibid., 306, where Climacus asks, "For an existing person, is not eternity not eternity but the future, whereas eternity is eternity only for the Eternal, who is not in a process of becoming?"

72. Ibid., 462.

73. Ibid., 56. See also ibid., 82, where Climacus writes, "the existing subject is eternal, but as existing he is temporal. Now, the illusiveness of the infinite is that the possibility of death is present at every moment. All positive dependability is thus made suspect."

74. Ibid., 67.

75. Ibid., 79.

Doubly Reflected Communication

What the art of "double reflection" seems to imply for Kierkegaard's Climacus is a form of communication that immediately negates whatever it offers positively, in an effort to be true to the uncertainty of an existing human being's relationship, in existence, to an eternal happiness. The relation to the eternal as the future is for an existing human being a relation to "infinite" uncertainty, not least because "the possibility of death is present at every moment."[76] In the instant the religious communicator would offer some positive confirmation of eternal happiness, then, he invokes the uncertainty that speaks with the voice of death, the voice by which "all positive dependability is made suspect."[77] Faith as a passion for eternal happiness is evoked precisely by remaining in this objective uncertainty of existence. The "subjective existing thinker" therefore pursues truth's positivity only while remaining mindful of the fact that every positive objectivity is at most an uncertain approximation to an eternal happiness, which aggravates the passion by which faith nonetheless chooses the uncertainty. Thus can we conclude that

> the genuine subjective existing thinker is always just as negative as he is positive and vice versa . . . And his communication corresponds to this, lest by being overly communicative he meaninglessly transform a learner's existence into something other than what human existence is on the whole. He is cognizant of the negativity of the infinite in existence; he always keeps open the wound of negativity . . . He is, therefore, never a teacher, but a learner.[78]

Such a communicator is never a teacher, in that the relationship of an existing human being to eternal truth is always one of becoming, never of the certainty of being and possession.[79]

This aspect of Climacus' argument contrasts starkly with Pickstock's claim that "contemporaneity" in Kierkegaard is a kind of quasi-Platonic nostalgia for the lost "origin." Pickstock's inclination is to read the historical accretions of the years intervening between Jesus and the present as an "obstacle" for Kierkegaard, which implies that he elevates the

---

76. Ibid., 82.
77. Ibid.
78. Ibid., 85.
79. Ibid., 86.

contextual contemporaneity of the disciples above our own situational poverty. But for Climacus and Kierkegaard both, the point is that the "ditch" of uncertainty intervenes between the disciples and their possibility of faith just as much as it does for us. In fact, then, for Kierkegaard the intervening history is a possible distraction *not* because it threatens us with distance from the "origin," but because it might persuade us, on the strength of these "eighteen hundred years," that we can have a *more* direct relation to the origin than a historical contemporary could have hoped for. Climacus thanks Lessing for being helpful on this point, since for Lessing, "contingent truths of history can never become the demonstration of necessary truths of reason."[80] This means that Jesus as a historical figure cannot function as a direct "demonstration" of the truth by which we are made free, and nor can any subsequent historical event demonstrate this truth, if demonstration means removing the difference in genus between the historical and the eternal (rather than paradoxically holding them together): "Understood in this way, the transition whereby something historical and the relation to this becomes decisive for an eternal happiness is a [shifting from one genus to another] . . . a leap for both the contemporary and the one who comes later."[81] The dialectical character of the Christian form of truth, then, does not imply that through some proficiency in dialectical reason, or some uniquely effective abstraction from one's historical situation, one may become more able to appropriate such truth. Rather it suggests that Christian truth eludes our communicative grasp, yet nonetheless stands before us, ever provoking our passion for living by appealing to our infinite interest in our eternal happiness, the satisfaction of which cannot be directly communicated to us, as *existing* beings. Thus the secret of the dialectical for Climacus is "the renunciation of the fancy that in his God-relationship one human being is not the equal of another, which makes the presumed teacher a learner who attends to himself and makes all teaching a divine jest."[82]

This jest is not meant to ridicule the human—far from it. Religiously speaking, truth is subjectivity; it pertains to the "how" of living.[83]

80. Ibid., 97.
81. Ibid., 98.
82. Ibid., 101.
83. See Caputo, *How to Read Kierkegaard*, 13, where he writes helpfully, "If Christianity is 'true' it is true in the sense that the Scriptures speak of when it is said of

Therefore the religious address, because it refers the human being to his eternal happiness but does so precisely *in existence*, must "make fun" of its own teaching in order to ensure that appropriation, rather than any possible objective discovery, remains the only possible honest relation to truth, because such is the only possible *living* relation. And this must mean that there is no confirmation for the learner via an "exemplar," but only via the learner's own appropriation of the task of living, momentarily and repeatedly. World-historically, one sees "effects," but the ethical/religious is all about the intention, the "life," rather than the ossified historical "works" of the human being:

> Just as one does not see the ethical in [history], so also one does not see God, because if he is not seen in the role of Lord, one does not see him. In the ethical he does play this role in that possibility-relationship, and the ethical is for the existing, for the living, and God is the God of the living.[84]

God is Lord in the inward relationship of the single individual to his own ethical possibilities. God is Lord of that inner *how* of living, the comportment of the single individual to the relative as relative, and to the absolute as absolute. Of this comportment there can be no direct historical exemplar. Here God is the sole teacher.

Persuasions and Provocations

For Climacus, to exist means to have thinking and being held apart; it means to be able to "be" only in virtue of one's subjective relation to truth.[85] It means in effect that no rhetoric can do your living for you. Here the Radical Orthodox concern might be that a rigid distinction between the supposed abstraction of language and the uncertain medium of existence only holds for the "metaphysically justified" discourses of secular reason, or in Pickstock's words, for the spatialization of sophistic reason. The power of rhetoric, by contrast, is that as a form of language it eschews from the start any mode of persuasion that asks the subject to abstract his "reason" from his living. By appealing to his aesthetic sensibilities rather than to his reason alone, rhetoric can espouse a truth

---

Jesus that he is 'the way, the truth, and the life,' meaning that its truth is a way of living in the truth."

84. Kierkegaard, *Postscript*, 156.
85. Ibid., 191.

that is "rationally absurd" while retaining a fuller persuasiveness. Does not rhetoric, then, and the inscription it offers to the subject, represent the possibility of a reconciliation of the objective/subjective poles that Climacus insists existence holds apart? Climacus anticipates such a question when he himself asks, "can mediation then help the existing person so that he himself, as long as he is existing, becomes mediation, which is, after all, *sub specie aeterni*, whereas the poor existing one is existing?"[86] In other words, can the subject not actually become the reconciliation of truth and existence, such that he would *be* the (rhetorical) accomplishment of the religious life? If not, then does the subject not remain at a despairing, abyssal remove from truth as such?

We can get at the problem with contemporary theology's offer of a rhetorical reconciliation of the eternal and the temporal by first asking what, if anything, *can* reconcile the subject with truth. For Climacus the answer is "passion": "Only momentarily can a particular individual, existing, be in a unity of the infinite and the finite that transcends existing. This instant is the moment of passion."[87] And what provokes such passion? For Climacus it is not rhetoric but *paradox*: "Truth as a paradox corresponds to passion, and that truth becomes a paradox is grounded precisely in its relation to an existing subject."[88] The existing subject lives by virtue of a continuance of this "passion of the infinite," which indeed becomes "a *striving* that is motivated and repeatedly refreshed by the decisive passion of the infinite, but it is nevertheless a striving."[89] Yet it remains crucial that even in this striving, the subject does not accrue an objective certainty, nor become something that might offer such certainty to his observer. Rather, here it is the case that "*an objective uncertainty, held fast through appropriation with the most passionate inwardness, is the truth*, the highest truth there is for an *existing* person."[90] A passionate holding fast to the objective uncertainty is the "way" of truth, and such passion is squelched rather than satisfied by a rendering of the infinite's relation to the finite that mitigates the uncertainty with plausibility or persuasiveness. Therefore Climacus offers this series: "the more risk, the

86. Ibid., 192.
87. Ibid., 197.
88. Ibid., 199.
89. Ibid., 203. Emphasis added.
90. Ibid., 203.

more faith; the more objective reliability, the less inwardness; the less objective reliability, the deeper is the possible inwardness."[91]

But why indeed should it not be inspiring to the passion of faith to be presented with an image in which it appears *more* certain that some exemplar has *actually succeeded* in living religious truth? What does it mean, in other words, to imply that the rhetorical form of communication favored by Radical Orthodoxy cannot so easily evade the abstracting tendencies of speculative thought, which remove the subject from the existence-medium rather than reconciling her with it, as is the pretension of theological rhetoric? The answer, for Climacus, is that a directly persuasive exemplar of the actuality of religious truth inevitably becomes an occasion for the observer to evade the religious calling in his own living, even while convincing himself he is not evading it, because he does not disparage it—indeed, he admires it. Thus, instead of presenting it in the form of actuality, "what is great with regard to the universal . . . should be presented in the form of possibility. Then whether the reader wants to exist in it is placed as close as possible to him."[92] The rhetorical, therefore, despite its ostensibly serious attention to religious truth as spiritual incarnation/incarnate spirituality, is, insofar as its persuasiveness is related to its narration of the accomplishment of this reconciliation of the eternal and the temporal, ultimately soporific: "Ethically understood, there is nothing on which one sleeps so soundly as on an admiration over an actuality. And, ethically understood, if anything is able to stir up a person, it is possibility—when it ideally requires itself of a human being."[93] To have religious/ethical truth presented as possibility uniquely enlivens the passion of faith because it maintains that nothing essential is settled before the single individual relates himself, in faith, to the exemplar in his own living. Thus it is not out of disdain for the human that God is the sole teacher in regard to religious truth, and that all human teaching, all historical exemplarity, is a "jest" by comparison. Rather, the anti-rhetoric of the form of Christian truth is rooted in God's love for the human; it expresses God's unwillingness to deceive,[94] his refusal to allow the single individual to mistake

91. Ibid., 209.
92. Ibid., 358–59.
93. Ibid., 360.
94. See ibid., 246.

the putative "persuasion" realized in admiration for one's own subjective appropriation, one's own enlivening enactment of the task.

What then is the meaning of "action," if it cannot be measured by its external effects? Climacus says that "the actuality is not the external action but an interiority in which the individual annuls possibility and identifies himself with what is thought in order to exist in it. This is action."[95] He asks us to imagine that the Levite who at first could not do what the Samaritan did for the wounded man on the road, later turned back in repentance after passing him by, but returned too late to help. Climacus asks, "had he, then, not acted? Assuredly, and yet he did not act in the external world."[96] Here it is the inner "how" of living, rather than the world-historical effect, that is the actuality of truth in the existing human being. Climacus admits that making "the subjective individual's ethical actuality the only actuality could seem to be acosmism."[97] Certainly this is how Pickstock reads Kierkegaard's indifference to the rhetorical power that can be attributed to the "eighteen hundred years" that intervene between Christ and the Denmark in which he writes. To make the individual's ethical actuality the only actuality would mean for Pickstock to render "the real" in a spatialized, inner realm, abstracted from the historical *synaxis* of genuine spiritual living. For Kierkegaard, however, to say that inward ethical actuality is "all there is" is not to say that the enactment of this actuality is atemporal and abstract. Rather it is to say that there is no possibility of a direct historical communication of the only actuality worth talking about—the actuality of spirit. If this actuality could be directly discerned in the world-historical, the result would *not* be an inexorably enacted spirituality, but a reversion to the soporific possibility of admiration, whereby one comes to know "*what* erotic love is, *what* faith is, and the question is only about their place in the system,"[98] even a "rhetorical" system.

The Thinker's Task

What then is the task of the thinker, if it is not to "know what faith is"? For Climacus, the crucial thought that the thinker must include in all

---

95. Ibid. 339.
96. Ibid. 340.
97. Ibid., 341.
98. Ibid., 344. Emphasis added.

his thinking is "the thought that he himself is an existing person."[99] At first this sounds very much like Pickstock's appeal to the Socratic practice of dialectic, the sort of thinking/existing which she says prefigures the mode of life ultimately grounded in Christianity's definitively "supplemental" conception of the primal origin of being. But Climacus continues in such a way as to distinguish the thinker's task from the genealogical task of theology as understood by Radical Orthodoxy. He writes, "instead of having the task of understanding the concrete abstractly, as abstract thinking has, the subjective thinker has the opposite task of understanding the abstract concretely."[100] The thinker's task, in other words, is not that of construing the historical in such a way that it becomes persuasive as the narrative of a spiritual agency, but rather of understanding the ideal, the absolute *telos*, as the end to which one can be related in one's own comportment to the concrete and relative. To deemphasize the task of understanding the concrete abstractly in this manner is another way of making ethical *possibility*, rather than actuality, the crucial factor in any relation to an "exemplar." In other words, to be convinced of the *actuality* of another existing human being's success in relating himself to the absolute *telos* is precisely to understand the concrete abstractly.

The fundamental tenet of Radical Orthodoxy, which is that one might be "persuaded" by the presentation of history as a "representation of the analogical blending of difference," is being called into question here. Climacus suggests, along with Lessing, that the pretension to "blend" two different categories of knowledge, even via rhetoric, is problematic—indeed, that any appeal to particular historical transitions that makes history "believably" spiritual *in virtue of the historical*, is already a deception. We must of course remember that it is not the objective reliability of his genealogy that Milbank hopes will make it persuasive. Rather, he believes that a presentation of history as possibly *lived* in the mode of spiritual reconciliation will resonate persuasively with the human being whose unique possibility, as Kierkegaard notes, is that of being "a synthesis" animated by a loving (rather than strictly aporetic) relation of its "parts." Milbank therefore does not hope to bypass the requirement of belief, but hopes to persuade the human being, as a synthesis, into the reconciling *way* of belief. For Radical

99. Ibid., 351.
100. Ibid., 352.

Orthodoxy, in other words, rhetorical persuasion, because it hopes to exceed the requirement of a "metaphysical justification," is also opposed to the problematic "objective certainty" Kierkegaard criticizes. Just as Climacus believes the attainment of such certainty would kill the passion which properly animates the human being as a synthesis, so too does Radical Orthodoxy believe that its rhetoric jettisons metaphysical argument so that the *movement* of its narrative will appeal not to the desire for certainty, but only to the passion in which belief arises. The difference, to clarify, is that for Climacus theological communication can never actually "appeal" to that passion except insofar as it makes the possibility of faith as difficult as it really is. In this way, the passion is not directly elicited so much as it is emphasized that only such a passion is adequate to the task of appropriation, for the task *is the continuance of passion*. There is nothing to say, in other words, that will make the task directly appealing, for the crucial characteristic of its object is that, directly speaking, it is totally uncertain, and even absurd.

Despite the fact, then, that Radical Orthodox rhetoric does not seek to persuade in the manner of objective certainty, there remains a significant tension here in relation to Kierkegaard's advocated response to direct theological communication. Radical Orthodoxy seeks to show that *all* human beings make "wagers" about the nature of historical transition—whether it is an unmediable "abyss," or a rationally transparent but utterly "routinized" transition—which determine differences in modes of life. Its theological imperative is then to demonstrate that the Christian wager, while not more "metaphysically justified" than the various secular possibilities, is more fundamentally *persuasive*. The force of this persuasion is felt, it is believed, in a human being's confrontation with narratives which are themselves believing wagers of the Spirit's historical irruption in transitions that can be narrated as "love." So while Radical Orthodoxy offers no direct metaphysical justification of its genealogies, it does assume that the human heart will be more ready to accept a theological account than it is to accept a secular one, especially when it is shown that the secular pretension to a metaphysical justification is dubious. The imperative of Radical Orthodoxy, in other words, is premised on the assumption that once it is shown that "objective certainty" is entirely a ruse, *the theological wager will be the most difficult to refuse*.

By contrast, for Climacus the ministerial task, or we might just say, the task of the Christian communicator, "must be to win them if possible by scaring them away."[101] So while Radical Orthodoxy seeks to win human beings to faith by scaring them away from their dubiously justified secular wagers, Climacus seems to indicate that human beings are not only "duped" in their despair, but also actively "polemical" against the participatory wager of faith.[102] The disagreement here seems ultimately to hinge upon the variation between Radical Orthodox and Kierkegaardian understandings of what the Incarnation makes possible for theological communication—whether it allows theology to "go further" than, and so "consummate" the Socratic, or whether it utterly complicates and shatters all other forms of religiousness. We know that for Radical Orthodoxy the Incarnation persuades us of the possibility of *Sittlichkeit*. In the next section we must pursue what it implies for Kierkegaard.

Incarnation and Christian Difficulty

A Primer on Decisiveness

Climacus writes that "the essentially Christian" has as its defining characteristic the claim "that an eternal happiness is decided in time by the relation to something historical."[103] This means that unlike the "eternal truth" to which Socrates refers—the learning of which causes time itself to "vanish" as the subject recollects that he already has the truth from time immemorial—the learning of Christian truth implies a decisive transition. That is, becoming a Christian, on a proper understanding, is "the most terrible of all decisions in a person's life, since it is a matter," not of recalling that one is already in the truth, but "of winning faith through despair and offense."[104] Christianity thus brings the subject to life, not through persuasion but by leaving open the possibility of offense; and the transition characterized here is every bit as decisive as that between "death" and "life."

Milbank in his reading of Kierkegaard attempts to reduce the "decisiveness" of this transition. Recall, for example, his effort to "problematize the rupture" between Kierkegaard's skepticism and his fideism. The skepticism of Kierkegaard inheres for Milbank in his account of

---

101. Ibid., 365.
102. See Kierkegaard, *Philosophical Fragments*, 15.
103. Kierkegaard, *Postscript*, 369.
104. Ibid., 372.

"the moment" as the introduction of something utterly "new" to being. Thus the possibility of achieving an "identity," consistent through time, or across many such moments, becomes the primary object of Kierkegaardian "skepticism." For Milbank, the rupture imposed by poststructuralism between skepticism and fideism has to do with poststructuralism's refusal to countenance faith in a "measure" of traversal between such abyssally separated moments. Milbank would like to persuade us that these poles can be held together, just as he holds together a superlative historicism (which, in its refusal of all metaphysical justifications, is akin to "skepticism") with an unabashed commitment to a particular historical series (by virtue of faith's possible continuance). Thus he argues that for Kierkegaard, we are "preinscribed" as subjects within a text that necessitates "the event of decision,"[105] which implies "an ineradicable 'subjectivity' that poststructuralism is not owning up to."[106] Milbank's point seems to be that as existing beings we are always engaged in the process of temporal transition, experiencing the arrival from the future of successive present moments. Each such arrival is an event of "decision" because of the sublimity of the future's "distance," or in other words, because of our inability to traverse that distance via any secure knowledge. This means that "we cannot, especially, 'see' that there is no finite/infinite, determinate/indeterminate proportion, which the tradition called 'analogy.'"[107] If we cannot see or *know* that the future does not arrive via a measure that is analogous to the charitable differentiation of the Trinity itself, then one can only *conclude* the impossibility of this proportion via the "ineradicable subjectivity" poststructuralism is keen to avoid. Thus the conclusion of poststructuralism, since it cannot be justified as genuine knowledge, indicates a subjective nihilism at its root. As Milbank writes,

> We can only "characterize" the determinate/indeterminate, "sublime" relationship, which includes "acting it out," either as monism in which the infinite process is indifferent to finite instances which it constantly negates—in the line of Eleatic denial of motion, despite its Heraclitean espousals. Or else as transcendence in which finite moments are absurdly repeated as "eternity."[108]

105. Milbank, "Sublime in Kierkegaard," 148.
106. Ibid., 134.
107. Ibid., 148.
108. Ibid.

That is to say, we cannot *know* the sublime relationship of the future to the present, or indeed, we cannot *know* the measure of temporal differentiation; we can only "characterize" it via a subjective choice. And on this logic, we can see that the first characterization is a self-contradictory "choice against choice for immanentism," the act of a subject who despairingly refuses to be himself as an existing human being in relation to the eternal.[109] In contrast to this choice against choice, then, it is simply "ordinary, but constitutively 'human' choice," to which Kierkegaard appeals. The Christian "characterization," in other words, is not necessarily a massive and absurd transition away from the "natural" course of life. Instead, "if it happens to us that we continue to choose at all, then this is the choice of faith."[110]

Of course, this revelation of poststructuralism's "mistaken" dismissal of Kierkegaard's fideism in favor of his skepticism only, is not the only possible "Christian" reading of Kierkegaard. It remains tenable that an emphasis on Kierkegaard's skepticism, as the determinative characteristic of a postmodern, "second phase" of critique, hinges upon an unwillingness to "reconcile" the two aspects of Kierkegaard's work speculatively. In fact, as I hope to show below, Milbank's own reading of Kierkegaard, which makes rhetorical hay of his "theological" predilections, ultimately results in a very un-Kierkegaardian response to postmodernism, precisely because it misses the distinction between "Religiousness A" and "Religiousness B." The refusal of poststructuralism to make Kierkegaard's "fideism" do any philosophical work, in other words, may be better attuned to "the essentially Christian" as absurd than is Milbank's transformation of philosophy, "without remainder," into theology. There is a sense one gets from Milbank and from all Radical Orthodox theology that the Incarnation makes religious existence *easier*, not just in the sense that Jesus' mission makes the Christian life possible, which of course Kierkegaard would affirm, but in the sense that Jesus' life becomes a direct confirmation of the possibility of inspired living as *Sittlichkeit*, already intimated by the ancients. For Kierkegaard, by contrast, the Incarnation is not the "consummation" of philosophy, nor the crowning of theology as a metadiscourse, so much as it is an infinite philosophical "complication," as we shall see.

---

109. Ibid., 149.
110. Ibid.

Religiousness A as Existential but not Christian

Climacus tells us that the implication of the transition into Christianity is that Christian truth cannot be directly communicated in any theology, even his. Thus he offers only an introduction, and notes that "even with the most prolonged introduction in the direction of decision, one does not come a single step closer to the decision, because in that case the decision is not the absolute decision, the qualitative leap."[111] Even when Christian rhetoric "succeeds," then, it misses or evades the essentially Christian: "Philosophy leads directly to Christianity; the historicizing and rhetorical introduction does likewise, and it is successful—because the introductions are to a doctrine, but not to becoming a Christian."[112] The "dialectical" nature of the essentially Christian "consists in this, that the eternal happiness to which the individual is assumed to relate himself with proper pathos is itself made dialectical by additional qualifications, which in turn work as an incitement that brings passion to its extreme."[113] These "additional qualifications" have everything to do with the Incarnation of God in Jesus and how this distinguishes the essentially Christian from "Religiousness A," which is not un-dialectical, but which remains more amenable to the rhetorical project of Radical Orthodoxy than what Kierkegaard calls the "paradoxical-religious."

Let us remain for a moment with Religiousness A, or at least with what is common to both A and B. Both forms of religiousness understand truth to be subjective, and so not "doctrinal." In this we can detect a resonance with Catherine Pickstock's critique of sophistic "writing" for the way it "spatializes" truth, abstracting it from the requirement of *living*. Similarly with Radical Orthodox rhetoric in general, as we have already mentioned that the persuasion it seeks is not entirely an "objective" one. Rather, it conceives of "inscription" in its narrative as participation in an existential mode of living. All parties would agree, therefore, with Climacus' comment that the truth is not "witnessed" in writing: "The pathos lies not in testifying to an eternal happiness but in transforming one's own existence into a testimony to it."[114] Yet in terms of how the testimony of one's own existence can "speak," Radical Orthodoxy "goes

---

111. Kierkegaard, *Postscript*, 384.
112. Ibid.
113. Ibid., 385.
114. Ibid., 394.

further" than Kierkegaard. For Climacus, the religious existence, while it "holds together" the absolute with the relative *teloi*, does not do so by "mediating" between them such that visible relations somehow "communicate" something of the existing human being's absolute relation: "It is true that the individual oriented toward the absolute telos is in the relative ends, but he is not in them in such a way that the absolute telos is exhausted in them."[115] This means that the religious discourse will *always*—not just at the beginning, before it has been "explained"—sound insane to the natural man and the sensualist. Hence Climacus' chagrin when the pastor uses mediation by saying that the path of Christianity "is narrow, stony, difficult in the beginning, but little by little . . . and little by little the two paths begin to resemble each other quite closely."[116] And what happens then? Exactly what happens in Radical Orthodoxy, where the secularist is shown to be "deluded," in such a way that it becomes obviously insane to continue in his "nihilist" wager, since Christianity more adequately gives him what he wants. As Climacus puts it, "then the sensualist (the eudaemonist) is not only lunatic because he chooses the path of pleasure instead of the path of virtue, but he is a lunatic sensualist for not choosing the pleasurable path of virtue."[117] By contrast, for Climacus, the merit of the truly religious discourse (which holds even for Religiousness A) is not that it makes the strenuousness of the religious venture more palatable and persuasive, but consists "in making the way difficult, because the way is the decisive thing—otherwise we have aesthetics."[118]

The religious task has to do with existing in the relative ends, not absolutizing them by willing their utter destruction, but voluntarily giving them up in their capacity to make you "something" before God. The task, then, as Climacus puts it, "is to comprehend that a person is nothing at all before God or to be nothing at all and thereby to be before God, and he continually insists upon having this incapability before him, and its disappearance is the disappearance of religiousness."[119] Yet Climacus does not hereby suggest abandoning existence; indeed, he adamantly resists what he calls the monastic movement of the Middle Ages precisely

115. Ibid., 400.
116. Ibid., 403.
117. Ibid.
118. Ibid., 428.
119. Ibid., 461.

because it "made a powerful attempt to think God and the finite together in existence but came to the conclusion that it could not be done, and the expression for that conclusion is the monastery."[120] For Climacus this conclusion is a problem because it lacks the comic earnestness of the properly religious. That is, the Middle Ages understood the difficulty of "holding together" the two poles in a life, but so clearly that it despaired of the possibility of actualizing faith in existence. For Climacus, by contrast, the "maximum" of the religious task for the individual human being is this: "to relate himself simultaneously to his absolute telos and to the relative—not by mediating them but by relating himself absolutely to his absolute telos and relatively to the relative."[121] To abandon the relative, to abandon the medium of existence, is, despite its "spiritualist" ring, to require a direct, *outward* expression for the inner relation, which bespeaks an utter lack of faith.[122] In other words, Kierkegaard, like Pickstock, recognizes the dubious possibility that a strenuous emphasis on the priority of the absolute telos can result in a refusal to believe that faith is possible *as a way of living, in the relative*. The difference seems to be that Kierkegaard would not say that the mistake of the monastic movement was that it had a "bad" conception of the absolute. Rather, "the monastery candidate" was certainly right to think that "the greatest danger was not to relate oneself absolutely to the absolute telos at every moment,"[123] but was wrong to despair of the possibility of actualizing this relation in existence. The greatest danger, therefore, which "mediation" approaches, is that of ignoring the peril of not relating oneself at every relative moment to the absolute telos. The contradiction is that while the truly religious person must live "just like other human beings," at the same time "resignation will see to it early and late that he works to maintain the solemnity with which he existentially gained the orientation toward the absolute telos the first time."[124]

The Radical Orthodox response to this rigor might be that a refusal to mitigate the absoluteness of the relation to the absolute telos via "mediation" with the relative ends will ensure that the human being leads an utterly strenuous, humorless, and scarcely enjoyable life. This

---

120. Ibid., 473.
121. Ibid., 407.
122. Ibid., 413.
123. Ibid., 416.
124. Ibid., 406.

impression is certainly at the root of David Bentley Hart's misgivings with Kierkegaard. Yet Climacus insists that such a person must *enjoy* himself: "And why does he enjoy himself? Because the humblest expression for the relationship with God is to acknowledge one's humanness, and it is human to enjoy oneself."[125] In other words, the strenuousness of the religious offers at the same time the possibility of resting in one's humanity, which is "the profundity and likewise the irony of existence, that the acting can be done *sensu eminenti* fully as well when the person acting is a very simple person and the feat is to go out to the amusement park."[126] Only when even enjoyment can be held together with the solemnity of the infinite relation is there true comic earnestness. The contradiction between the two accentuates the comedy and arouses passion, whereas any mediating cancellation of the contradiction, while it might seem to make "reconciliation" more likely, reduces the passion of a *lived* reconciliation to a subjectively soporific (even if persuasive) construal. The proper enthusiasm of the religious person is that his outward activity, while not outwardly different from that of the next person, is inwardly deepened by "cutting off every teleological relation to what is directed outward, all income from it in finitude, even though he still works to the utmost of his ability."[127] This would cease to be religious enthusiasm if the religious person were to "mediate" between the absolute relation and his finite income, if he were to become certain, in other words, of his *success* in "holding together" the contradiction.

Religiousness B and Sin

Let us move now to the difference between Religiousness A and Religiousness B. For Radical Orthodoxy, to recall, the Incarnation and Jesus' sending of the Spirit combine to ensure that Christianity is the series most able to sustain human existence as a *living* inscription. That is, the Incarnation justifies a "constitutively supplemental" conception of the primal origin of being, in Pickstock's or Hart's terms, and thereby confirms the possibility of spiritual life, insofar as it reconciles the eternal and the temporal. The functional link here is "analogy," which is to say that the Incarnation demonstrates the possibility that the very

125. Ibid., 493.
126. Ibid., 497.
127. Ibid., 506.

movement of time might be both utterly unexpected in the newness it brings, and at the same time believably determined by the spiritual measure of "agape"—analogous, in this measure, to the eternal supplementation of the immanent Trinity itself. The Incarnation, in other words, validates the possibility of "going further" than Religiousness A, via theological doctrine. Let us keep this in mind as we follow Climacus' discussion of the uniqueness of Religiousness B.

Climacus writes that Religiousness A, which becomes attuned to the existential task of relating itself to the absolute telos by holding this absolute relation together with existence in the relative ends, is characterized by an inward pathos or passion, as we have seen. This relation is characterized as passion because it must hover in the objective uncertainty of the absolute telos, and relate itself to that telos by grasping its certitude only in faith, which does not cancel, but passionately overcomes, the objective uncertainty. Climacus says this existential pathos is moreover characterizable as "guilt," which is not the result of particular misdeeds in relation to the fundamental existential requirement, but is a "qualitative" guilt, which goes all the way "backward":

> This is how it goes backward: the task is given to the individual in existence, and just as he wants to plunge in straightway, and wants to begin, another beginning is discovered to be necessary, the beginning of the enormous detour that is dying to immediacy. And just as the beginning is about to be made here, it is discovered that, since meanwhile time has been passing, a bad beginning has been made and that the beginning must be made by becoming guilty, and from that moment, the total guilt, which is decisive, practices usury with the new guilt.[128]

The guilt is total or qualitative, and thus continues to characterize the existential pathos of religiousness, precisely because "to relate oneself existentially with pathos to an eternal happiness is never a matter of occasionally making a huge effort but is constancy in the relation . . . and in this, perhaps most of all, human beings fall short."[129]

What addition can Religiousness "B" make to this existential pathos, which recognizes the task of enacting, in the continuance of faith and precisely in the medium of existence, its relation to an eternal happiness, and which understands itself as qualitatively guilty before this

---

128. Ibid., 526.
129. Ibid., 535.

fundamental requirement? Perhaps the easiest way to begin to state the difference between the two is to emphasize that for Climacus, the consciousness of Religiousness A still lies entirely "within immanence," which can be seen in the fact that Religiousness A does not need the Incarnation. The human being who is attuned to existence in the mode of Religiousness A discovers the task within himself, in that he discovers the possibility within himself of passionately holding together his inward relation to an absolute telos with the medium of existence. He discovers, thereby, an "immanental underlying kinship between the temporal and the eternal,"[130] discovers that in existence, "the eternal is continually hidden . . . and in hiddenness is present."[131] But this sort of religiousness is only distinctively "Christian" if we can allow a movement from the immanent Trinity to the economic Trinity—i.e., if we can allow Christian thought, like secular reason, to be premised on a metaphysical *a priori*. That is, for this religiousness, which already understands, or discovers within itself, the possibility of a "constitutively supplemental" conception of being, the Incarnation of God in Christ does not appear as an inexorable paradox, but instead as the confirmation of a theological *a priori*, the rhetorical justification of an immanently discovered possibility of the *analogia entis*. The Incarnation thus becomes the possibility of "going further," of supplementing Religiousness A with "doctrinal" confirmations. On this understanding, then, Jesus does not increase the difficulty of the human being's achievement of true religiousness, does not "offend" this religious consciousness, but instead, in the telling words of David Bentley Hart, Jesus comes as "a delightful 'surprise.'"[132]

Climacus, by contrast, while he does not conclude that Religiousness A is absent of existential pathos, does indicate that the essentially Christian, or Religiousness B, adds further qualifications in such a way that it uniquely preserves the passion of the religious life. Religiousness A may be "dialectical," but Religiousness B is "paradoxical-dialectical." More specifically, "in Religiousness *A*, the eternal is *ubique et nusquam* but hidden by the actuality of existence; in the paradoxical-religious, the eternal is present at a specific point, and *this is the break with immanence*."[133] In Religiousness B, therefore, the possibility of relating

130. Ibid., 573.
131. Ibid., 571.
132. Hart, "Laughter of the Philosophers."
133. Ibid., 571. Emphasis added.

oneself to the eternal is not discoverable in oneself, because the eternal is proclaimed as present in a particular historical life. The actuality of one's own religious consciousness hereafter depends, paradoxically, upon one's relation to something historical—the man Jesus. That the eternal becomes incarnate precisely *here* moreover accentuates guilt as *sin*, because it suggests that there is no immanently discoverable "kinship" with the eternal of which I fall short, but rather emphasizes that I do not possess even the condition of this kinship. I am so far outside the possibility of this relation that the eternal had to become historical in order *to establish the possibility*. Therefore Jesus is not a delightful surprise but the sign of offense by which I am made conscious of my sin and forced to look outside myself for salvation: "There is no immanental underlying kinship between the temporal and the eternal, because the eternal itself has entered into time and *wants to establish kinship there*."[134]

The Annihilation of Possibility as the Annihilation of Theology

At this point a key difference becomes apparent between the "dialectical" as Kierkegaard articulates it and the "rhetorical" suggestion of Radical Orthodoxy, according to which Christianity offers a "consummation" of philosophy. The difference can be stated as that between the presumption of an underlying analogical kinship of eternal and temporal "supplementation," of which Jesus is the ultimate persuasion, and the claim that the proclamation of Jesus as the Word made flesh does not "consummate" our immanental discovery of kinship (allowing us to go further with Religiousness A) so much as it shatters our presumption in this regard:

> when the historical is outside and remains outside, and the individual, who was not eternal, now becomes eternal, and therefore *does not reflect on what he is but becomes what he was not* . . . What is inaccessible to all thinking is: that one can become eternal though one was not eternal.[135]

The difficulty that is unknown to Religiousness A, then, despite its existential pathos, is that one would find one's eternal happiness, not by reflecting on oneself, but in relation to something "outside" of oneself, something that, as historical, is but an approximation and thus by its

---

134. Ibid., 573. Emphasis added.
135. Ibid. Emphasis added.

very nature inadequate to the certainty of an eternal happiness. Here is the contradiction present in the Christian requirement of faith in Jesus Christ, that one is asked "to base one's eternal happiness on an approximation, which can be done only if one has no eternal qualification in oneself . . . which is why this in turn is coherent with the paradoxical accentuation of existence."[136]

It would be a mistake to read Kierkegaard's articulation of Religiousness B as the accentuation of a "metaphysical" or structural incompatibility. Instead, the accentuation of Religiousness B is meant to exacerbate the difficulty of becoming a Christian, which is always an existential difficulty. In other words, the "contradiction" clarified by the Incarnation ensures not that the essentially Christian remains utterly "sublime," and in this sense immanently inaccessible, but that the individual human being can *only* relate to it in the passion of faith. The Incarnation infinitely accentuates the difficulty of religiousness precisely in order to ensure that the religious life *will not become an objective state but will remain an inexorably passionate, and so spiritual, existence.* Kierkegaard believes this passion is only maintained in relation to the contradiction: "to require the greatest possible subjective passion, to the point of hating father and mother, and then join this together with historical knowledge that at its maximum can become only an approximation—this is contradiction."[137] Radical Orthodoxy wants to "go further" and claim that the Incarnation has persuasive and liberating implications for the historical as a "mere" approximation—that the Incarnation *confirms* a presupposition that the historical figures, at worst, as an "analogical approximation" to eternal supplementation. Kierkegaard will not suggest that this analogical possibility is simply wrong, but he implies that moving so easily from the exemplar who is Jesus to a general affinity between time and eternity easily forgets that the Incarnation means God wants to make the human being into something she presently is *not*. In other words, it forgets that the Incarnation does not confirm the actuality of "constitutively human choice" as *already* "analogous" to the movement of *caritas*, so much as it offers this movement to the human being as a new possibility, which we must therefore assume she has previously forfeited.

136. Ibid., 574.
137. Ibid., 576.

For Kierkegaard, to use Jesus as a confirmation of the "identity of eternity with time"[138] is indeed to make the Incarnation into the "consummation" of Religiousness A, but it is also to remain within its parameters, and thus to risk reducing religious discourse to objectifying chatter. As Climacus puts it, the accentuation of existence effected by Religiousness B is such that "every Christian is Christian only by being nailed to the paradox of having based his eternal happiness on the relation to something historical,"[139] which means above all that Christianity is not a metaphysical doctrine. On this point Kierkegaard and Radical Orthodoxy reach a putative agreement, though Kierkegaard is ready to show how even a rhetorical response to secular metaphysics remains all too systematic:

> If . . . the coming into existence of the eternal in time is supposed to be an eternal coming into existence, then Religiousness B is abolished, "all theology is anthropology," Christianity is changed from an existence-communication into an ingenious metaphysical doctrine addressed to professors, and *Religiousness A is prinked up with an esthetic-metaphysical ornamentation that in categorical respects neither adds nor detracts.*[140]

This does not exactly mean that for Kierkegaard such an eternal coming into existence or an "identity of eternity with time" is impossible, but that for him the essentially Christian does not come to confirm or persuade us of this possibility, but *to "annihilate" it as a possibility, and to demand a decision about it as an actuality*—the actuality of Jesus. While it might seem to Radical Orthodoxy that an actuality is not so much the annihilation as it is the persuasion or confirmation of a possibility, for Kierkegaard Jesus' actuality exposes the speculative possibility as an illusion that allows the individual to presume he is relating himself to the paradox, when in fact he remains in a "fantasy-medium" and does not yet know the absolute paradox:

> The person who understands the paradox will, misunderstanding, forget that Christianity is the absolute paradox precisely because it annihilates a possibility (the analogies of paganism, an eternal becoming-of-the-deity) as an illusion and turns it into actuality . . . *In the fantasy-medium of possibility, God can very well*

138. Milbank, "Sublime in Kierkegaard," 138.
139. Kierkegaard, *Postscript*, 578.
140. Ibid., 579. Emphasis added.

> coalesce with humankind in the imagination, but to coalesce in actuality with the individual human being is precisely the paradox.[141]

For Climacus, then, the consequence of the Incarnation is not that Religiousness A's immanently discovered presence of the eternal in existence is confirmed and rendered more persuasive by Jesus' initiation of a particularly "reconciled" historical series. We could very well assent to religiousness as the "possibility" of coalescence with the god, but that the god actually coalesces with us as a particular human being forces a disclosure of our hearts via a decision about this Jesus. Thus, the result of the Incarnation is that "for the believer, *offense comes at the beginning*, and the possibility of it is the continual fear and trembling in his existence."[142]

What then is left for the religious discourse, or "theology," to communicate? The theologian's inclination at this point might be to speak about the Incarnation in such a way that he or she would help others get *past* their offense. For Climacus, however, we ought to look at Jesus as historical only to increase the paradox and thus to heighten the passion of faith, for "direct recognizability is paganism; all solemn assurances that this is indeed Christ and that he is the true God are futile as soon as it ends with direct recognizability."[143] But is it not part of the Christian task to reflect on, and exposit, what it means to be a Christian? Climacus replies that, "since the highest is to become and to continue to be a Christian, the task cannot be to reflect on Christianity but can only be to intensify by means of reflection the pathos with which one continues to be a Christian."[144] Thus Climacus himself refuses to make reflecting on Christianity as a "doctrine" the same thing as heeding its existential call, and tries at all times, if not directly to intensify his reader's pathos (which would be self-defeating), at least to keep before his reader Christianity's requirement of such pathos.[145] The ultimate theological consequence of the Incarnation, then, is that a distinctly "theological" form of commu-

---

141. Ibid., 581. Emphasis added.
142. Ibid., 585.
143. Ibid., 600.
144. Ibid., 607.
145. Ibid., 619. Here Climacus says that "just as in Catholic books," which come with a statement of ecclesiastical approval, "so also what I write contains the notice that everything is to be understood in such a way that it is revoked, that the book has not only an end but has a revocation to boot."

nication becomes utterly irrelevant to the fundamental Christian task, and that no form of communication with the goal of becoming a metadiscourse ought to call itself "theological," though it may be a compelling expression of that more "natural" theology called Religiousness A.

The Invitation: Kierkegaard's *Practice in Christianity*

Given that we have arrived at this point through a consideration of the accentuation of existence brought about by the Incarnation, and have gathered that for Kierkegaard the possibility of "offense" is what characterizes the essentially Christian, I propose that we now turn to his discussion of Christ as the reconciling inviter, such that we might reiterate and clarify just how this invitation is mediated or possibly received.

Practice in Christianity is another pseudonymous work, this time penned by "Anti-Climacus," whose name obviously refers to and appears even to oppose the author of the *Postscript*. However, as Howard and Edna Hong write in their historical introduction to the text, the "anti-" "does not mean 'against' but 'before,' a relation of rank, the higher."[146] As with all of Kierkegaard's pseudonymous works, we can assume that the importance of his using another name is "in wanting to have no importance, in wanting, at a remove that is the distance of double-reflection, once again to read through solo, if possible in a more inward way, the original text of individual human existence-relationships."[147] The difference in "rank" of these two pseudonyms in particular becomes clear in their distinct "tones"—Johannes is the crafty dialectician who does not pretend to be a Christian, and Anti-Climacus is much more the preacher, given to a presentation of the Christian requirement which forces it up "to a supreme ideality."[148] This does not mean, of course, that Anti-Climacus is a rhetorical mediator in the vein of those preachers with whom Johannes takes issue; and in the other direction, Johannes' portrayal of the essentially Christian is not so far off a "supreme ideality," insofar as he makes it his task to make it "difficult" to become a Christian. While neither could write in the voice of the other, it is also clear that each works within the same Kierkegaardian ken.

---

146. *Practice in Christianity*, xiii.
147. Kierkegaard, *Postscript*, 629.
148. Kierkegaard, *Practice in Christianity*, 7.

Anti-Climacus begins with the invitation rather than the offense, yet ensures from the beginning that we do not become so enamored with being "invited" that we imagine we conceived this reconciliation in our own hearts; most especially this means he makes sure we do not forget the difficulty of achieving contemporaneity with the inviter. Just as for Radical Orthodoxy the Incarnation is an invitation to and a demonstration of reconciliation, so too for Kierkegaard, Jesus' invitation is a reconciling one. In saying "come here, all you, and I will give you rest," Jesus offers, in himself, a reconciliation of man to God. Moreover he offers a reconciliation with all other human beings, insofar as the scope of his invitation implies a decisive leveling: "The invitation blasts away all distinctions in order to gather everybody together; it wants to make up for what happens as a result of distinction: the assigning to one person a place as a ruler over millions . . . and to someone else a place out in the desert."[149] This blasting away of distinctions is not akin to the nihilism of a metaphysical opposition to reconciliation, save through the cold abstraction of a "death" to existence. But insofar as one can only "reconcile" the religious truth of equality with the distinction of existence not by "mediating" them but by inwardly *dying to distinction*, then this invitation, this leveling, *is* like the call of death in Heidegger: "The invitation stands at the crossroad, where death distinguishes death from life."[150]

The call from the crossroad of death, the call "out" of worldly distinction, is a call to both the distinguished ones and to those "whose residence has been assigned among the graves." And as a call out of distinction it is nonetheless—indeed, all the more—a call and an invitation to find rest in true life.[151] The invitation is to a life that moves freely among and across all the "differences" that mark life and loss in terms of possession. It is an invitation to a living *in* those differences, via a movement which immeasurably exceeds them. How is this invitation, then, from the one who is the way and the truth and the life, in the flesh, not a "persuasion," in the sense that Milbank calls the Incarnation "the best possible *reason*" to have faith?[152]

Anti-Climacus does not make such a claim because, as he puts it, this invitation provokes an inevitable "halt." He clarifies that it is not so

149. Ibid., 17.
150. Ibid.
151. Ibid., 18.
152. Milbank, "Sublime in Kierkegaard," 139.

much before the invitation that one halts (for *on its own*, the invitation is but another declaration of Religiousness A) as it is before the inviter. And who is the inviter? "Jesus Christ. Which Jesus Christ, the Jesus Christ who sits in glory at the Father's right hand? No. From glory he has not spoken a word. So, then, it is Jesus Christ in his abasement, in the situation of abasement, who has spoken these words."[153] But can we not "go further" than Christ's abasement, we who live in the "knowledge" of resurrection and ascension? No again, for we have no access to the Christ in glory except by believing on him in the form of abasement: "He does not exist in any other way, for only in this way has he existed."[154] Resurrection and ascension are only "relevant" for the one who believes that precisely *this particular abased man* is the elected and exalted one.

A rhetorical theology might respond by suggesting that too much is being made of this halt. Jesus himself seems to "verify" his promise of true life through his manner of treating those whom he touches and heals. But as Anti-Climacus points out in this regard, Jesus does not "heal" by any but an offensive measure. Indeed, to any human wisdom, his offer to "help" by promising the forgiveness of sins seems like cruelty. In this particular offer, Jesus suggests, as no "Religiousness A" could discover on its own, that *"sin is a human being's corruption."*[155] Jesus' apparent cunning is that he speaks of and with compassion but at the same time seems to say, "I acknowledge only that there is one sickness—sin—of that and from that I heal all of those . . . who labor to work themselves out of the power of sin . . . but manage only to be burdened."[156] At this point, Christianity becomes "madness" to the one who wants to be rhetorically persuaded by Religiousness A, or in other words, to the "sensate person." For not only does one become a Christian at the risk of a consciousness of sin, but also at the risk of a martyrdom that is continual even in a tolerant age, when the martyrdom of one's own understanding precedes each repeated moment of willing to be contemporary with Christ in abasement. Anti-Climacus writes:

> Christianity came into the world as the absolute, not, humanly speaking, for comfort; on the contrary, it continually speaks about how the Christian must suffer or about how a person in

---

153. Kierkegaard, *Practice in Christianity*, 24.
154. Ibid., 24.
155. Ibid., 61.
156. Ibid.

order to become and remain a Christian must endure sufferings that he consequently can avoid simply by refraining from becoming a Christian.[157]

But our own generation, one might be inclined to object, is qualitatively different from Christ's. We do not face the same sufferings, because Christianity now has a "history" initiated by this invitation, a "body" that has carved out a space in the world that is accommodating to the would-be sufferer. But to Anti-Climacus, such an objection is "nonsense and un-Christian and muddled thinking, because whatever true Christians there are in any generation are contemporary with Christ, have nothing to do with Christians in past generations but everything to do with the contemporary Christ."[158] In other words, to think that the "history" of the church makes Christianity more accommodating because it has ensured that those who profess faith do not face physical violence is to miss entirely the meaning of Christian suffering and martyrdom, which inhere in faith's inward willing to be contemporary with Christ. If this is not possible for you, "if you could not go out into the street—and see that it is the god in this dreadful procession and this your condition if you fell down and worshiped him—then you are not *essentially* Christian."[159]

What then ought you to do? Ought you to find or even invent assurances to the effect that the god is seen precisely in this man? Is there any possibility of such assurance? The answer to both questions is of course "no," and the Christian task in this regard is finally to "learn and to practice resorting to grace in such a way that you do not take it in vain; for God's sake do not go to anyone in order to be 'reassured.'"[160] To resort to grace authentically means to confess with honesty where you stand in relation to the requirement of ideality: "Honesty before God is the first and the last, honestly to confess to oneself where one is, in honesty before God continually keeping the task in sight."[161] This implies a life that rests even in its failure to live, "resting" not because it "mediates" or synthesizes the failures with authentic living, but because it confesses them in honesty and therefore is related in truth to the

157. Ibid., 63.
158. Ibid., 65.
159. Ibid.
160. Ibid.
161. Ibid., 66.

need for grace. The refusal to "mediate," or to seek to be "reassured" that one is a Christian, does not therefore imply morbid self-loathing, even if it does mean self-mortification for the sake of truth (martyrdom). Christianity comes into the world in order to spiritually awaken human beings in time, which means to allow them to admit without shame their tendency to seek objective security in direct, speculative assurances of "life." Beyond this honesty, "nothing further; then, for the rest, let him do his work and rejoice in it, love his wife and rejoice in her, joyfully bring up his children, love his fellow beings, rejoice in life."[162]

With the invitation, then, comes this crucial injunction: "Examine yourself: what if you had lived contemporary with him!"[163] Kierkegaard reminds us of this requirement especially in the presence of Christendom's suggestion that "the truth that once was contending is now the established order. To be in the truth can no longer mean to have to suffer, and the more one is in the truth the more suffering. No, here is congruity."[164] But the requirement of contemporaneity with Jesus as the god-man, Kierkegaard argues, never becomes "congruous" with membership in the established order. The established order as such seeks its own deification, its own ability to confirm, by turning itself into direct "evidence" of, the divine nature of the particular man in question. For Kierkegaard, however,

> Every human being is to live in fear and trembling, and likewise no established order is to be exempted from fear and trembling. Fear and trembling signify that we are in the process of becoming; and every single individual, likewise the generation, is and should be aware of being in the process of becoming.[165]

The essentially Christian religious individual thus refuses to appeal directly to the established order for his criterion of truth and life, and instead appeals above it, to his God-relationship, which he does not have in conjunction with any other human being. Such an individual hereby belongs to the established order but does not participate in its deification, which makes him, of course, always its enemy. This is part of the suffering which the religious individual endures on the basis of his being

---

162. Ibid., 67.
163. Ibid., 39.
164. Ibid., 89.
165. Ibid., 88.

in the process of becoming a Christian, through honest self-examination in relation to the requirement of contemporaneity with God in Jesus Christ. This is also his imitation of Christ's suffering, in the sense that it was out of love for the established order as, in truth, a *human* order, that Christ had to become for it the sign of offense. So too at all times the Christian, in relation to any established order defined objective-historically, must express in his life a loving indifference to its efforts of self-deification, and must therefore appear to others as if *he* is the one trying to be *more* than human. The possibility of contemporaneity with Christ does not become less difficult as an object-historical order, such as the church, becomes a more "direct" testimony to the Incarnation, for the humility of "fear and trembling" should cause any such order to remain indifferent to its own directness in the first place. Thus, "the possibility of offense in relation to Christ *qua* God-man will continue until the end of time."[166]

All of this raises certain questions about Radical Orthodoxy's proposal of the necessity of cultural inscription. That is, Radical Orthodoxy suggests that in order for theology to resist the objectification of the religious life proffered by secular reason's boundary between transcendence and immanence, it must make the persuasive counter-offer of a peaceful tradition or series of historical transitions in which we can become inscribed as characters, alive to incarnate spiritual truth. Kierkegaard's account of the established order calls into question any supposedly direct relationship between one's inscription in a particular social order and "conversion" to life in the spirit. We shall have occasion in the next chapter to pursue Milbank's critique of accounts of Christian sociality that are putatively as vacuous in terms of their material recommendations as Kierkegaard's is at this point. The work of René Girard in particular will prove helpful here, since Girard develops a way of reading texts and cultures that aids us in seeing the established order's falsehood, "brought about by ignoring its own origin,"[167] as Kierkegaard puts it. In the final chapter, however, we shall find ourselves turning again to Kierkegaard, and specifically to *Works of Love*, in order to develop an account of Christian love that is opposed to preference (and also to rhetoric) even as it refuses the metaphysical dualism of immanent and transcendent

---

166. Ibid., 94. See Kierkegaard's comments about the possible misunderstanding of his position as "anarchism" in *For Self-Examination/Judge For Yourself!*, 19–21.

167. Kierkegaard, *Practice in Christianity*, 88.

that characterizes all secular reason. In this move, finally, we shall come to the culmination of our critique of Radical Orthodoxy, which begins here with the revelation of its attempt to *consummate* "Religiousness A" via Christian theology, and will eventuate in the suggestion that Radical Orthodoxy comes up short of its own hope to defend Christianity as an unwaveringly existential mode of sociality.

Conclusion

We began this chapter by asking why it makes sense at all to pursue a conversation between Radical Orthodoxy and Kierkegaard, given the decidedly dismissive treatment the latter receives from some quarters. First we heard Catherine Pickstock's critique, according to which Kierkegaard propounds a "contemporaneity" whose relativization of historical mediation equates with a predilection for truth unmired by any temporal deployment. Second we explored David Bentley Hart's chastisement of Kierkegaard for his lack of humor, which Hart says concerns the ability to receive all of finitude's suffering and yet to "transcend despair through jest."[168] Kierkegaard ultimately fails in such comedy, Hart argues, because he remains unwilling to allow that Christianity might have a direct, cultural effect in the world.

Next we considered John Milbank's more sympathetic treatment of Kierkegaard, wherein he resists the easy alignment of Kierkegaard's "skepticism" about historical continuity with the more characteristically postmodern proposal of an irreconcilable "abyss" between Being as such and its temporalization. For Milbank, rather, Kierkegaard's intention is to reconcile the "absurdity" of repetition with the possibility of a historical consistency-through-faith, even on the basis of the "absurd," which for him means the Incarnation. Milbank thus relates the Kierkegaardian notion of "absurdity" to the Radical Orthodox postulate that historical commitments are mediated aesthetically (and so rhetorically) rather than via dialectical reason. This propelled us into a much more productive conversation between Radical Orthodoxy and Kierkegaard, whose guiding question was whether or not Kierkegaard's refusal to hypostasize skepticism in opposition to faith provides an opening and even an injunction to communicate the possibility of faith rhetorically. When we turned specifically to Kierkegaard, then, we were asking whether the

---

168. Hart, "Laughter of the Philosophers."

"difficulty" of conversion, which Kierkegaard undeniably stresses, is the result of residual sympathies with secular reason, or of existential qualifications that Milbank's theology ignores.

We saw the realization of this possible critique of Milbank in our discussion of the importance and effect of the Incarnation in Radical Orthodoxy and in Kierkegaard. For Radical Orthodoxy, the Incarnation does not infinitely complicate all former religiousness, but "consummates" an already redeemable, if pagan, philosophy of supplementation. In effect this means that Radical Orthodoxy seeks to "go further" than Religiousness A on the power of "theology" alone, which limits it, ironically, to the realm of a kind of pre-Christian natural theology. By contrast, the Incarnation of God in Christ is for Kierkegaard no "delightful surprise," but the point at which the "dialectical-religious," or religion as the *task* of temporal enactment, to which Radical Orthodoxy appeals in its best moments, becomes "paradoxical-dialectical." With the Incarnation it is revealed that all immanently discovered religiousness is a ruse; the fact that the eternal had to become temporal at a specific point means we have a need for a teacher, that we do not have the condition of the religious life within ourselves, but that we are even "polemical against the truth" and must therefore relate ourselves to the actuality of another, this God-man, and thereby "resort to grace." We are not "persuaded" by the actuality of Jesus of the reality of our own previously intimated kinship with the divine; rather are we shown, by the appearance of the teacher, that we are in sin, that we have forfeited and are continually forfeiting the condition of such kinship, and that even our previous intimations of religiousness were in the mode of this forfeiture, the mode of a refusal to be given our lives by God.

Mindful of the fact that this "complicating" Jesus nevertheless *invites* us to come and receive rest, we turned finally to Kierkegaard's *Practice in Christianity*. There we tried to understand how the kindness and love of Christ's invitation could be held together, not with the pseudo-absurdity of a rhetorical persuasion, but with the genuine "absurdity" of needing to be for each and every believer the sign and possibility of offense. Specifically we saw how this understanding of Jesus' redeeming action implies an irreconcilable confrontation between the inwardness of faith's passion and the "authority" of the established order, which continues "until the end of time." That is, with this Christianity, the requirement of contemporaneity with Christ provokes faith as *irreducible* passion, which, as contemporaneity with God in Christ, requires in every age an indifference to the established order's pretension to any direct or rhetorical alignment with the criterion of eternal truth. It implies, in other words, a decidedly anti-cultural Christianity, or at least an indifference to the effect of religion as a direct, "cultural" effect.

This implication provokes a final objection from rhetorical theology, which is that such an emphasis upon Christianity's indirect form of truth extends to the evacuation of Christian sociality of any content, in such a way that secular metaphysical presuppositions about the incompatibility of "religion" and "the social" are allowed to creep back in. This is the predictable outcome, Radical Orthodoxy suggests, of any overemphasis on the "indifference" of religiousness to the historical, which is that it does not transfigure the meaning of history so much as it loses its seriousness about the Incarnation altogether. Thus we must now turn, in the fourth chapter, to a particular articulation of such a "vacuous" ethic, namely that of René Girard, and to Milbank's critique of the same, which ultimately proffers a "synthesis" of Christian *agape* with preferential *eros*. We shall then have occasion to offer a rebuttal to this account of love in the fifth and final chapter.

4

Cultural Logic and Christian Sociality

Introduction

As we have seen in previous chapters of this book, John Milbank's theological project culminates in a construal of Christianity as the unique possibility of a peaceful mode of life. In the first chapter we saw that for Milbank, theology alone is fit to become a "metadiscourse" because it alone "remains the discourse of non-mastery."[1] Theology's non-mastery consists in its refusal to offer "metaphysical justifications" for its wager of a possibly lived reconciliation of transcendent and immanent, spirit and nature. This refusal means that Christian *Sittlichkeit* does not require that the subject who would appropriate it first "master" his passions via reason. When we considered Milbank's reading of Kierkegaard in the previous chapter, we were able to clarify how theology's wager of the possibility of intra- and inter-subjective reconciliation implies an opposition to any sociality determined by "sacrifice." Milbank helps to show that the ostensibly religious practice of sacrifice inheres even and perhaps especially in secular social orders. For in order to maintain the immanence of the immanent, secular reason institutes a "boundary" between immanence and transcendence that cannot be traversed except by violence. Thus, to secure its city *as secular*, secular reason must establish the necessity of sacrifice, even if perhaps unbeknown to itself. On Milbank's reading of Kierkegaard's *Fear and Trembling*, Abraham

1. Milbank, *Theology and Social Theory*, 6.

opposes precisely this necessity when he wills to give up Isaac (not one element of the city, but the whole of it) to God. Abraham's gesture indicates a refusal to institute a "boundary" between the human city and the economy of divine justice in the name of falsely "securing" the former. Radical Orthodoxy opposes sacrifice in a similar way, for in its appeal to a particularly Christian sociality, it suggests that human participation in the divine measure of love does not require the violent expulsion of anything in particular. Rather than sacrificing "the one" in order to maintain the city's self-security, Christian sociality requires one to give up "the whole," which means to act upon the promise of reconciliation without fear and in self-denial.

In the present chapter we shall pursue the concrete meaning, for Milbank, of such a non-sacrificial reconciliation of divine and human economies of love. We will contrast this project of reconciliation with the work of René Girard, to whom Milbank is at least partially indebted for his analysis of the manner in which non-Christian political formations are predicated upon the necessity of sacrifice. Yet Girard does not appeal to Christianity's alternative as a "new social mechanism," as Milbank does. Eventually, we shall pursue the critique that Milbank levels at Girard for this ostensible deficiency, and show how it extends to a dismissal of characteristically "dialectical" differentiations of the purity of *agape* from the fundamental corruption of human *eros*. We shall see, therefore, that Milbank's Christianity does not seek to mortify human *eros* so much as woo it toward an object that exceeds its current persuasions. My own critical claim in this chapter shall be that Milbank's corresponding tendency to appeal directly to concrete social practices as decidedly "Christian" misses the possibility of a "rupture" between divine and human economies of love that is due, not to what he calls a "univocal ontology," but rather to a sensitivity to the manner in which sin pervades the erotic as preference. In the final chapter, we shall build on this and try to show how a Christian ethic that inexorably "ruptures" and mortifies the erotic, and therefore remains empty of direct appeals to ostensibly Christian practices, does not thereby fail Christianity as a unique mode of sociality, a "way" that exceeds the objective binaries of secular reason.

Milbank's *Altera Civitas*

In the final chapter of *Theology and Social Theory*, Milbank argues that Christian theology is only distinct from secular reason as social science "because there is also a distinguishable Christian mode of action, a definite practice."[2] This indicates that theology's task is not to out-speculate secular reason's objective definitions of the parties to any social order, but instead to reflect on "a distinct society, the Church."[3] Granting the contingency of its "ontological" wager, Christian theology can and even must begin not with "pure reason" but with the aesthetics of the church's history. So Milbank says that Christian theology's threefold task is prioritized as follows: "counter-history," "counter-ethics," and "counter-ontology."[4] He believes that through the first task one comes to see the *ecclesia* as an historical "interruption," and that upon describing the particular ethical practices that animate this history, "Christianity starts to appear—*even 'objectively'*—as not just different, but as *the* difference from all other cultural systems."[5] The crucial difference, however, comes to light in theology's third task, that of articulating Christianity's "counter-ontology," through which one sees that all the concrete differences are rooted in a wager of faith whose distinction makes up the "'total' difference" from secular reason and sociality.[6]

Augustine Versus Nietzsche

Crucial to the manner in which theology as a rhetorical discourse opposes secular social theory is the priority of its "genealogical" task. The Christian wager, as the sole possibility of *Sittlichkeit*, cannot hope to "persuade" in a rhetorical and thus reconciling manner if it appeals first to a speculative construal of reality.[7] That is, a discourse is only

---

2. Milbank, *Theology and Social Theory*, 380.
3. Ibid., 381.
4. Ibid. Notice how this prioritization mirrors Hans Urs von Balthasar's progression from aesthetics to drama to logic, and reverses Kant's own order—pure reason, practical reason, judgment.
5. Ibid. Emphasis added.
6. Ibid.
7. On this point, see also Milbank, "Invocation of Clio," where Milbank writes, "for us, in the present, the epiphany is always-already repeated by traditional interpretation, and indeed *traditio* is itself the only epiphany, which is not, however, to deny its vertical ecstasy" (7).

truly post-metaphysical if it eschews the objectifying rationalisms upon which secular reason bases its separation of immanent from transcendent. If the "idea" of a discourse is to be really *viable*, then it "of its own nature demands a return to the concrete, narrative level."[8] To put it in a way that more clearly distinguishes theological allies from enemies, "if Jesus really is the word of God, then it is not the mere 'extrinsic' knowledge of this which will save us, but rather a precise attention to his many words and deeds and all their historical results."[9] Milbank's suggestion here targets especially modern Protestant theology, whose ostensibly pious assertion that the Christ event is totally paradoxical vis-à-vis human history does not adequately account for how this interruption may determine a new historical *series*. If the Christ event cannot be read as having such a continuing and "legible" relevance, if it cannot be seen as an interruption with a possibly narrated *continuance*, then the religiousness of Christianity remains a mere instance of "charisma" in a Weberian history. Consequently, the narrative which orients genuine Christian theology, for Milbank, "is *not* just the story of Jesus, it is the continuing story of the Church, already realized in a finally exemplary way by Christ, yet still to be realized universally, in harmony with Christ, and yet *differently*, by all generations of Christians."[10]

At this point, Augustine's story of the unique *civitas* originated by the Christ event becomes crucial for Milbank. Augustine narrates the movement of a new spirit in history, the Spirit of the Christ for whom, uniquely, suffering violence in obedience cancels the ontological purchase of that violence. Nietzsche too recognized this interruption, recognized that Christianity's "peculiar mode of difference, the celebration of weakness (as Nietzsche inadequately described it) showed up by contrast a *common* element in all other cultures, namely, a heroic ethical code celebrating strength and attainment."[11] For Milbank, Augustine maintains the "peculiarity" of the Christian mode of difference precisely because his historiography does not pit the *civitas Dei* against the earthly

---

8. Milbank, *Theology and Social Theory*, 385.

9. Ibid. Here we see how uncomfortable must be Milbank's expression of sympathy for Kierkegaard in "The Sublime in Kierkegaard," as his whole statement here is about an attention to historical results that "will save us."

10. Milbank, *Theology and Social Theory*, 387.

11. Ibid., 389.

city, nor see it as "emerging" from one of the conflicts that animate the *civitas terrena*. In contrast, then, to both Hegel and Marx, Augustine

> puts peaceful reconciliation in no dialectical relationship with conflict but rather does something prodigiously more historicist, in that he isolates the codes which support the universal sway of antagonism, and contrasts this with the code of a peaceful mode of existence, which has historically arisen as "something else," an *altera civitas*, having no logical or causal connection with the city of violence.[12]

As historicist, Augustine's narrative is not an "explanation" of the Christian process so much as it is a repetition and a new instantiation of Christianity's interruptive wager of "the ontological priority of peace over conflict."[13] Its guiding speculative principle is not an *a priori* claim but is necessarily grounded "in a narrative, a practice, and a dogmatic faith."[14] To offer such a historicist account, a genealogy rather than a metaphysics, is to be grounded in "faith" because it is to remain related in one's living to the historical *as infinite uncertainty, which also means infinite possibility*. This is to remain in the true, anxious situation of every historical "present," from which the pretension to a "metaphysically justified" truth hopes to escape, and which naught but faith can abide. To be historicist in Augustine's sense is therefore to have a "dogmatic"— i.e., metaphysically uncertain—faith that the particular tradition of the church, determined by a willingness to forego the violent deployment of rigid conclusions about supposed "offenders," makes possible a comportment to the future as uncertainty that nevertheless wagers a viable continuance.

"Supernatural Materialism" and Christian Socialism

In the case of Christianity's counter-ethics, which is tied to its counter-history, Milbank stresses its interruptive difference from "*both* modernity *and* antiquity."[15] In other words, for Milbank there can be no residue in the theological articulation of Christian praxis of either the "the protestant view of the Church, which understands it as an association

12. Ibid.
13. Ibid., 390.
14. Ibid.
15. Ibid., 399.

of individual believers who possess, outside the social context, their own direct relationship to God,"[16] or the ancient supposition that one's political virtue is won through a conquest of the *oikos*. Both of these ethical paradigms suggest that the realm of true freedom, be it that of "politics" or of "faith," is in a dialectically opposed relationship to the "social." Therefore, the Christian ethical difference must be felt in terms of its elevation of that which both ancient and modern reason deem "irreconcilable." Milbank focuses on the domestic realm as the primary locus of this elevation—an emphasis he claims to retrieve from the self-understanding of the early church, in which "the 'household' became a metaphor for the Church itself, indicating that association between its members, and mutual support, was a vital aspect of its life."[17]

In any case, the critical matter is to be able to construe Christianity as concerned with an irreducibly spiritual goal, but without suggesting thereby that it is unconcerned with material arrangements, or without suggesting that material arrangements do not "matter" spiritually. Milbank thus emphasizes that for Augustine, while the *ecclesia* has no objectively definable *telos*, this does not mean that the Christian ruler is "indifferent to the fate of the celestial city on pilgrimage, insofar as the true 'rule' of charity is being enacted, and not simply a *usus* being made of earthly things."[18] That is to say, just because the celestial city is not concerned in its pilgrimage with the "end" of the *civitas terrena* as mere "use," still its "rule" has much to say about the arrangement of those objective ends, insofar as every such arrangement speaks to and reveals a "way" of being. So this pilgrim city "continually *is* the differential sequence which has the goal beyond goal of generating new relationships, which themselves situate and define 'persons.'"[19] On the Augustinian understanding, then, Christianity is distinct not in virtue of its *indifference* to social order, but in its comportment to social order *as the possibility of generating and preserving relationships of charity*, rather than the mere possibility of "accumulating" the objective. In this respect, Milbank concludes, "more than is usually recognized, Christianity implies a unique and distinctive structural logic for human society."[20]

16. Ibid.
17. Ibid.
18. Ibid., 404.
19. Ibid., 405.
20. Ibid., 406.

Milbank finds it helpful at this point to contrast Augustine with Aquinas on the relationship of properly Christian concerns to the "logic of human society." Aquinas, Milbank argues, makes the problematic suggestion that social life is in some manner "natural," which correspondingly "opens the way to regarding the Church as an organization specializing in what goes on inside men's souls; his affirmation, for example that the new law of the Gospel adds no new 'external precepts,' seems to tend dangerously in this direction."[21] Milbank believes this move is more "Cartesian" than Augustine even in his worst lights, in that its chief effect is "the tendency to see the finite/infinite relation as something 'inwardly' encountered."[22] A concession that governance is in some manner "natural," that it is effective in a realm whose concern can be delimited to the achievement of finite goals, thus fails in the intended reconciliation of *oikos* and *polis*—or more generally, the reconciliation of virtue with difference—because it assumes that the "means" of the essentially Christian life, the deployment, in other words, of the finite/infinite relation, has no "social" relevance. Indeed, it assumes that the category of "social relevance" cannot be receptive to such a measure, since it necessarily proceeds according to its own natural machinations.

Such a nature/supernature distinction seems on the one hand to operate on the basis of a profound seriousness about the material—a willingness to understand it "on its own terms." Thus does Aquinas understand the passions as "natural," pertaining transparently or directly to their finite, material objects. But this allows for a conception of contemplative pursuits as belonging to a different "genus" than that of the passions, and thereby leaves open the (ancient Greek) conclusion that because the infinite/finite relation is known or contemplated inwardly, it therefore does not apply essentially to the passions. For Milbank, Augustine's "materialism" is therefore superior to that of Aquinas, since Augustine does not allow the "material" an exclusively natural domain. That is, Augustine does not speak of passionate *and* of contemplative pursuits, but only of desire, which animates *both* aspects of the soul.[23] For Augustine, then, it may be finally improper even to speak of two aspects of the soul, since whereas Aquinas subordinates appetite to

---

21. Ibid., 407.
22. Ibid., 408.
23. Ibid., 415. Augustine, *Civitas Dei*, XIV 6, 7.

apprehension (in classic Greek fashion), for Augustine "all apprehension occurs through appetition."[24]

Since Augustine presupposes a reconciliation of passionate experience and "knowledge" of the finite/infinite relation via the common medium of *desire*, he does not need to assume either that there "is" a realm in which finite ends are pursued unto themselves, or that the sphere of explicit concern with the finite/infinite relation excludes a definite concern with the material arrangement of finite ends. For Augustine, these finite ends may become, through a *charitable* arrangement, part of the finite/infinite measure that is the form of creation as such. In short, then, Augustine's reconciliation of apprehension with appetition allows him to articulate an "ethics" that is essentially Christian, while retaining a materially distinguishable structural form. For Milbank, this form is especially captured in a kind of "socialism," which leads him to express a (somewhat reserved) sympathy for

> the first Christian socialists in France, the group round Pierre Buchez, who . . . considered that Augustine had discovered a "social" realm (which, nonetheless, under the influence of St Simon, they understood in far too positivist a fashion) and that "socialism" would restore and extend it, through a proliferation of self-managing, egalitarian and cooperative groups. *Like medieval guilds, these groups were also to be religious associations, "orders" within the Church, although by no means subordinate to clerical control.*[25]

Such socialism captures what Milbank is trying to say here about Christianity's reconciliation of virtue with difference because the "guild" system embraces a distinct model of cooperation, whose egalitarian arrangement of finite ends aligns harmoniously with the meaning of a "religious" association. Indeed, this arrangement brings the pursuit and sharing of material ends decisively within the realm of charity, thus incorporating the material itself, in virtue of a particular structured deployment, into the very spiritual proportion of the finite/infinite relation.

This socialism, and the "supernatural materialism" by which it is animated, Milbank derives from Augustine's suggestion of the necessity of right worship in any truly just society. That Augustine makes worship fundamental to the justice of society "does not mean," however, "that

---

24. Milbank, *Theology and Social Theory*, 415.
25. Ibid., 408. Emphasis added.

Augustine's real criticism lies solely at the level of religious practice,"[26] as if the Romans could have redeemed their politics simply by spending more time at church. Instead, Milbank argues, "Augustine believes that the form taken by true worship of the true God is the offering of mutual forgiveness in the community," and therefore, "the pagans were for Augustine unjust, because they did not give priority to peace and forgiveness."[27] This communal conception of worship applies directly to the socialism Milbank espouses because that structure is based on a "wager" of the non-necessity of competition and retaliation in the processes of production and attainment of material ends. Milbank's socialism, in other words, aims to be a sphere of reciprocity, which implies that it will think of matter as primarily significant only in terms of its possible arrangement in accord with that aim. And for Milbank, only worship of the true God, which assumes that even the "material" of creation only *is* through an arrangement that facilitates relationships analogous to those among the persons of the Trinity, can forego retaliation for an offense whose goal is possession of the material as mere "matter." That is, only such worship can dispose members toward the offender in such a way that they do not "see" the offense, since for them an offense like greed or theft does not register as a rival accumulation of "being" (which is the offender's thought), but as the offender's self-punishing exclusion from the true being of charitable relations, an action that is therefore "rectified" only by an extension of charity as forgiveness in the direction of the offender. Thus does Milbank conclude that charity for Augustine is not "a matter of mere generous intention: on the contrary, it involves that exact appropriateness of action necessary to produce a 'beautiful' order, and, in this sense, charity is the very consummation of both justice and prudence."[28]

This implies also that there *is* no element of the sinful human being that must be mortified in order for God to make him a "new creation." Instead, for Milbank, God's atoning work is one of re-ordering the sinner's desire, and therefore it is not an exclusively vertical, divine act, but happens through the offender's incorporation into a body that "is" because it forgives. Such a body communicates itself to the offender as life

26. Ibid., 409.
27. Ibid.
28. Ibid., 411.

and reconciliation only insofar as it is inextricably bound to a tradition that makes harmony a livable structure:

> Although "the goal beyond goal," (the non-telos) of charity, is the creation of difference, and in consequence, liberty and equality, it aims also in this creation to reproduce itself as love and friendship. It follows that charity has to be a *tradition*, that new moves must locate themselves in the tradition, be accepted within the tradition, even though such a tradition must also be radically open-ended.[29]

This is the hope residing at the heart of a distinctively Christian social vision, which is that through a precise and beautiful ordering of the material, new creations will be made of those who did not previously consider that the "radical open-endedness" of the future as such could be approached in the mode of a continuing "friendship." So Milbank says the church "should be a space where truly just economic exchanges occur, in the sense that the equivalents of value are established between product and product, service and service," and that a serious effort to deploy such a mode of exchange in the world will correspond to a hope "that the space of arbitrary exchange, motivated by the search for maximum profit, and dominated by manipulation . . . can be made to recede."[30] Such is the uniquely Christian possibility of *Sittlichkeit*, its capacity to "reconcile virtue with difference," in the sense that it is able to see differences as the material for the supernatural arrangement of charitable and thus virtuous relations. Christian charity *is* a process of differentiating, and "only because it allows difference does [Christianity] truly realize *Sittlichkeit*, whereas the antique closure against difference meant that it really promoted a heroic freedom which was only for the few."[31]

Christianity's Unique Speculation

Christian theology finally offers a counter-ontology, in addition to its counter-history and counter-ethics. The ontology, which consists in Christianity's doctrine of the Trinity, articulates the ultimate difference of Christian thought from both ancient and modern reason, in that a

---

29. Ibid., 416.
30. Ibid., 422.
31. Ibid., 417.

conception of the origin of all being as three-in-one, united by love, prohibits from the outset any hypostasization of "unity" or "difference," and likewise any irrevocable boundary between infinite Being and its temporalization. Rather, according to the Trinity, God is "the God who differentiates."[32] The eternal itself is therefore a movement "from unity to difference, constituting a relation in which unity *is* through its power of generating difference, and difference *is* through its comprehension by unity."[33] What, if anything, does this have to do with the *creatures* of such a differentiating God? Milbank argues that, "just as an infinite God must be power-act, so the doctrine of the Trinity discovers the infinite God to include a radically 'external' relationality."[34] This "discovery" leads Milbank to conclude, in turn, that "the created world of time participates in the God who differentiates; indeed, it *is* this differentiation insofar as it is finitely 'explicated,' rather than infinitely 'complicated.'"[35] As we have heard before, then, creation itself is not a collection of discrete "things" at all. Rather, the God who differentiates *creates* by generating persons who, made in his image, only "have" a personhood through their own analogical possibility of further, charitable differentiation. What *is* means what *moves* in the way of this differentiation, and "creation is therefore not a finished product in space, but is continuously generated *ex nihilo* in time."[36]

In virtue of this difference in ontology—according to which creation is not related to its origin of being only insofar as one can discern "objective" similarities between finite and infinite "things" (think "ideas" versus "copies") but through the creature's possibility of a dynamic analogical alignment with God's own movement of differentiation—the fundamental human task is utterly reconfigured. Whereas for the ancients contemplation was the goal of a good life—since it seems to remove the human being from realm of objective dissimilarity and make him as much as possible "like an idea"—for Christianity, "the task of human creative differentiation is to be charitable, and to give in 'art' (all human action) endlessly new allegorical depictions of charity."[37] Theology's

32. Ibid., 423.
33. Ibid., 423–24.
34. Ibid., 424.
35. Ibid.
36. Ibid., 425.
37. Ibid., 426.

"counter-ontology" hereby gives rise, Milbank believes, to a discernibly *socialist* practice, for the task of giving new "allegorical depictions of charity" implies the enactment of a certain kind of exchange that can, through love, generate and situate "persons." Being situated by a loving, just form of exchange, as in Milbank's socialism, means becoming a "person" because as the initiation of a *way* of being in relation to others, it opposes the human being's former life as objectively defined by the accumulation and possession of mere "things." Christian speculation thus becomes, in virtue of the peculiarly generative character of its object, another enactment of the reconciliation of virtue with difference. That is, contemplation of this object cannot mean becoming more objectively similar to an idea, but instead becoming increasingly "constituted" by this object, in one's corresponding enactment of the measure of charity. Thus, derived from Augustine, Milbank writes, "truth, for Christianity, is not correspondence, but rather *participation* of the beautiful in the beauty of God."[38]

Reserving the difference of Christian ontology for the end of his book, Milbank prefigures the way in which Catherine Pickstock articulates the most essential distinction of Christian thought as a kind of speculative "going further," an articulation we examined in the second chapter. Consider Milbank's characterization of Christian speculation:

> Building on the neo-Platonic recognition of the One as itself "without limits" . . . both Augustine and Dionysius (in their Trinitarian theologies) *went further* by situating the infinite emanation of difference within the Godhead itself, and in this fashion overcame the "third antimony" of antique reason, between the "gods" of truth and the "giants" of difference.[39]

Here again, Christianity is introduced as a speculative difference from, but also a consummation of, ancient Greek reason. Neo-Platonism could go *as far as* conceiving of an ontological principle that did not necessitate an understanding of created, temporal reality as a fundamental "negation" of being. And yet, just as Pickstock discovers a residual "tragedy" in the Platonic conception of creation as the temporalization of the good, so too Milbank argues that the "emanation of difference"

---

38. Ibid., 427. Note the resonance here with Balthasar's claim, in *Seeing the Form*, that Christian contemplation is not an exclusively noetic practice but "a life-form which indissolubly unites the aesthetics of faith with the mystery of suffering" (524).

39. Milbank, *Theology and Social Theory*, 428. Emphasis added.

in which creation participates must be situated in the Godhead as such (Pickstock calls this Christianity's conception of a "constitutively supplemental" origin of being). The doctrine of the Trinity therefore implies a more direct relationship between creation and its principle or "idea," since no "objective" criteria separate them; and at the same time it makes unity with that idea ostensibly far less abstract, since the desired reconciliation is not with an objectified monad, but with the "interval" of a particular relation. We are, for Radical Orthodox theology, both closer to the "idea," *and* utterly disabused of any ideal*ism*; for the Christian "idea" is only *had* in the *way* of our living.

Milbank's later treatment of Kierkegaard is already implied in this connection between speculation and its necessarily repeated and therefore uncertain "confirmation." Milbank's appeal to the Baroque, in particular, suggests his later appropriation of Kierkegaard's putative "reconciliation" of fideism and skepticism. Noting Christianity's task of differentiation as resonant with the Baroque trait of stressing the possibility of temporal difference "to its limits," Milbank argues nonetheless that "the path of dissonance is not embarked upon."[40] Yet Milbank will not tolerate the suggestion that in its ultimate opposition to dissonance, Christianity simply does not have the stomach for the "gaps" of temporal differentiation that threaten "repetition" as consistency.[41] Instead, "one should say, it is always possible to place dissonance back in Baroque 'suspense'; at every turn of a phrase, new, unexpected harmony may still arrive."[42] To be unwilling to admit such suspended harmony as a *possible* shape of temporal life is to be too "metaphysically" certain about the putative necessity of dissonance. Thus, Milbank will suggest that retaining the possibility of harmony is more genuinely connected, not to a self-assuredness about the "metaphysical justification" of such a wager, but to a skepticism which can only be traversed by faith: "Between the nihilistic promotion of dissonance, of differences that clash or only accord through conflict, and the Baroque risk of a harmony stretched to the limits—the openness to musical grace—there remains an undecidability."[43]

40. Ibid., 429.

41. This being, in effect, Slavoj Žižek's critique of Milbank in *Monstrosity of Christ*. See especially 248–49.

42. Milbank, *Theology and Social Theory*, 429.

43. Ibid.

Going Further with Rhetoric

While this emphasis upon the undecidability between the two alternatives seems to stress the "objective uncertainty" that Kierkegaard emphasizes in order to maintain faith as an inexorable *passion*, Milbank is not content to leave the matter as undecidable as all that. In fact, because he believes the "nihilist" option, which reifies what we have been calling a Kierkegaardian skepticism, is inextricably bound to an untenable "metaphysical" presupposition of an "ontology of difference," he can make a rhetorical case for "deciding" on a Christian ontology instead: "The thought of God as infinite Being, as difference in harmony . . . *ends and subsumes all philosophy*, just as the Christian counter-ethics ends and subsumes all politics."[44] This "end" of philosophy is realized only when theology *refuses to stop* with its own moment of "skepticism," which would be to capitulate to secular reason's reification of the sublime "distance" of temporal difference, the sacrificial "leap" between successive moments. Theology's thoroughgoing historicism means it is able to "go further," and construe those leaps not as the inevitably repeated treachery of beings against Being, but as the compelling possibility of achieving peaceful harmony through the repeatable enactment of charity. Thus Milbank can claim, in relation to theology's own task, that *"the aesthetic reconciliation of the sublime with the beautiful is the same task as the ethical reconciliation of virtue with difference."*[45]

I emphasize this last statement because it captures with succinctness the connection between Milbank's claims about Christianity as the unique possibility of *Sittlichkeit* and the urgency of his concern to usher in Radical Orthodoxy's "new theological imperative."[46] The meaning of this statement is effectively that the task of living Christian *Sittlichkeit* can be identified with the task of writing "aesthetically compelling" theology. In the previous chapter we saw that the reconciliation of skepticism and fideism Milbank advocates is based on an understanding of sin as one possible response to anxiety. As Milbank notes, the existing

---

44. Ibid., 430. Emphasis added.
45. Ibid., 431. Emphasis added.
46. This sentiment is succinctly captured by Graham Ward's defense of Christian apologetics, which he says grounds "the Christian mission not only to disseminate the good news, but *to bring about the cultural and historical transformations concomitant with the coming of the kingdom of God.*" Ward, "Barth, Hegel, and the Possibility for Christian Apologetics," 43. Emphasis added.

human being's relationship to the future as a "dizzying infinity" is what provokes anxiety. The possible responses to anxiety are fear (with all of its concomitant possessive results) or faith, which Milbank says is action toward a future still construed as distance, but a distance that is "beguiling," even erotically so. The Christian task of living is therefore to "build" upon Jesus' action, which for Milbank means to continue the tradition he initiates and sustains—a tradition that does not reduce the contingency and uncertainty of repetition, but lives toward that contingency with a faith in love's capacity to be the "interval" between present moments. This implies that virtuous actions are those that take temporal intervals to be utterly undecidable, but in the direction of openness, rather than closure. Good actions thus "compel" us to recognize the possibility of a reconciliation of love and sublime distance: "A well-made deed should be like a picture which *admits the sublime within the scope of its beauty*."[47] The theological imperative, by extension, enjoins a rhetoric that "beguiles" the reader toward the sublime as an opening rather than a dead end—a sacrificial gap. Secular reason, in its reification of the gulf between being and its temporalization, is always directed *away from living*, always concluding that temporal continuance is impossible. Milbank therefore tries in his own theology to connect the concession of uncertainty intrinsic to an act of faith with an unabashedly persuasive presentation of the possibility of living temporal uncertainty via *caritas* rather than fear. In contrast to faith, fear resolves *not* to traverse the "gap" of temporal differentiation, and thus not to *live*. Therefore it should not surprise us that the "difficulty" of the essentially Christian does not figure prominently in Milbank's work. For him, instead, "the beautiful form taken by the opening of the sublime gulf *ought to make the gulf appear attractive*, must seem to manifest, be suspended by, the gulf itself."[48]

In this ontology, evil is not a "real" adversary of God, but stems from "a will to the inhibition and distortion of reality."[49] Such a will is rooted in "a free subject" who fails to recognize the possibility of hope in the situation of anxiety, and therefore wills not to give herself to others, nor "back" to God, but instead concludes in her fear that a possessive independence is the only possible defense against the future's "dizzying infinity." Evil thus becomes a rejection of being as such, a will to the

---

47. Milbank, *Theology and Social Theory*, 431. Emphasis added.
48. Ibid. Emphasis added.
49. Ibid., 432.

closure of temporal life from the possibility of a "differing" analogous to that of the Trinity:

> If nothing is evil insofar as it exists, then it is only evil in terms of its failure to be related to God, to infinite peace, and to other finite realities with which it should be connected to form a pattern of true desire. Evil becomes the denial of hope for, and the present reality of, community.[50]

Here we begin to see an explicit connection between evil and secular reason's failure of *Sittlichkeit*. *Sittlichkeit*, to recall, implies a direct relation to the "absolute" criterion of goodness, but which does not preclude a serious attention to "customary" directives inherent in particular situations. Christianity is capable of such a way of communing because its "absolute" criterion, as determined by its counter-ontology, is not an "objective" criterion at all, which means the Christian *way* of action is not violated even when it is deployed differently in an external sense. Christian charity can wend its way through all kinds of terrain, because it is not defined by any monadic, "pre-existing" realities, but brings genuine differences as such into being. Evil, by contrast, implies fear in relation to eternity as the sublime distance of the future, which generates a refusal to give oneself to the eternal movement, a decision instead to control and reify temporal economy as predictable and therefore radically separated from genuine anxiety. Evil thus coincides with a materialism that refuses the supernatural, and stipulates that any incursion of the eternal into temporal economy will require "sacrifice."

The differing intrinsic to temporality itself can indeed only be "known" objectively as the "sublime," which accosts all knowing. Yet Christianity's Trinitarian ontology asserts that one can possibly "see" this sublime differing as time's suspension by a beguiling "beauty," or in other words, by a measure that makes objective uncertainty compelling as an opening onto infinite being, rather than a final closure against the possibility of repetition. Thus do we arrive at a crucial point for this book, for here we see that any insistence on the part of a "dialectical" theology that Christianity's form of truth is necessarily *indirect* is seemingly ill-equipped to counter secular reason's despairing refusal to traverse the distance of the sublime. Of course, Milbank himself does not advocate direct communication in the sense of appealing to a sort

---

50. Ibid.

of "rational" security of the Christian wager. But for Milbank, the jettisoning of metaphysical justifications, which he associates with an emphasis on objective uncertainty, does not increase the "difficulty" of Christianity, but instead *removes* certain obstacles to one's acceptance of the religious life. That is, it frees all of the passions, not only the exclusively "rational" ones, to be enlivened in relation to *caritas* as a material form of beauty. Any theology that goes as far as "objective uncertainty," or Kierkegaardian skepticism, without "going further" in order to woo the human being with its beautiful traversal of that very uncertainty, ultimately remains precariously and even damnably close to secular reason's fearful relationship to the sublime. For any communicative refusal to give human desire something to "latch onto," any conclusion that the possibility of peace is at most indirect in its appeal, becomes, like evil itself, "the denial of hope for, and the present reality of, community."[51] Let's keep this in mind as we turn now to René Girard's characterization of Christianity's unique opposition to sacrifice.

Desire and Sacrifice in Girard

René Girard's account of the "necessity" of sacrifice in human societies develops in a distinct way from that of Milbank—though there remain, as we shall see below, many significant similarities between the two. Girard begins from a "fundamental anthropology" that is both more and less "empirical" and more and less "ideological" than forms of modern thought which have not been able to adequately conceptualize the origins of culture and religion. In *Things Hidden Since the Foundation of the World*, Girard says he is interested in developing a "science of man" from which an authoritative account of religion and the uniqueness of the Gospels would emerge.[52] This aim bears an obvious resemblance to the attempt at "metaphysical justification" that Milbank so often criticizes, which is to say that it seems to eschew the persuasion of "unjustified" rhetoric, and thus also theology's appeal to "faith." Girard's argument about the historical mediation of the gospel is a good example of this, where the Hegelianism that Milbank refutes in *Theology and Social Theory* seems to rear its head. Girard writes:

---

51. Ibid.
52. Girard, *Things Hidden*, 7.

> Under the pressure of circumstances that we ourselves have brought about, we are being irresistibly compelled to correct the mistakes of the sacrificial reading ... The only advantage that we have is that we happen to be at a more advanced stage in the same historical process, which is accelerating and leading toward an increasing revelation of the truth.[53]

At the same time, however, Girard does not suggest that the progressive revelation of gospel truth is immanently discoverable. That is, the "scientific" verification of his theory is meant to oppose *both* the *a priori* metaphysical postulates of those who, like Hegel, "already know" how to read history, without sufficiently attending to the "data," *and* those who, like Milbank's Weber, pretend on a more serious attention to the data to be able to read history's utter difference from any "transcendent" determinants. Thus, in a way that resonates with Milbank's own "historiographical" rather than "explanatory" engagement with human history, Girard characterizes the true spirit of science and knowledge as follows:

> The scientific spirit is, in effect, a rather crafty kind of *humilitas*, which agrees to depart from the data and to look far afield for what it has not discovered near at hand. But for the philosophical spirit, moving away from the data in this way is to abandon the only conceivable form of knowledge—the knowledge that seizes upon its object straight away, without intermediaries. *A departure that rules out one kind of certainty (in fact, a deceptive one) paves the way for the only kind of* verification *in which science is interested.*[54]

I emphasize this last sentence in particular because it could be taken straight out of *Theology and Social Theory*, where Milbank argues that theology's eschewal of metaphysical justifications opposes secular reason's pretension to make the immanent "transparent" to reason, and precisely in doing so, becomes supremely "persuasive" as a metanarrative. Thus the Radical Orthodox ring of Girard's concomitant claim that his hypothesis "has scientific status *because it is not directly accessible to empirical or phenomenological intuition.*"[55] That is, Girard's peculiarly "scientific" spirit abandons the immanentism on which a Weberian

---

53. Girard, *Things Hidden*, 436.
54. Ibid., 437. Emphasis added.
55. Ibid. Emphasis added.

approach to history might turn. It is in this spirit that he develops his account of the necessity of "sacrifice" in human culture.

Imitation and Sacrifice

Girard begins in this effort with his "fundamental anthropology," which is oriented by the supposition that "there is nothing, or next to nothing, in human behavior that is not learned, and all learning is based on imitation."[56] Therefore, he continues, "to develop a science of man it is necessary to compare human imitation with animal mimicry, and to specify the properly human modalities of mimetic behavior."[57] On this score one may notice immediately that human cultural formation consists in the institution of prohibitions directed at imitation, in spite of the fundamental role imitation plays in all human behavior. Thus Girard says cultural formation begins with an apparent "absurdity." Traditionally, ethnologists have explained the role of prohibitions related to imitation by reducing their "fundamental" character—which is effectively to say, by failing to account for the "absurdity" of human culture:

> Imitation doubles the imitated object and produces a simulacrum that can in turn become the object of types of magic. When ethnologists comment on such phenomena, they attribute them to a desire for protection against so-called imitative magic. And this is also the explanation they receive (from the natives) when they inquire into the *raison d'être* of prohibitions.[58]

Girard believes this explanation of prohibitions against imitation is inadequate because it does not account for their inclusion with prohibitions that have a more obvious social function, such as the universal prohibition against "violence among those who live together."[59] The question for a fundamental anthropology therefore concerns, first of all, the relationship between imitation and violence, and secondly, the uniquely human possibility of generating a "culture" that must be at once founded upon imitation, and in equal measure opposed to it.

Girard believes that Plato is distinguished among other ancient philosophers for "his fear of mimesis," or his understanding that

56. Ibid., 7.
57. Ibid.
58. Ibid., 11.
59. Ibid., 10.

imitation, so fundamental to human behavior and therefore to cultural formation, is also dangerous. Yet for Girard, "Plato is also deceived by mimesis because he cannot succeed in understanding his fear, he never uncovers its empirical reason for being."[60] What Plato primarily ignores here is the relationship of imitation to conflict; he does not get beyond what Girard calls a "representational" understanding of mimesis, where the imitator tries to present a "copy" of his model. This understanding of mimesis does not yet uncover the "empirical reason" to *fear* imitation, because it does not recognize how imitation functions in relation to *acquisition*. Similarly, Girard writes, "the modern use of [imitation] . . . is restricted to modalities of imitation in which there is no risk of provoking conflict and which are representational only, on the order of the simulacrum."[61] What is missing here is the ability to relate "conflict to acquisitive mimesis, that is, with the object that the two mimetic rivals attempt to wrest from one another because they designate it as desirable to one another."[62] This failure prevents philosophy in general from discovering how imitation can be "both a force of cohesion and a force of dissolution," even if it does, like Plato, intimate an appropriate "fear" of mimesis. What Girard is after, however, is an *explanation* of "the contrary effects of one and the same force."[63]

The need to deal with this contradiction becomes especially clear when we consider that any attempt to understand the distinctly human elements of mimesis must come to terms with the paradoxical combination in human culture of prohibition and ritual. The paradox appears when one considers that in the case of ritual—which is, like law, a force of social cohesion—"the concern is not to avoid, but to reproduce the mimetic crisis."[64] It is clear from diverse ethnographic accounts that rituals encourage the violation of prohibitions, and thus encourage mimetic behavior: "at an acute point in the crisis men violently dispute objects that are normally prohibited; ritual incest, meaning fornication with women one ordinarily has no right to touch, is therefore more frequent."[65] Girard adds that in the case of rituals that refrain from overt

60. Ibid., 15.
61. Ibid., 17.
62. Ibid., 15.
63. Ibid., 17.
64. Ibid., 19.
65. Ibid., 20.

violations of prohibitions such as those against incest, what is retained is still the "doubling" of the self that such prohibitions are meant to prevent: "In order to reproduce a model of the mimetic crisis in a spirit of social harmony, the enactment must be progressively emptied of all real violence so that only the 'pure' form is allowed to survive."[66] This pure form, it seems, "is always a matter of *doubles*, that is, partners in reciprocal imitation."[67] In this reading of the "progression" of violent rituals to a more "aestheticized" form, it follows that what societies really fear is not the battle over goods or property as such, but the "doubling" of the self and its tendency toward conflict and violence. Girard therefore concludes that in ritual, "communities throw themselves deliberately ... into the evil they fear most and believe that by doing so they will somehow escape it."[68]

If we can discover how the enactment of this feared evil can provide the possibility of an escape from the *actual* social dissolution it seems to suggest, then we shall come closer to an account of how human imitation is paradoxically both fundamentally conflictual and at the same time a required element in social genesis. Girard argues that the explanation of this paradox lies in the most crucial, culminating element of ritual, the performance of sacrifice. The fact that rituals characteristically conclude with sacrifice indicates that such an act is the likely conclusion of the crisis of "undifferentiation" caused by mimesis. The community must be both "unified" *and* once again "differentiated," extricated somehow from the way of being as a double that finally becomes "pure" rivalry. It is important, then, that the performance of ritual sacrifice typically involves the whole community: "Where previously there had been a chaotic ensemble of particular conflicts, there is now the simplicity of a single conflict: the entire community on one side, and on the other, the victim."[69] The accomplishment of unity here is obvious, but how exactly does this allow for a "redifferentiation" of human beings in the community, a defusing of mimesis as conflictual?

In order to understand this one must come to terms with Girard's characterization of the full course of mimetic desire. Let me try to cast his argument in simple terms: 1) imitation is fundamental to all human

66. Ibid., 21.
67. Ibid.
68. Ibid., 22.
69. Ibid., 24.

behavior; 2) acquisitive mimesis engenders conflict as human beings desire the same object because they imitate the desires of their neighbors; 3) the rivalry or competition occasioned by acquisitive mimesis becomes self-propulsive as the subjects in question begin to imitate *the antagonism* of their doubles as such; 4) any *object* of conflict beyond the antagonists themselves drops out of the picture; 5) sooner or later a particular antagonist will arbitrarily "win" unanimous support, via mimetic contagion, against his particular rival; 6) the murder of this rival will bring about the "end" of conflict.[70] Girard characterizes this murder as the "end" of conflict by suggesting that here "the community satisfies its rage against an arbitrary victim in the unshakable conviction that it has found the one and only cause of its trouble. It then finds itself . . . purged of all hostility against those for whom, a second before, it had shown the most extreme rage."[71] All of this means that sacrifice and its maintenance in ritual is a necessary element in the arising of human culture, if the imitative desire fundamental to human behavior is not to end in utter disintegration.

It is clear then that mimesis as conflict escalates toward a violent event that paradoxically has the capacity to restore "peace" to the community. But how, if the ritual practice of sacrifice recalls a *real* "founding murder," does such an act become "religious"? For Girard, this question concerns the connection of violence and the sacred, which he suggests has everything to do with the murderers' misunderstanding of their own act:

> The return to a calmer state of affairs appears to confirm the responsibility of the victim for the mimetic discord that had troubled the community. The community thinks of itself as entirely passive *vis-à-vis* its own victim, whereas the latter appears, by contrast, to be the only active and responsible agent in the matter. Once it is understood that the inversion of the real relation between victim and community occurs in the resolution of the crisis, it is possible to see why the victim is believed to be *sacred*.[72]

Culture arises from this act as the "calmer state of affairs," and is naturally attended by the inclination to do whatever is necessary to maintain "the miraculous calm apparently granted to it by the fearful and benign being

---

70. See especially ibid., 26.
71. Ibid., 27.
72. Ibid.

that had somehow descended upon it."[73] Therefore the community must both prohibit mimetic desire for its disintegrating and antagonistic effects, and at the same time institute the repetition of the "miraculous event," so as to partake, periodically and unconsciously, in its relief. Such is Girard's explanation of the contradiction between culture's simultaneous prohibition and encouragement of mimesis among human beings, which is at the same time a revelation of the foundation of culture upon violence.

The necessity of sacrifice in any mimetically sustained social order is therefore both mitigated and guaranteed by religion, in virtue of religion's concealment of its own and society's origins. The concealment is directed toward the victimage mechanism and its utter arbitrariness. A sacrificial order therefore offers the community an "inversion of agency" through the mechanism of sacralization. The victim is worshipped for sacrificing *himself*, while the community is exonerated of guilt. This mechanism of the "founding murder," as well as the duplicitous peace to which it gives rise, constitute the distinctly *human* characteristics of mimetic desire:

> At the point when mimetic conflict becomes sufficiently intense to prohibit the direct solutions that give rise to the forms of animal sociality [i.e., the rise of a "dominant" individual to curb further disintegration], the first "crisis" or series of crises would then occur as the mechanism that produces the differentiated, symbolic, and human forms of culture.[74]

Here the crucial or distinguishing aspect of human imitation is finally identified. In animal societies, Girard believes the capacity of "dominance patterns" to organize communal behaviors relates to the way imitation remains in some measure objective—rivalry remains rivalry over *things*. With human beings, however, imitation proceeds beyond competition for identifiable goods, and therefore beyond the relevance of an objective "victor." In human beings, acquisitive mimesis gives way "to antagonistic mimesis, which eventually unites and reconciles all members of a community at the expense of a victim."[75] At this point, mimesis attains a power that goes beyond a desire directed at the objects of "opaque, mute instinct," and we reach what Girard calls "the threshold

73. Ibid., 28.
74. Ibid., 94.
75. Ibid., 95.

of hominization."[76] The implication is that this threshold is a spiritual one, something that goes beyond instinct and refers instead to a certain non-objective "image" in the human being, though in this case from the angle of its perversion by sin.[77] As Girard puts it, the rise of the victimage mechanism "should be seen as an exceptionally powerful means of creating a new degree of attention, the first non-instinctual attention."[78] Thus the threshold is at once a discovery of humanity's elevation and, because we only discover it insofar as it is directed not toward spirit and life, but toward a unanimously designated victim, indicates the human being's downfall: "Beyond the purely instinctual object, the alimentary or sexual object or the dominant individual, there is *the cadaver* of the collective victim, and this cadaver constitutes the first object for this new type of attention."[79] What are the exact means of concealing the baselessness of this violence?

On Girard's account, "the ability of the victimage mechanism to produce the sacred depends entirely on the extent to which the mechanism is misinterpreted."[80] More specifically this implies that a direct inscription in cultural practices always implies the subject's unconscious acquiescence in the duplicitous *writing* of his innocence of the "founding murder." In order for the founding event to continue to be *reconciling*, its effect must remain that of the unconscious sacralization of what is really the victim of an arbitrary violence. For Girard, this means that religious ritual is always buttressed by "myths" that memorialize the sacred victim as an agent of reconciliation. Indeed, language itself, Girard argues, has its origin in the massive human effort to obfuscate the origins of violence, for the sake of its pseudo-peace:

---

76. Ibid.

77. One must concede, at this point, that Girard is sometimes confusing or confused in his desire to be "scientific," as the scientific spirit causes him, at one moment, to urge a reading of the human that goes beyond instinct and so beyond the immediacy of scientific immanentism, and yet he cannot stop himself at other moments from inviting someone like Milbank's critique of his scientific pretensions. Consider that he writes that it would be a mistake to attribute the threshold of hominization to something immediate to instincts, but continues by suggesting that distinctly human violence is attributable to "the growth of mimetic activity linked to the increase in brain size" (ibid., 95).

78. Ibid., 99.

79. Ibid. Emphasis added.

80. Ibid., 33.

> Since we understand that human beings wish to remain reconciled after the conclusion of the crisis, we can also understand their penchant for reproducing the sign, or in other words for reproducing the language of the sacred by substituting, in ritual, new victims for the original victim, in order to assure the maintenance of that miraculous peace.[81]

Girard argues that the victim itself is the primordial "signifier," and that "the signified constitutes all actual and potential meaning the community confers on to the victim and, through its intermediacy, on to all things."[82] This means that human language as such arises in the event of reconciliation brought about by the death of the victim, out of the need to have such reconciliation signified. And thus the victim becomes the first sign, its effect the first cohesive moment to which the community will take recourse repeatedly in ritual. Girard concludes that "the imperative of ritual is therefore never separate from the manipulation of signs and their constant multiplication."[83]

Language as we know it therefore bears such a problematic relationship to the victimage mechanism of human mimetic desire that any social existence as "inscription" in cultural idioms becomes perhaps inexorably fraught with difficulty. One is tempted to reply to this that while some of our language may arise in ritual practice and sacred sign, much of it, especially in the modern West, seems directed *against* violence, in that it seems to tend in an entirely *secularized* direction. Somewhat like Milbank, however, Girard is not inclined to take secularism at face value. He sees in our ostensibly non-violent tendencies a strong disavowal of the violence of former cultures' rituals, to be sure, but at the same time, insofar as these disavowals are self-congratulatory rather than deeply personal acts of confession, they inevitably re-enact the victimage mechanism vis-à-vis those former cultures. And even if secularism could come close to a total abandonment of ritual, its failure to *know* it as the outcome of mimetic desire means secularism would only invite the undifferentiation of that very same desire. Thus it would invite the crisis without the "barbaric," but effective, salve of ritual. Girard therefore acknowledges that "the moment arrives when the original victim . . . will be signified by something other than a victim," but argues that it

---

81. Ibid., 103.
82. Ibid.
83. Ibid.

will "continue to signify the victim while at the same time progressively masking, disguising, and failing to recognize it."[84]

The Bible as Text

What can awaken us, then, from our characteristically human slumber, in which sacrifice is carried out again and again precisely in our act of convincing ourselves that *we* would never sacrifice individuals to the community? The answer, for Girard, comes by way of the Bible. On Girard's account, as we have heard, all cultural peace founded upon religion is "organized around a more or less violent disavowal of human violence,"[85] which signals the danger inherent in aligning oneself with this truth. Girard believes it is precisely this dangerous subjective awakening which the Bible both enjoins upon us and makes possible. That is, the Bible uniquely enjoins our extrication from cultural inscription, from the textual fabric by which violence is disavowed in the name of a false peace. The Bible traces the well-worn mythical/sacrificial paths of human-generated ritualistic religion, but uniquely takes the side of the victim, a perspective that culminates in the portrayal of Jesus in the Gospels, who is unanimously persecuted even while being portrayed as innocent. Here the violence of culture is revealed as what it is—baseless and arbitrary—and Jesus is revealed as uniquely alive, in separation from the mimetic cultural existence that despairs of its true self. This indicates in turn that "culture" as such cannot accommodate a fully human existence, in the sense of a subjectivity awakened to consciousness:

> Violence, in every cultural order, is always the true *subject* of every ritual or institutional structure. From the moment when the sacrificial order begins to come apart, this subject can no longer be anything but the *adversary par excellence*, which combats the installation of the Kingdom of God.[86]

Thus it is clear that for Girard the objective of the Kingdom of God is to bring into existence individual human beings whose source of life is independent of the cultural order in which they are situated. This is not to say that human beings are to be sheared off from all "communion" with others, but only that they cannot acquire their true selves through

---

84. Ibid.
85. Girard, *Girard Reader*, 165.
86. Ibid., 183.

association with any humanly instituted and so mimetically sustained order. The Biblical injunction to love one's neighbor, requiring as it does that one extricate oneself from murderous rivalry with that neighbor, is therefore precisely an injunction to become *a self*.

To align oneself with the truth that the "peace" of the current order is founded upon a recurring violence is to court a differentiation from the unanimously unconscious "subject" of culture, which cannot believe in the possibility of a peaceful differentiation—so bound is it to the "doubling" of mimetic desire—nor tolerate the suggestion that the differentiation it does sustain is inauthentic. As Girard explains, human beings "must kill and continue to kill, strange as it may seem, in order not to know that they are killing."[87] The difference of the Gospels, which indicates their composition through divine agency, is that they do not offer any self-justifying affirmation that subjective differentiation comes only through a "necessary" sacrifice (of which "we," like the Pharisees of Luke 11:47–48, would be exonerated). The Gospels in fact disable ritual and even religion itself, by telling of a Word who speaks things formerly hidden, and by *being* this Word, insofar as they do not write Jesus' death into a sacrificial economy. It is because the Gospels are still misunderstood as representations of a sacrificial economy that they are "today rejected with contempt," and yet they are destined to be revealed as "the only means of furthering all that is good and true in the anti-Christian endeavors of modern times: the as-yet-ineffectual determination to rid the world of the sacred cult of violence."[88] Modern culture resists building itself upon a necessary and ritualized sacrifice; but the irony, from Girard's perspective, is that this enterprise requires a recognition that Christ alone can mediate, an interpretation of the "rejected stone" of Psalm 118 that only he can give, by "becoming the rejected stone, with the aim of showing that this stone has always formed a concealed foundation."[89] In order to move past the founding of culture upon this rock of rejection, one must recognize in the Gospels not just one more instantiation of "sacrifice," but an exposure of the unanimous will to expel that is intrinsic to even the best human desire to "overcome" it. In Jesus alone, therefore, "the stone is revealed and can no longer

---

87. Ibid., 162.
88. Girard, *Things Hidden*, 177–78.
89. Ibid., 178.

form a foundation, or, rather, it will found something that is radically different."[90]

A Radically Different Sociality

For Girard the "radically different" sociality made possible by the Gospels begins, quite like Milbank's alternative to the violent ontology of secular reason, with the premise that the revelation of God in Jesus Christ shows God to be utterly distinct from the mechanism of human violence. God as the origin and giver of true life can have no part in a violence that the Gospels demonstrate to be utterly baseless. In the Gospels, we witness the escalation of conflictual mimesis, and its selection of Jesus as the object of the community's need to be reconciled. The texts show us, moreover, that Jesus is able to *live* in separation from mimetic desire—indeed, his distinction is not that he is uniquely parasitic on true social life, but that he alone refuses to buy into the community's "pharisaical" righteousness. More specifically, Jesus will not exist in the false "peace" of the Pharisees, which turns upon their confidence that "*we* have not killed the prophets." Such a claim is offered in the same spirit as modern secularism's denouncement of all sacrificial cultures. Jesus, uniquely, can force such a declaration to the crucial moment of enactment—the moment in the Gospels at which all human beings are demonstrably willing to kill in order to avoid admitting their complicity in violence—because he alone believes that true life transcends the power of bodily death wielded by violence. For Jesus, therefore, self-protective desire is finally *nothing* to fear. And thus, "in the Gospels, this violence is always brought home to men, and not to God."[91]

Girard's premise here bears an obvious resemblance to Milbank's suggestion of Christianity's fundamental "ontological" difference from secular reason. This resemblance is complemented by Girard's articulation of Christian sociality in a way that mirrors what Milbank says about Christian action as giving "priority to peace and forgiveness."[92] Girard writes that "to leave violence behind, it is necessary to give up the idea of retribution."[93] For him this means not just "leaving retribution to the

90. Ibid.
91. Ibid., 186.
92. Milbank, *Theology and Social Theory*, 409.
93. Girard, *Things Hidden*, 198.

Cultural Logic and Christian Sociality   185

courts," but acting as if the offense itself registers *nowhere* in the order of creation. One must act as if the offense gives *nothing* to "imitate," as if it does not appear as a rival power to the power of true life:

> People imagine that to escape from violence it is sufficient to give up any kind of violent *initiative*, but since no one in fact thinks of himself as taking this initiative—since all violence has a mimetic character, and derives or can be thought to derive from a first violence that is always perceived as originating with the opponent—this act of renunciation is no more than a sham, and cannot bring about any kind of change at all.[94]

The renunciation that is really required is a renunciation of what modern culture holds dear—its ability to identify violence in others. The revelation of the Gospels itself makes possible all that is good—all that recognizes violence—in modern culture, but the evil of violence cannot be genuinely transcended except when the judgment of the Gospels is turned radically inward. As Girard writes, interpreting Matt 7:1–5:

> No mere chance places the log in the eye that is quick to spot the speck . . . The speck is certainly there, but the critic fails to see that his own act of condemnation reproduces the structural features of the act deserving condemnation, in a form that is emphasized by the very inability of the perspicacious critique to see its own failings.[95]

In other words, it is not as if Jesus in Matthew 7 simply chanced upon a judge who was indeed guilty of the sin he recognized in another, as if a different judge might have had clear eyes. Rather, the inclination to judge itself reduplicates the act of sacrificial expulsion that is condemned, an expulsion that in this case guarantees the "peace" of the current community by allowing it to remain unconscious of its own mimetic cohesion. All of this is to say that for Girard, like Milbank, what characterizes the "radical newness" of the Gospels is their common offer of a sociality that proceeds according to the priority of forgiveness. For Milbank this ethic is rooted in an "ontology" that need not treat offenses to charity with an adversarial spirit, but sees them instead as mere privations upon Being. The spirit of true life need not "rival" the non-entity of sin as if it were a "real" power—for this would be to adopt the way of sin itself—but can

---

94. Ibid.
95. Ibid., 427.

always respond in love, in an effort to disarm and initiate the offender into a new way of being. For Girard too, the only way to oppose the economy of sacrifice is to count the antagonism of sin as what it truly is—i.e., as "nothing" to be imitated.

Conversion

Yet Girard is less likely to suggest, as Milbank does, that the refusal of reciprocal antagonism itself composes a new "tradition," or a new "social idiom" that appeals to the very same subjective desire which the offender presently turns to bad ends. Girard speaks instead about the movement of renunciation or repentance as one that must be undertaken in separation from all cultural idioms. This is not to say that Girard rejects all hope of such a conversion, only that for him it is radically disconnected from any cultural mechanism: "Mankind can cross this abyss . . . The decision to do so must come from each individual *separately*, however; for once, others are not involved."[96] Others cannot be involved in a true renunciation of violence, a conversion to true life, because of "the fundamental human situation of a mimetic rivalry that leads to a destructive escalation."[97] In order to be converted, one must give up everything in oneself that can be chalked up to imitation of other human beings:

> It is quite literally true, when we are concerned with the confrontation of *doubles*, that he who wishes to save his life will lose it; he will be obliged, in effect, to kill his brother . . . He who agrees to lose his life will keep it for eternal life, for he alone is not a killer, he alone knows the fullness of love.[98]

In order to *love*, one must give up one's very life. There is no mitigation of the radical newness of the sociality founded hereby with another "object" of the very same mimetic desire. Rather the conversion demands a relinquishment, a mortification, of the entirety of what one "is" according to one's fundamental desire. How then does this conversion occur?

Girard's confidence in the originality of his theory at times strikes the reader as a declaration that mimetic theory itself is the holy grail of learning, and that the knowledge it offers is one and the same with conversion. Or, on the other hand, he sometimes seems so certain of the

---

96. Ibid., 199.
97. Ibid., 214.
98. Ibid., 214–5.

"apocalyptic" character of the present age that it sounds as if the immanent historical process itself will bring about humanity's conversion. As we have seen, Girard finds it noteworthy that in our "secularizing" age we have reached a denial of our own implication in mimetic violence that is so strong it seems destined to succeed in purging culture of sacrifice, or at least seems destined for an imminent encounter with the gospel, an encounter humanity was "not ready for" previously: "we have carved out such a strange destiny for ourselves so that we can bring to light both what has always determined human culture and what is now the only path open to us—one that reconciles without excluding anyone."[99] This obviously resonates with the reading of Hegel that Milbank offers in *Theology and Social Theory*, which says that Hegel has the right sense of Jesus' accomplishment of *Sittlichkeit*, but finally subsumes the possibility of our own participation in such an ethic to a "necessary" historical process that gets rid of those elements in nature that are "indifferent" to true peace.

I suggest there is much in Girard's work that gives us reason to discount the Hegelian resonances of some of his descriptions of historical progress. Chief among these is his willingness to make conversion an utterly existential process, which his theory can identify as the requirement of any true peace, but which it cannot actually describe or bring about. Ultimately, he says, "the peace that passes human understanding can only arise on the other side of this passion for 'justice and judgment' . . . *But I do not know how to speak about these matters.*"[100] This is as far as his anthropological discourse can take us. The knowledge that is required in order for one to "arise on the other side" of judgment does not come as a direct result of one's introduction to a theory. Instead,

> [Love] alone can reveal the victimage processes that underlie the meanings of culture. There is no purely "intellectual" process that can arrive at true knowledge because the very detachment of the person who contemplates the warring brothers from the heights of his wisdom is an illusion. *Any and every form of human knowledge is illusory to the extent that it has failed to submit to the decisive test, which is the test of the warring brothers.*[101]

99. Ibid., 445.
100. Ibid., 446. Emphasis added.
101. Ibid., 277. Emphasis added.

Even if one "agrees" with Girard's theory, even if one is "persuaded" that Jesus uniquely reveals the violence of all human mimesis, one's conversion occurs on a different plane from that of persuasion, the plane on which knowledge means consciousness of one's own sin, and where persuasion concomitantly means enactment: "for there to be even the slightest degree of progress, the victimage mechanism must be vanquished on the most intimate level of experience."[102] There is no "essential" knowledge—no persuasion, in other words—outside of the existential movement of conversion, a movement that, because it begins with the consciousness of sin, is certainly not fostered by one's "persuasion" by a discourse. Rather, the Word of God "works" insofar as it first persuades a person, "at the most intimate level of experience," that he is *not* persuaded of the truth that life inheres in the movement of self-renunciation. Such a movement, obviously, must be initiated by an agency that is wholly "other" than that behind even the best "progress" discernible in human history—indeed, an agency that is wholly opposed to the tendency to call the self-justifying denunciations of sacrifice *"progress"* at all. Rather than articulating the uniquely Christian possibility as a new "social idiom" then, and appealing directly to human desire, Girard adopts a theological mode of *silence*. Theological rhetoric would be inappropriate at this stage precisely because "desire is always using for its own ends the knowledge it has acquired of itself; it places the truth in the service of its own untruth, so to speak, and it is always becoming better equipped to reject everything that surrenders to its embrace."[103] Girard hereby lumps in any appeal to a sociality directly transmittable in the idiom and practice of the church with the dangers of pacifying desire with the only salve it knows—self-protective sacrifice. Jesus himself remained incomprehensible to even the best of human desire, such as that of his apostle Peter, and thus "mortifies" this desire by uniquely refusing to compromise with it. But while we can see in the Gospels how the world rejects the Word that is Jesus, to go beyond this recognition, to the realm where this knowledge can become repentance and then love, would be to "become involved in questions of *faith* and *grace*, which our anthropological perspective is not competent to address."[104]

102. Ibid., 399.
103. Ibid., 304.
104. Ibid., 216.

Does this mean, then, that for Girard there is no possibility of a real temporal enactment of an alternative social ethic? Is Jesus the lone accomplishment of *Sittlichkeit*, as he is for Hegel? In fact, Girard argues that the union of Jesus with the Father "does not imply that this union is an exclusive one, or prevent us from envisaging the possibility of mankind becoming like God through the Son's mediation."[105] Specifically, this means envisaging the possibility of realizing and then repenting of our tendency to divinize our own violence, and turning in love to God's non-violent advocacy for his creation. Christ is the true "form" of this creation, and his mediation of that form to us means that in our living "there can be no victim who is not Christ, and no one can come to the aid of a victim without coming to the aid of Christ."[106] Yet this enactment of the distinctly Christian ethic, however it may be "mediated" by Christ, is not quite the *sittlich* reconciliation of the world to God that Milbank envisages, insofar as it seems not to identify Christ's agency in conversion with "the continuing story of the Church."[107] Does this not suggest that true life is so very removed from ordinary human arrangements that it cannot be continuously temporally present? Actually, Girard does not at all rule out the possibility of a continuation of the Incarnation in the story of the church, but only refuses to say directly how the church accomplishes this. For any direct description of the church's role, as the body of Christ, in provoking others' consciousness of sin and conversion would come with the risk of placing members of that body in the judgment seat. Thus conversion *cannot* be directly ascribed to inscription in *any* culture's tradition, even that of the church. Indeed, for Girard one cannot make direct appeals to the church for the same reason one cannot make such appeals to Jesus himself. That is, Jesus is a complete offense to fundamental human desire, which seeks an object of rivalry, for he offers nothing to rival, no selfhood to "possess," only a new *way to live*: "There is no acquisitive desire in him . . . With him, we run no risk of getting caught up in the evil opposition between doubles."[108] Therefore Jesus himself, and similarly his body, the church, is the "sole model who never runs the danger . . . of being transformed

---

105. Ibid.
106. Ibid., 429.
107. Milbank, *Theology and Social Theory*, 387.
108. Girard, *Things Hidden*, 430.

into a fascinating rival."¹⁰⁹ But this means conversion is one and the same with "giving up mimetic desire."¹¹⁰ Jesus' self is only "had" in the movement of giving it up, the movement of giving up the sense of "self" that inheres in the simulacra produced by desire. To the desiring subject, this giving up seems to eviscerate all that is compelling in life as such. This, Girard says, characterizes "the road to the Kingdom, which may seem arid but in reality is the only fruitful one."¹¹¹

Whither the Resurrected Sign?

We ought not to conclude from the foregoing that Girard finally sides with the postmodern evacuation of "life" from the sign, as an *a priori* determination of the objective incompatibility of true life with temporal, material reality. In fact Girard opposes his own "scientific spirit" to the conclusiveness of the ideological *a priori*s that determine "metaphysics." Thus he argues that "the end of philosophy brings with it a new possibility of scientific thinking within the religious domain," and that "however strange this may seem, it brings with it a return to religious faith."¹¹² Indeed, the "scientific" spirit that Girard means to call upon is in keeping with the very spirit of faith. That is, for Girard, "the scientific spirit is pure expectancy."¹¹³ Instead of modernity's language of pure correspondence, or postmodernism's language that cannot possibly signify, Christianity offers a language that we can only speak in expectancy of its being filled. Such expectancy understands the congruence of postmodern despair with modern epistemological certainty, and therefore it remains equally opposed to both the modern prioritization of epistemology—which, as we have seen, is naïve to the violent, sacred roots of its need to have reality signified—*and* to the postmodern inclination to a language evacuated of meaning. The self-certainty of postmodernism about the death of the sign amounts to a reduplication (even though it is more "knowing" about violence) of the sacrificial move, insofar as its conclusion about language is again a sacralizing expulsion of former cultures (think of how it is

---

109. Ibid.
110. Ibid., 431.
111. Ibid., 430.
112. Ibid., 438.
113. Ibid.

precisely the relativism of the postmodern that makes it still too "metaphysical," according to Milbank). Girard writes:

> Present-day thought is the worst form of castration, since it is the castration of the signified. People are always on the lookout to catch their neighbors red-handed in believing something or other . . . a form of Puritanism far worse than [that of our parents]—a Puritanism of meaning that kills all that it touches.[114]

In Girard's understanding, the Gospels address both the problem of the violence of any human cultural-linguistic "solutions" to rivalry ("there is no *pharmakon* any more"), and the problem of meaninglessness courted by an exclusively human rather than divinely transformative rejection of the cult of violence: "Recipes are not what we need, nor do we need to be reassured—our need is to escape from meaninglessness."[115] We must therefore make this escape without a "recipe," which is to say, without reverting to the variety of signification that is rooted in the sacred violence of the victimage mechanism. What this implies is that we must learn to understand "significance" in a way that undercuts what normally happens in our persecutory signifying. We must understand that the signification of mythical patterns in the service of concealing our nihilistic violence has "significance" not in the way we thought, but "only because at each moment [the persecutors] are open to the ironic reversal of the judgment against the judge that recalls the implacable functioning of the gospel law in our world."[116] In contrast to "*all* modern ideologies," therefore, which Girard says "are immense machines that justify and legitimate conflicts,"[117] the knowledge and meaning offered by the Gospels does not allow us to grasp at a "significance" that will put us at ease. Instead, we must "learn to *love*" the justice that reverses judgment against the judge, a justice "we both carry out and fall victim to."[118]

For Girard, therefore, our opening to the true significance of all of our signifying acts, our movement towards the "functioning of the gospel law in our world," consists not in our being persuaded or placated by this law, but in our learning to love it. This love implies an *inexplicable*

---

114. Ibid., 442.
115. Ibid., 446.
116. Ibid.
117. Ibid., 31.
118. Ibid., 446.

persuasion, for it expresses a commitment to justice *without* the self-justifying significations that usually accompany our commitments. Such a claim determines love as such as the dedication of one's whole self, even in the *absence* of any concessions the object might make to our desires. We must not participate in an economy of "meaning," in other words, that would see us inscribed in any relations that directly accommodate our desires, in any relations that do not "scandalize" our fundamental tendency toward a "reconciliation" founded upon violence. This allows Girard to be at once utterly serious about the gospel's provision of meaning to language and communication—its "resurrection of the sign" that neither modern nor postmodern reason can understand on their own—and at the same time opposed to theological rhetoric, as another dangerously direct appeal to human desire. Thus he claims that he has always "cherished the hope that meaning and life were one," and that while this union is threatened on all sides by the death of meaning, which also means the deathliness of human language, it "simply awaits the breath of the Spirit to be reborn."[119] It is the expectancy of this breath which characterizes the Christian possibility of "inscription," which means more explicitly that it is characterized by a willingness to live in *any* cultural text "as if not," as Paul puts it in 1 Corinthians 7. The resurrection of meaning does not occur as the direct production of a new cultural rhetoric, but as the initiation of a way of living that invites, accepts and suffers the gospel judgment that, for the sake of true life, is turned against the judgment deployed by *any* direct consonance between human desire and its signification in an "idiom." Meaning and life are one where the human being lives an inexplicable love for the gospel's continuous undoing of his direct relationship to his cultural inscription, which would always implicate him in sacred violence. This means the Christian ethic for Girard is characterized especially by a love that exceeds the peace and reconciliation that ritual mediates directly to the subject's mimetic desire. It is an ethic recognizable, then, by its unreserved love, which means also its indifference to all that the culture determines as "necessary" for reconciliation. In his or her truly unbounded love, the Christian will therefore appear presumptuously self-assured to every cultural order, when such love is truly the epitome of self-renunciation, of resting not in one's own power, mimetically sustained, but inexplicably in the only power that transcends the power of

119. Ibid., 447.

death—a power that scandalizes precisely because it does not represent itself directly as power at all.

Milbank's Rejection of Girard and its Consequences

Girard's account of human beings' commitment to a "necessary" sacrifice aligns with that of Milbank in a couple of significant ways. For Milbank as for Girard, the subjective wager of "the secular" (for Girard, "all modern ideologies") is unconsciously despairing of its true, spiritual self, and precisely therein assumes the necessity of intra-and intersubjective violence. Second, just as Milbank's appeal to the wager of a charitable historical interval is meant to "convert" subjects to what more authentically persuades and enlivens them, so too for Girard the subjective wager of the Holy Spirit's historical advocacy for all victims is a "conversion" from the blind, self-protective violence of humanly orchestrated cultural order, to a way of living that is fully alive to the possibility of reconciliation without murder.

But Girard's appeal in this regard refuses to supply the Christian ethic with positive cultural "content," and here Milbank must raise objections.[120] This is also the point at which Milbank's Kierkegaardian account of anxiety, which we outlined above, becomes crucial. That is, here Milbank will force us to wrestle with the possibility that Girard's reluctance to convey Christian sociality as a "distinct structural logic" for society, an alternative "idiom" to the inscriptions offered by mythological language, leaves the anxious subject without recourse before the sublime distance of the future. A refusal in this way to propel the subject toward the future via the presentation of a *desirable* measure of repetition is effectively to leave him or her open to conclude in fear, as postmodernism does, that a reconciliation of time and eternity is impossible without sacrifice. This charge would mean that the existential rigor we have detected in Girard foregoes rather than safeguards the character of the essentially Christian as inexorable temporal enactment. Let us try to work this out briefly.

According to Milbank, our inscription in a particular narrative of ontological difference (as "love" or as violent aporia) actually *is* our "being." Thus only a text that is *direct* in terms of its application to the whole, rational/passionate human person can remedy the divide

---

120. See Milbank, *Theology and Social Theory*, 392–98.

between faith and its temporal deployment, and thereby maintain life as a *way* rather than a reified "thing." If the mystery of the Christian imperative to *caritas*, then, is taken to imply its radical distinction from the mundane economy of the passions, if it offends rather than arouses the subject's economic desire, it will remain incapable of propelling that subject into a series of (non-identical) repetitions of such love, and thus will present no viable alternative to secular reason's ontology of violence. In *Theology and Social Theory* Milbank therefore says that while Girard is correct to emphasize the refusal of violent means as definitive of the Biblical account, the problem remains that he "allows little place for the concrete 'form' taken by Jesus's nonviolent practice," which goes hand in hand with his "denial of the possibility of an objective desire or a benign *eros*."[121] If there is no possibly "benign" objective desire, which for Girard would be the same thing as a desire that could resist the violence of mimesis and its obfuscation of the Kingdom's objective of forming selves, then there is no possibility that an "erotic" turn toward the unique objective form of Jesus' nonviolent practice can equal salvation from the divided kingdom of human culture. For Milbank this means it is finally "difficult to see what 'the kingdom' could really amount to"[122] in Girard's account. Briefly stated, for Milbank Christian truth can only become for us a *form of existence* when it takes the shape of "*a new social mechanism in which we can be situated*."[123]

In the first place, Milbank's conclusion here is obviously ungenerous, since we have seen already that the real difference between Milbank and Girard is not that Girard makes Christian sociality unimaginable (recall his "envisaging the possibility of mankind becoming like God through the Son's mediation"), but that he criticizes the inclination to put the content of this imagining to direct theological use. Yet this is where a proponent of a rhetorical form of truth like Milbank will have to disagree about the putatively "aporetic" nature of conversion, and claim instead that "only the *attraction* exercised by a particular set of words and images causes us to acknowledge the good and to have an idea of the ultimate *telos*."[124] Without appealing to the attraction exercised by such a "social mechanism," Girard apparently leaves us with

121. Ibid., 395.
122. Ibid.
123. Ibid., 397. Emphasis added.
124. Ibid., 398.

no adequate existential alternative to violence. As I have put it above, however, Girard leaves us with *only* an existential alternative. That is, for him, a true "persuasion" by the Christian way of living involves extrication from the unacknowledged rivalry that is the end of desire. And on this score he claims that "there is a resistance to shedding light on the role of rivalry in our lives," which means that "knowledge of mimesis is really tied to conversion."[125] Here conversion means "breaking away" from mimesis, by "changing your personality"—or indeed, *becoming* a person through the mortification of your desire. James Williams asks Girard if a "good mimesis" is required for such a conversion, and Girard is reluctant to name or explain it—his most direct reference is to "the idea of Kierkegaard, the idea of subjectivity as passionate inwardness."[126]

The opposition Girard hereby draws between Christian love and fundamental human desire, from which one must unequivocally "break away," Milbank identifies as the primary danger in all so-called "dialectical" theology. Such a dialectic between *agape* and *eros*, which implies that the Christian ethic will be one of indifference to any "distinct cultural logic" mediated to human *eros*, for Milbank amounts to a refusal of the existential challenge of Christianity, which is the challenge of a *living reconciliation* of time and eternity. In his essay, "Sublimity: The Modern Transcendent," Milbank suggests in effect that the Protestant idea "of loving God for himself alone, quite apart from any questions of one's own salvific destiny and the regard of God towards oneself,"[127] is subject to the same nihilism as are modern philosophy's epistemological conclusions about God's utter unknowability.[128] Such a "purity of love," that is to say, only *annihilates* what it means to purify. For Milbank, by contrast,

> Every charm, every attractive feature of anything radiates outwards, rendering things apprehensible and thereby specifically lovable only in the measure that they affect the state of the observer in a positive fashion . . . it therefore follows that to love anything *purely* for itself, in abstraction from the quality of its influence upon oneself, is not at all to love that thing in its

---

125. Girard, *Girard Reader*, 268.
126. Ibid.
127. Milbank, "Sublimity," 265.
128. Ibid., 259.

specificity, but rather to love it for that mere abstract quality of "being" that it shares with anything else whatsoever.[129]

Milbank thus reads the Protestant "reform" of love as but a "modern reworking of the antique (pre-Christian) concentration on a private war of reason with the passions, in which sacrificial pain is the mark of authenticity."[130] For Milbank, genuine Christianity transcends paganism by *elevating* the objective-erotic life, affirming the participation in truth of the "common," domestic life of passions suffered and fulfilled independently of properly philosophical—i.e., gnostic—truth.[131] Precisely at the point of its "agapeic" purity, then, Protestant—and by extension, pagan and philosophical—ethics "discloses its secret truth to be *absolute self-sacrifice without return*."[132] The "return" of all that Protestantism sacrifices—which is to say, the world itself—is only possible via the reintroduction of *eros*, and by extension the possibility of a rhetorical form of divine truth, into the Christian ethic.

We can understand that such a reading of dialectical theology is possible. In Luther's "Heidelberg Disputation" the Reformer claims, as Milbank would expect, that any truly Christian love must not be enlivened by the attraction exercised upon it by particular objects, but instead must "extinguish" this attraction as its animating force.[133] However, it is also true that for Luther, only this love, excised of its erotic quest for pleasure, allows for something like a human *participation* in God; for it is God's love especially that is not dependent upon "attraction":

> Rather than seeking its own good, the love of God flows forth and bestows good. Therefore sinners are attractive because they are loved; they are not loved because they are attractive . . . This is *the love of the cross*, born of the cross, which turns in the direction where it does not find good which it may enjoy, but where it may confer good upon the bad and needy person.[134]

Is this what Radical Orthodoxy perhaps fails to understand—that a love "born of the cross" might be both non-objective, and yet at the same time

---

129. Ibid., 265.
130. Ibid., 274.
131. See Milbank, *Theology and Social Theory*, esp. 364–72.
132. Milbank, "Sublimity," 279.
133. Luther, "Heidelberg Disputation," 53–54.
134. Ibid., 57. Emphasis added.

"participatory" in God, inasmuch as it exists in the mode of the Spirit's outpouring, articulated in both creation and redemption as God's loving forth beings from nothingness?

We can by now anticipate the response of a rhetorical theology, which would be to claim that a "love of the cross" articulated as a turning in the direction where no enjoyment is to be found, where no objective attraction is exercised, is but the outworking of an epistemological dilemma about God's infinite being that inheres only in a world construed according to a "univocal ontology." *But it is precisely at this point,* I want to emphasize, when Protestantism's (or any theology's) anti-imagism, which connects naturally with a suspicion of human *eros*, is cast as an epistemological rather than an existential rigor—a problem related to the incompatibility of ontic structures rather than to the pervasiveness of sin—that rhetorical theology goes fatally wrong. For it hereby insulates itself from theology's need to grapple with the existential problems posed by human desire. Mindful of the danger of failing in this reflective task, which a scholarly tracing of historical philosophical mistakes would certainly allow us to avoid, let us pursue in the final chapter the possibility that the "dialectic" of dialectical theology is something other than a simple gnostic ignorance of created particularities, and that it might in fact offer the only alternative to the nihilism of despair, precisely in its refusal to be found "charming."

Conclusion

In this chapter we have considered the relationship between human cultural arrangements and the practice of sacrifice. Furthermore, we have asked the question of Christianity's capacity to address and perhaps transcend the "necessity" of sacrifice in human cultural formation. That is, we have asked whether and how Christianity's promised "reconciliation of the world to God," and its "peace to men on earth" can be deployed in the world. We found that for both Milbank and Girard, the question of this deployment is at some level an "existential" question. That is, we found that for both thinkers, Christianity's distinction from "secular" or "pagan" cultures consists in its refusal to reify the meaning of "life" in *a priori* ideologies. For Milbank, this means more specifically that Christian truth is never "had" except in the *living* of that truth. Such an approach to truth reconciles the subject's passionate and rational natures, and moreover enables "objective" differences among human beings or people groups to be traversed by the measure of charity. This approach is reflected also in Milbank's theological methodology, which is characterized by a primarily "historiographical" or "genealogical" strategy. In this way theology avoids the "hypostasization" of temporal and eternal realities that is the basis of secular reason's inexorable violence. For Milbank, the institution of this boundary can ultimately be chalked up to despair, or the subject's unwillingness to believe that temporality might be both sublimely mysterious and yet still traversable via a consistent, charitable measure. Such a boundary leads to sacrifice because it does not see being as fundamentally a *way among differences*, but instead sees it *as objective difference*, which means that any peace requires an objective "unification" that spells the sacrifice of all "contradictory" elements.

In a similar vein, for Girard, Christianity interrupts all other cultural logics by unmasking the ideological commitments that sustain those orders as grounded nowhere but in a collective refusal to believe in the possibility of reconciliation without violence. Girard therefore has an account of myth and even of the development of human language in general that resonates with Catherine Pickstock's critique of language as writing. That is, just as Pickstock reads the longstanding "sophistic" understanding of truth as fundamentally abstractable, in writing, from the temporal site of its enactment (as a "gesture of security" against death), so too does Girard see human cultures' justifying, ideological myths as rooted, not in a real, "scientific" approach to truth, but in the fundamental human inclination to self-protection. Thus Girard's reconfigured account of "scientific" methodology begins not with *a priori* ideological commitments, but with an attention to "the data" that ought to be aligned more closely with Milbank's historiography than with any objectifying empiricism. Hence also Girard's reluctance to "write" us into Christianity as a distinct but equally "ideological" sociality. In order to safeguard the possibility, to which Milbank is also committed, of reconciliation as a "way" among differences rather than the periodic elimination of difference, Girard prefers not to engage in a communicative discourse about the "structure" of Christian sociality, fearing such a discourse would remain too "mythological" in its function, and thereby fail Christianity as inexorable existential movement.

At this point, important differences begin to emerge between Girard's opposition to sacrifice and that of Milbank. On the surface, the crucial difference concerns the role each thinker gives to the discourse of theology in bringing about a new, distinctly Christian sociality. As should be clear from previous chapters, Milbank believes that theology can and must adopt a form of discourse that opposes all forms of secular reason. It can do this by "out-historicizing" every discourse, which means by remaining unabashedly rhetorical, and thereby showing up the residual "dialectics" in all secular discourses—some of which claim to be historicist, but none of which finally succeeds in becoming "anti-metaphysical." This means that theology can advocate a robust "interestedness" in a particular historical series that is not premised upon any *a priori* metaphysical justifications; and nor is it, like postmodern nihilism, radically "indifferent" to commitment as a result of its unjustifiability. In this way theology *can* speak in a unique fashion about the merits of the social history from which it emerges.

That it *must* speak in this way is a second, albeit related point, which gets to the crux of the tension between Girard and Milbank, and also to what has emerged as the crucial question in this book. As we have seen, in this and prior chapters, Milbank's claim that Christianity offers the sole possibility of a genuine *Sittlichkeit* is the basis of our ability to describe his Christianity as "existential." That is, for Milbank *Sittlichkeit* implies the reconciliation of universal and particular truth, not in a new ideology, but in a life. The relationship of theology as a discourse to the deployment of a *sittlich* way of being finally hinges, as we see especially in the last chapter of *Theology and Social Theory*, on an account of temporality and anxiety that is always implied, if not always explicated in Milbank's thought. In short, the account suggests that the existing human being is situated in the "present," at the edge of a future whose impendence is utterly unpredictable. Such a mysterious impendence of the future represents to human beings a relationship to the eternal, and the character of the "mystery" is the "how" of the eternal's determination of the historical. The anxiety provoked by this situation leads modern thought to its conjecture of a reified and more manageable—i.e., predictable—temporal economy. Postmodern thought, by contrast, being more attuned to the self-deception of this modern move, "deconstructs" it and leaves us with an account of temporal differentiation that is more honest in its conclusion of the "sublimity" of the future's advent. Yet this response to anxiety is no less "despairing," because it is equally fearful of the mystery of time's relation to the eternal. In this case subjective fear, which Milbank identifies with sin, concludes that because the distance of the future is so great, traversing it is utterly impossible. This too is an anti-existential move, because in its despair over repetition, postmodern thought concludes that there is no *way* of being that can reconcile temporal movement with eternal supplementation. Obviously for Milbank Christianity offers an important counter to this despair in virtue of its "Trinitarian ontology," according to which the eternal itself is characterized by a measure of spiritual "motion," which therefore does not preclude time from participation in its measure even in virtue of its objective inconsistency. But it is also important for Milbank, who does not want only to be a Christian metaphysician, that Christianity not only *can* give a different account of time, but also that it *must*, precisely in order to transform the subject herself into a living, breathing analogue of Christian speculation. Ultimately this means countering not just the conclusions of fear embodied in all secular reason, but countering the possibility of fear itself, by "figuring" the distance of the sublime as a compelling offer of true life. Thus theology, in its uniquely anti-metaphysical methodology, must become the instrument of the subject's inscription in a new and uniquely historical tradition of existential enactment.

In this chapter we have heard most strongly Milbank's opposition to those "dialectical" theologies that, out of what he calls elsewhere a "false humility," refuse to go further than presenting the existential task of Christianity as an unmediable "leap." Most succinctly, his argument is that such a refusal to appeal directly to human *eros* aligns with the skepticism of postmodernism and so leaves the subject as a temporal "impossibility," rather than inspiring it to life in the eternally consistent movement of charity. These varieties of theology are finally too "Heideggerian" in their existentialism, we might say, making their conclusions on the "faithless" basis of an asserted aporia between time and eternity. And according to Milbank, by cutting out the direct appeal of distinctively Christian sociality to human *eros*, "dialectical" theology effectively disregards the very real neighbor for whom the "purity" of its love was intended. In the next and final chapter we shall return to Kierkegaard, in order to develop an account of Christian love that will figure as a response to Milbank precisely on this point. There we shall see, I hope, that the existential rigor of an anti-rhetorical theology more adequately addresses the authentic concerns of Radical Orthodoxy than does any theological metadiscourse. Precisely in its refusal to "woo," the essentially Christian ethic alone leaves open the possibility of a way of living in the world, "as if not." Let us turn now to Kierkegaard's *Works of Love*.

5

Love's Obstinate Hope

Introduction

IN THE PREVIOUS CHAPTER we saw that for Milbank, Christian theology's capacity to move subjects toward a true *Sittlichkeit* via rhetorical persuasion indicates its unique opposition to the necessity of "sacrifice." By contrast, all forms of secular reason are rooted in a fearful subjective response to temporal anxiety, which presupposes that any traversal of the sublime distance of futurity cannot be undertaken but for a sacrifice of the sublime itself to the predictability of a reified temporal economy (Weber), or a sacrifice of the subject to the void of temporal disharmony (Heidegger, Derrida). Uniquely, Christianity suggests that neither the eternal nor the subject is necessarily sacrificed by entering into the process of temporal differentiation, for the "gap" that seems so problematic to secular reason is for Christian "fideism" a beguiling distance—pregnant with the promise that the subject will get everything back, will receive his or her true self in the self-sacrificing movement of *caritas*.

Given the centrality of Christianity's opposition to sacrifice in Milbank's theological imperative, at this point I recommended that we move to a consideration of the cultural analyses of René Girard. We saw that for Girard, like Milbank, all cultural orders premised upon sacrificial mythologies are unable to countenance "reconciliation" without violence. Such cultural idioms are so fixated on objective difference that they cannot conceive of life as a peaceful *way* among differences.

Milbank is keen to expose the ontological assumptions of such a sacrificial posture as unnecessary—to suggest, in other words, that one does not have to ascribe a fundamental "reality" to all "conflictual phenomena." Christianity's prescribed way of forgiveness disabuses the subject of precisely this tendency, suggesting that regardless of the objective contradiction of a particular "offense," one can respond not in kind but instead without registering the contradictory nature of the offense at all—i.e., one can always extend love rather than retribution. Similarly for Girard, all human conflict is rooted in the tendency of human desire to imitate the very antagonism of its rival, and therefore is premised upon a difference that literally amounts to "nothing." This means that a true reconciliation is possible if only one can "give up" the founding of one's selfhood upon such rivalry, which effectively removes the obstacle to reconciliation for one's former antagonist—i.e., it gives him "nothing" to rival.

Despite the resonances between their accounts of Christianity's unique opposition to sacrifice, however, we saw that the ultimate difference between Girard and Milbank turns upon the fact that Girard's analysis of the foundation of culture upon mimetic rivalry also gives rise to an account of "signification" as complicit in sacrificial violence. This account leads Girard to a suspicion of cultural "inscription" as such, which extends to an implicit critique of any direct communication of the Christian possibility of true peace. For Milbank, as we saw in the last part of the previous chapter, this refusal on Girard's part to persuade us of the "idiom of peaceable behavior" is his ultimate failing of the Radical Orthodox theological imperative and by extension of the possibility of *Sittlichkeit*. Upon pursuing this critique, we found that for Milbank the apparent dialectic in Girard between *eros* as "fundamental human desire" and *agape* as the uniquely Christian mode of sociality resonates in problematic ways with the Protestant "reform" of love. Such an account "purifies" love of erotic attractions, which makes it akin, on Milbank's account, to secular reason's refusal to reconcile infinite and finite economies of differentiation. That is, it indicates a refusal to believe that the interval of temporal differentiation might be analogous to the charitable relations of Father, Son, and Holy Spirit, and that Christianity might therefore be the infinite truth, precisely *as a temporal way of living*. The putative existential rigor of such a radical "Religiousness B" hereby leads to the opposite of enacted love, allowing the subject to evade the real and present task of incorporating *caritas* into temporal life.

Thus have we arrived at the present and final chapter, which aims to be attentive to Radical Orthodoxy's concerns about the debasement of love accomplished by secular reason, but also to offer a final measure of resistance to its suggestion that only a rhetorical construal of the possibility of Christian living ensures that the subject will respond to his anxiety in love rather than fear. Here we shall undertake a reading of Kierkegaard's *Works of Love*, in which Christian love is relentlessly distinguished from erotic love as preferential. In all of Kierkegaard's distinctions between the erotic and the "agapeic," we shall try to discern in preferential love a constant deferral of living that goes unnoticed by rhetorical attempts to beguile the human subject into action. Ultimately we shall see that for Kierkegaard, only a love that inexplicably "hopes all things" can keep being in motion, and that this hope is secured not when the subject is finally *persuaded* to let go of his mistrust, but when he banishes this mistrust because he *shall* love. Kierkegaard's refusal to "aestheticize" possibility as the possibility of the good therefore bears within it a critique of both secular reason and of rhetorical theological communication as complicit in the same despair of mistrust. The love that Kierkegaard ultimately champions, then, despite its indifference to rhetoric and its necessary mortification of human *eros*, will nonetheless be shown to be the last bastion of a genuine *Sittlichkeit*—that is, *if one* takes up the task of love.

Erotic Love and Friendship in *Works of Love*

The Difficulty of Reading *Works of Love*

In *Works of Love*, Kierkegaard celebrates the possibility of true life in the way that is Christ as available *right now*, and at every moment. At the same time, the book indicates that the celebration only "holds," so to speak, insofar as *the reader* in fact takes up the essentially Christian task, which is love; and it does everything to suggest there is no time for delay. Its rigor in this regard is compounded by the fact that the love it praises offends everything one might have thought was loving about one's life. In these quite basic ways Kierkegaard's book seems decisively opposed to Milbank's account of love as responsive to the charms or immediately attractive features of its object.¹ Indeed, Kierkegaard's account is more closely aligned with that of Martin Luther, which I cited in the previous chapter as saying that Christian love "turns in the direction where it does not find good which it may enjoy, but where it may confer good upon the bad and needy person."² As Kierkegaard himself puts it,

> The beloved and the friend are the immediate and direct objects of immediate love, the choice of passion and of inclination. And what is *the ugly*? It is the *neighbor*, whom one shall love. One shall love him; that simple wise man knew nothing at all about this... Yet the true love is love for the neighbor, or it is not to find the lovable object but to find the unlovable object lovable.³

Here we are confronted once again with Christianity's distinction from the Socratic, or from Religiousness A. Given that we learned in the third chapter that the newness of Christianity constitutes an infinite complication of Religiousness A, we should expect that here too, in the matter of love, Christianity does not just "consummate" the love that already knows how to love the beautiful, but complicates it. That is, just as Religiousness B, which proclaims the Incarnation of the eternal in a particular human being, calls into question even the best of Religiousness A's intimations of the religious task, so too Christian love, as the love that finds the unlovable lovable, will not function to "confirm" the power native to selective *eros*, but will dethrone the erotic as such. The first moment in this reconfiguration of love consists in the revelation of human *eros* as, in fact, polemical against true love, just as the first moment in the transition to Religiousness B is to become conscious of sin.

Thus Kierkegaard's *Works of Love* poses necessary challenges, as we will see in greater detail, for any mindset that wants to "synthesize" Christianity's defense of love with what *eros* "already knows" about love. It proves difficult even for Kierkegaard scholars, some of whom must finally reject much of his account of love.⁴ Such rejections most often take offense at what seems to be Kierkegaard's unreserved critique of ways of being that we usually assume make up what is "best" about human life. My general sense of such responses is that they are well attuned

1. See Milbank, "Sublimity," 265.
2. See Luther, "Heidelberg Disputation," 57.
3. Kierkegaard, *Works of Love*, 373–74.
4. See, for example, George, "Something Anti-Social about *Works of Love*," and Løgstrup, "Settling Accounts with Kierkegaard's *Works of Love*."

to the rigors of *Works of Love*, and moreover that one should not try to show how Kierkegaard might avoid their disgust. In this respect I disagree with Stephen Evans, for one, who offers a defense of Kierkegaard's "humaneness" in his 2004 book, *Kierkegaard's Ethic of Love*. Evans uses Kierkegaard's *Works of Love* to make a case for divine command theory as a reasonable option in contemporary philosophical and theological discussions of moral obligation. He believes Kierkegaard provides a compelling rejoinder particularly to those who suggest that divine command theory utterly disregards what we might call the realm of human flourishing, in which the discernment of natural goods can help autonomous human subjects to determine "moral" courses of action. This means Evans must persuade his reader, on the basis of his reading of Kierkegaard, that "humans have *good reasons* to obey God's commands ... because God has created them, graciously showering them with many goods."[5] Moreover he must emphasize what he says are Kierkegaard's arguments "that such a divine command theory of moral obligation is humanistic in the sense that it views moral obligations as successfully directed towards human flourishing."[6] Thus, while making use of a different form of communication from that of Radical Orthodoxy—in that he works within and responds to a tradition of analytic philosophy, whose means Milbank would oppose to his own "rhetorical" strategies—Evans' enterprise should be nonetheless familiar to us by now. That is, Evans attempts specifically to reconcile the "sublime" offense of religious obligation with the "natural" inclinations felt in relation to what he calls "special loves," an aim that resonates with Milbank's rhetorical effort to persuade us of the unique reconciliation of universal and particular afforded by a Christian *Sittlichkeit*.

The difficulty of construing such a reconciliation with Kierkegaard's help begins with the fact that love for Kierkegaard is not an "inclination" whatsoever, but a "duty," and when Evans tries to get around this opposition, his argument loses credibility as a reading of Kierkegaard. Evans makes such an attempt by beginning not with love's transformation into *duty*, but with something we "already know" about love—that love "is an *emotion*."[7] Thus, for him the transformation of love accomplished by Christianity resides in its command to have an "emotion" for the neigh-

5. Evans, *Kierkegaard's Ethic of Love*, 299. Emphasis added.
6. Ibid., 300.
7. Ibid., 190. Emphasis added.

bor. This reading of Kierkegaard's comment that "love is a passion of the emotions"[8] gives Evans just the sort of entry-point he needs for an explanatory reconciliation between love of the neighbor and natural inclination. Emotions, Evans tells us, are rooted in the "construals" we form of people and situations. In regard to his own teenage son, then, who always has a messy room, Evans writes that he might "choose to perceive him as an emerging adult who is attempting to demonstrate some independence by making his own decisions about 'his' space. Which way I see him and the room will determine the emotional response I have."[9] In relation to his cranky neighbor, Evans adds, "I must construe him as a child of God, made in God's image. If I love God unconditionally I cannot be indifferent to that which God has made, particularly not to that which he has made that resembles himself."[10] In such cases, *if* I can form such a construal and *if* I do indeed love God, Evans affirms that the "construal will indeed ground an emotion."[11] But what is lacking in Evans' analysis, here and elsewhere in his book, is a proper account of how love as duty *dethrones* preference, rather than "expanding" it—and how it does this precisely in order to *secure* love. Evans' "explanation" of dutiful love with reference to construal-based emotions only brings back the uncertainty of a love grounded in the attractiveness of its object. For Kierkegaard, by contrast, only when your love does *not* depend on whether or not the neighbor evokes a certain "feeling" can it be eternally secured. This means that love eternally secured by duty does *not* work within the machinations of natural feelings, but remains indifferent to them—precisely so that you may love the neighbor! Let us now move to give our own consideration of Kierkegaard on the problem of preference in the erotic, remaining mindful that it would be better honestly to take offense than to attempt to defend Kierkegaard to the humanists.

Love and Earthly Wisdom

From the beginning of *Works of Love*, Kierkegaard does indeed suppose that love, like the analogical measure of *caritas* for Radical Orthodoxy,

---

8. Kierkegaard, *Works of Love*, 112.
9. Evans, *Kierkegaard's Ethic of Love*, 192.
10. Ibid., 194.
11. Ibid.

is above all that which "connects the temporal and eternity."[12] Thus love on Kierkegaard's account is like Radical Orthodoxy's measure of *caritas* insofar as love *is* this reconciling "connection," but perhaps unlike that measure in that love for Kierkegaard does not by any means give rise to "persuasive" analogies between temporal movement and eternal differentiation. Instead, Kierkegaard wants to hold together the "connectivity" of love with its jarring opposition, not to temporality as such, but to the wisdom that would presume only upon a temporal economy. As he puts it, "precisely because temporality and eternity are heterogeneous, love can seem a burden to temporality's earthly sagacity, and therefore in temporality it may seem to the sensate person an enormous relief to cast off this bond of eternity."[13] Does this mean that love is "irrational" or utterly "sublime" vis-à-vis the sensate, as Milbank would charge?

Here it is important to call to mind the connection between Kierkegaard's construal of love as a burden to earthly wisdom and the relationship of the passion of faith to the conclusions of human knowledge. For Kierkegaard, as we may recall from the *Postscript*, the passion of faith is elicited by the pairing of objective uncertainty with the subject's infinite interest in eternal happiness. Faith then becomes a passionate choosing of that which is objectively uncertain—specifically, the affirmation that Jesus, a historical person, is the appropriate "point of departure" for one's eternal happiness. The tendency of human beings is to refuse this affirmation in order to remain resolved in ostensible objective certainty. Yet in no case where the human being so concludes does Kierkegaard believe that his or her conclusion is "valid." That is, like Milbank, who argues that secular reason's supposition of a "boundary" between the temporal and the eternal is not based on irrefutable knowledge of the temporal, but on a subjective wager that resolves its anxiety in *fear*, so too for Kierkegaard, the anti-faith "conclusions" of knowledge are in fact subjective "resolutions" *not* to banish doubt through belief. In the same way that Milbank argues that Weber's hypostasization of a "routinized" history is naught but a subjective wager, Kierkegaard suggests in *Philosophical Fragments* that honesty would have us admit that belief (or disbelief), rather than knowledge, is "the organ for the

---

12. Kierkegaard, *Works of Love*, 6.
13. Ibid.

historical" as such.[14] In the section of *Works of Love* titled "Love Believes All Things," Kierkegaard puts it this way:

> The deception is that *from* knowledge (the pretense and the falsity are that it is by virtue of knowledge) mistrust concludes, assumes, and believes what it concludes, assumes, and believes *by virtue* of the disbelief inherent in mistrust, whereas *from* the same knowledge, *by virtue* of belief, one can conclude, assume, and believe the very opposite.[15]

Therefore Kierkegaard does not interpret the opposition of Christianity to "sagacity" as the opposition of the sublime to the immanent, the unknowable to the knowable, but as the opposition of two equally unjustified subjective dispositions, one believing, and one mistrustful. This means, in turn, that Christian love for Kierkegaard does not eschew the "known" charms of the present object for the proper unknowability of the divine life, or of "pure" agape. Rather, it substitutes an imperative to love *every* neighbor for erotic love's tendency to evade love in relation to the most difficult objects. Thus, "love is as knowledgeable as anyone, knows everything that experience knows, yet without being mistrustful."[16]

The crucial point of contention between Milbank and Kierkegaard, which this chapter is devoted to addressing, concerns the relationship between "persuasion" and certainty. For Milbank, rhetorical persuasion is to be distinguished from "dialectical" or exclusively rational persuasion, which therefore distinguishes it from the despairing resolution of what Kierkegaard would call "earthly sagacity." Rhetorical persuasion is thus an existential passion insofar as it is "wooed" even in the absence of, or in virtue of a refusal to offer, its own "metaphysical justification." In this way, then, for Milbank the passion proper to the Christian life is compatible with, and even requires, an integration of the subject's erotic "preferences." The *way* that is Christian truth in fact elicits the subject's passion precisely *by "persuading"* him or her, in the absence of any dialectical justification. For Kierkegaard, by contrast, the play of preferences upon human inclinations is closely connected to the self-protective desire of earthly sagacity for certainty. That is, in his discussion of *eros*,

---

14. Kierkegaard, *Philosophical Fragments/Johannes Climacus*, 81.
15. Kierkegaard, *Works of Love*, 227.
16. Ibid., 228.

Kierkegaard tries to show that preference does not arouse or enliven true Christian passion, but allows one to evade it. Thus *a refusal to have one's preferences "crucified" constitutes for Kierkegaard an evasion of the uncertainty upon which the whole of the Christian life turns, and in which alone its passion is sustained and sustaining.*

Whither "the Other"?

According to conventional wisdom, it does seem that to love the one whom one prefers is to love the other in all his or her specificity, that it is to love one who is truly *other*. Yet Kierkegaard argues that "to love someone who in the sense of preference is nearer than anyone else *is self-love*,"[17] which implies that he takes Christianity's primary opposition to paganism from Jesus' question in Matt 5:46: "do not the pagans also do the same?" No connection between preference and *self*-love ever occurs to paganism, which opposes self-love to preference in this way: "self-love is abhorrent because it is love of self, but erotic love and friendship, which are passionate preferential love, are love."[18] Thus, any account of Christianity that wants to read it as a consummation would say that Christian love takes pagan love and *expands its domain*. Christianity would then be the *integration* of that which "persuades" you even in the enemy with a preference no longer limited by the "boundaries" set up by an ontology of violence. For Kierkegaard, however, Christianity does not appeal to the same mechanism of preferential love whatsoever, suggesting instead that "self-love and passionate preferential love are essentially the same, but love for the neighbor—that is love."[19]

To love passionately on the basis of preference seems least of all to be contained within the circle of self-love—it appears instead that such love means being gripped by the other, "taken" with that other as if obliged from out of nowhere and beyond one's choosing. At the same time, however, such love is of necessity limited to objects of *admiration*; that is, a worldly understanding of love stipulates that at no time should one ask a person to rise to the heights of love in relation to something random. Thus the claim of the preferential lover that "love arises when it will and commands me even to forget myself" means also, "love does not arise

---

17. Ibid., 21.
18. Ibid., 53.
19. Ibid.

except when I determine that the object is worthy of it." Unsurprisingly, then, if one asks the poet to describe one in the throes of erotic love, "he will add: 'and then there must be admiration; the lover must admire the beloved.'"[20] This already deflates the question we are likely to ask at this point, since by now we can anticipate the response: "but how can *devotion* and *unlimited giving of oneself* be *self-love*? Indeed, when it is devotion to the *other I*, the *other self*."[21]

Honest self-reflection would have me admit that admiration in fact serves as a device by which my love is always returned to me, in my despairing effort to secure myself by my own power. That is, on Kierkegaard's reading, what preferential love "prefers" is *not* the other in all her specificity, but rather the lover's own criteria of lovability: "erotic love and friendship are the very peak of self-esteem, the *I* intoxicated in the *other I*."[22] In the throes of admiration, then, the subject does not really love the beloved. But nor does he love himself as he truly *exists*, by the very breath of God; for his admiration casts even his own selfhood as a preferred compilation of objective qualities, to which he relates his spirit with infinite passion in a comedy one can only call despair. My dispossession of erotic preference therefore does not strip me of anything that could be called "real love," but in fact makes possible a different love, which does not honor only the charms I would like to possess, but instead loves forth beings from the nothingness of their own despairing immediacy to their objective attributes. Only thus can I love the particular neighbor according to her true, spiritual self.

The undeniable passion of preferential love is hereby revealed as a mere cover for its insecurity. Its passion is provoked by anxiety over its own and its beloved's changeability, but it cannot overcome this anxiety because it is already an expression of fear's self-deceptive conclusion that it has nothing to be anxious about—and it can prove it! Therefore, preferential love, in all its passion, is moved not by love as such, but by the anxiety it does not know how to surmount, even as it pretends to surmount it through its own power: "the anxiety is hidden, and the only expression is the *flaming craving*, whereby it is known that the anxiety is hidden underneath."[23] Interestingly, the anxious nature of

20. Ibid., 54.
21. Ibid.
22. Ibid., 56.
23. Ibid., 33.

this craving makes this most passionate love also uniquely susceptible to the seductive sleepiness of habit. This is first of all because all particular beloveds, whose immediacy to the lover's preferred distinction first awakened his or her love, will not always be so immediate. Thus it makes sense that such love eventually "loses its ardor, its joy, its desire, its originality, its freshness. Just as the river that sprang out of the rocks is dissipated further down in the sluggishness of the dead waters, so also love is dissipated in the lukewarmness and indifference of habit."[24] But habit, which is a continuance in this "lukewarmness," is in the first place the utter perversion of erotic love's flaming passion. How then does such a love ever give in to the cooling of habit?

Habit's cunning power vis-à-vis the erotic is that it offers the fulfillment of erotic love's desire for a self-made security against change. By appearances, then, habit forsakes preferential love as rooted in the power of passion's discovery of its preferred distinction. Yet beneath appearances, habit whispers to this anxious love that perhaps it can continue to call itself love even in the routinized patterns of the dead waters farther downstream. Thus habit lulls the passion of preferential love to sleep and at the same time "sucks the blood of the sleeper while it fans and cools him and makes his sleep even more pleasant."[25] Habit knows how to make this lover sleep soundly because it knows that what fires the passion of preferential love is precisely its insecurity. Therefore habit's suggestion that love can remain love, even without being "new every morning," becomes attractive precisely to the one whose passion should be opposed at all times to habit's drowsiness. Now such love can sleep—if not rest—in freedom from its exhausting and interminable testing. In habit, therefore, preferential love is secured—though *not as love*. Similarly, in habit the self is secured—*though not in love*. And insofar as habit protects such a lover from recognizing his or her anxiety, insofar as it removes him or her even from the *thought* of insecurity, it becomes the very worst of enemies, ensuring that the subject will cease even to look for true security.[26]

---

24. Ibid., 36.

25. Ibid.

26. This is why Augustine is retrospectively pleased that God never allowed him to be lulled to sleep by the habits of his preferential passions, instead "sprinkling bitter gall over [Augustine's] sweet pursuits." See Augustine, *Confessions*, Book III.

Self-love and Sociality

It may be suggested that such a construal of all preferential love as fundamentally self-love does not adequately account for the socially constructive nature of this love. That is, it seems undeniable that preferential love forms and sustains bonds between lovers, families, local communities, and larger bodies. How can the ostensible divisiveness of a love that never gets beyond the *I* (even when it "extends" to the *other I*) achieve such social cohesion? Interestingly, Kierkegaard discusses the connection between self-love and sociality in a way that resonates with René Girard's suggestion that human culture is organized around a more or less violent disavowal of human violence.[27] For Girard, to recall, despite the spiritual capacity of human desire, the fundamental human unwillingness to surrender to a true spiritual power expresses itself in the perversion of imitative self-protection. As human beings, we become fascinated with the "selfhood" of our neighbors, who consequently become rivals that offer "nothing" but reflections of our own violence. The fundamentally cohesive character of imitation therefore always threatens to lead to rivalry and itself become the need for reconciliation. The only solution to this need that is not external to the subjects' own power is the periodic murder of a representative "double" to restore cohesive differentiation. Thus Girard argues that true peace requires a solution that completely interrupts the repetitive crises of human desire. And therefore what passes for love in human culture on this account does not really mean giving oneself to the other, but agreeing with the others to allow each to seek his own self-protection.

To surrender oneself to an interruptive power, by contrast, would mean ceasing to reflect the selfhood desired by "the others," and thus courting a differentiation they are bound to find intolerable. In a similar vein, Kierkegaard writes that

> The distinction the world makes is namely this: if someone wants to be self-loving all by himself, which, however, is rarely seen, the world calls this self-love, but if he, self-loving, wants to hold together in self-love with some other self-loving people, particularly with many self-loving people, then the world calls this love

---

27. Girard, *Girard Reader*, 165. For more on this connection, see Bellinger, *Genealogy of Violence*.

> ... What the world honors and loves under the name of love is an alliance in self-love.[28]

For Kierkegaard too then, love as understood by the world is honored in such a way that it gives rise to a sociality dedicated to protecting the mere appearance of genuine, self-denying love. Neither does Kierkegaard hesitate to connect such sociality, as an "alliance in self-love," with violence. That is, for Kierkegaard as for Girard, there is the self-sacrifice of true neighbor love, the willingness to "give up" your very self to a movement that you do not control, and on the other hand there is the violence of the world, which asks that you "sacrifice" your true self to the crowd, for which you will receive the "security" of imitative self-protection: "the sacrifice that people understand has its reward, after all, in popular approval and to that extent is not true sacrifice, which must unconditionally be without reward."[29]

But what could possibly be wrong with receiving friendship in return for one's self-sacrifice? Would one not need to hate the human good in order to disparage this reward? Perhaps this would be true if friendship truly was what it claims to be—i.e., honest, self-sacrificing devotion. But Kierkegaard argues it is entirely more likely that your friend will "not care for your conviction that truly to love yourself is to love God, that to love another human being is to help him to love God."[30] If this is your conviction, and if your life reflects it, then your friend will recognize in your life "an admonition, a requirement for him—this is what he wants to remove. The reward for this is friendship and the good name of a friend."[31] That is, your friend wants to maintain a relation of preferential love, by which each of you can forget, in the passion of your preference, the requirement of any true eternal security—the requirement that you surrender yourself to God unreservedly. This corruption, inherent in friendship, is not obvious to the world, for it is not as if such a friend wants to make off with all your belongings—indeed, he may very well want to see you flourish. His relatively unremarkable offense is only that he "wanted to defraud you of the God-relationship and wanted you, as a friend, to help him defraud himself—in this fraud

---

28. Kierkegaard, *Works of Love*, 119.
29. Ibid., 119–20.
30. Ibid., 127.
31. Ibid.

he would then hold together with you in life and death."[32] Such is friendship as preferential love in a nutshell, for Kierkegaard. Its intrinsic wish clarifies that "the world prefers not to hear anything about the eternal, God's requirement of love,"[33] since this requirement undoes—and asks the individual human being to help in undoing—the machinations of self-love that give rise to the whole of what the world knows about sociality. Violence follows soon after any expression of God's requirement in a life, for "what, then, does the world do? Then the world says of the person who wants to hold to God that he is self-loving. *The expedient is an old one: to sacrifice one person when all the others can profit from it.*"[34]

The connection between Kierkegaard's analysis of preferential *eros* and Girard's discussion of sinful human mimesis becomes still more striking in Kierkegaard's discussion of how preferential love practices rejection. Preferential love wants so badly to prove itself secure; but it can only do so via a passion in relation to the preferred, such that part of its very craving is directed toward the rejection of those who are not worthy of its love. And this it must of course chalk up to a deficiency not in its love but in "others":

> People bemoan humanity and its unhappiness, bemoan finding no one whom they can love, because to bemoan the world and its unhappiness is always easier than to beat one's breast and bemoan oneself . . . And what is it that is wrong, what else but their searching and rejecting! Such people do not perceive that their words sound like a mockery of themselves, because *the inability to find any object for one's love among people amounts to denouncing oneself as totally lacking in love.*[35]

This analysis runs parallel to Girard's suggestion that modern cultural criticism is attuned to the bankruptcy of what has been called love in the past, as a vehicle for truly peaceful reconciliation, but it is not attuned to the fact that its condemnation of past ages retains the very impoverishment of love it praises itself for having "overcome." Kierkegaard writes of the anxious and despairing lover that "his eyes are sharpened and armed, alas, not in the sense of truth but rather in the sense of untruth; therefore his outlook becomes more and more prejudiced so that, infecting, he

32. Ibid.
33. Ibid., 128.
34. Ibid. Emphasis added.
35. Ibid., 157.

sees evil in everything, impurity even in the purest."[36] Preferential love wants to be secured by its own selectivity, which means that rather than believing a good in the other for love's sake, it bets upon its power of "discovery," which finds sin in all but the "other I." Hereby we come to see definitively that spontaneous, preferential love, which promises to deny itself by loving the beloved even *more* than itself, is but an exercise in self-protection. This love must become allied with "the others," such that each can be unto himself while remaining ignorant of his nihilism for being this way. Thus, Kierkegaard writes, "the world continually sees to it that there is a sufficient number of forged notes of counterfeit self-denial in circulation."[37]

True Christian sacrifice, by contrast, does not sacrifice the human being for the sake of the city, or what Kierkegaard would call the "established order." Instead, Christian love wills to stand in the position of one who offends the established "security" of a sociality based upon preferential love: "the inwardness of Christian love is to be willing, as reward for its love, to be hated by the beloved."[38] Worldly self-denial also "casts off" pleasantries, but only in order to be "elevated" in the eyes of human culture. Christian sacrifice promises an elevation through sacrifice, but not elevation to esteem; one must forego the possibility of esteem as such:

> But to stand on this elevated place (inasmuch as sacrifice truly is elevation) accused, scorned, hated, mocked almost worse than the lowest of the low—that is, superhumanly striving to reach this elevated place and to stand on that elevated place *in such a way that it appears to everyone that one is standing on the lowest place of contemptibility*—this, in the Christian sense, is sacrifice; moreover, in the human sense it is *madness*.[39]

For Kierkegaard, moreover, it is not as if this "mad" sacrifice is a one-time enactment that afterward begins to accrue income for the lover as his neighbors recognize his true elevation. Rather, the task of Christian sacrifice is to practice the continuance of this total disenfranchisement. The requirement, as Kierkegaard puts it, is "simultaneously and at every

36. Ibid., 286.
37. Ibid., 195.
38. Ibid., 131.
39. Ibid. Emphasis added.

moment lying at death's door and, upright, having to walk forward."[40] To refuse to "secure" one's love via the insecurity and incessant testing of preferential love is indeed to be "dead" to the world. But it is also, as we shall discover in the next section, to be able to "seek the confidential relationship with God,"[41] and thus to be secured by a love that is commanded in relation to every neighbor, a love that no worldly conditions can defeat.

Eros as Interested Indifference

All of this brings us, finally, to the distance of preferential love from the task of living—its "indifference," despite the fact that it is secured by "interest," to the immediacy of love's need to love. This indifference consists in the fact that erotic love and friendship, as preferential, rely upon "good fortune."[42] That is, if love is determined by preference, then it must hope to get lucky enough to come across the preferred one. "At most, then, the task is to be properly grateful for one's good fortune."[43] For even when the task is to seek this preferred one out, it is still the case that fortune alone determines the task, since the *seeker* of the preferred one is not yet a *lover*. And as most of us surely know, "if someone goes out into the world to try to find the beloved or friend, he can go a long way—and go in vain, can wander the world around—and in vain."[44] On the logic of preferential love, therefore, which suggests that to love what one finds charming is to love truly, much time can be spent on *not loving*—ostensibly *in the name of love*. By contrast, Christian love disregards preference or aversion as determining factors in love, and therefore it is "immediately involved in the task because it has the task within itself."[45]

Milbank implies an objection at this point when he comments that a love purified of *eros* cannot love the beloved "in its specificity,"[46] which is to suggest that Christian love as Kierkegaard articulates it is so "blind" to the particularities of its object that it cannot be said to be a temporally enacted task at all, but only the operation of a spatialized

40. Ibid., 133.
41. Ibid., 195.
42. Ibid., 51.
43. Ibid.
44. Ibid.
45. Ibid.
46. Milbank, "Sublimity," 265.

logic, the abstraction from material circumstances of a supposedly actualized "disposition." To offer such an objection is effectively to claim that preferential love, while not as immediate to love as a task, is certainly more immediate than Protestantism's pure neighbor-love to the beloved as the real, visible object of love's task. But for Kierkegaard, to purify neighbor-love of preference as a determining factor is actually to make it *less* prone to the abstraction of love than is preferential *eros*. Kierkegaard clarifies this in his chapter "Our Duty to Love the People We See," where it becomes clear that the command to love without regard for preference in fact frees the lover to "see" the beloved with a clarity that preference could scarcely imagine. For in order to love the person one sees, it is critical above all "*that one does not substitute an imaginary idea of how we think or could wish that this person should be.*"[47] Kierkegaard's implication here is that the criteria of preference constitute such an "idea," which neighbor-love alone can excise from love, since neighbor-love *does not need to see the beloved as something fantastic* in order to love him or her. This is what erotic love cannot imagine:

> It is worthy to wish and to pray that the one we love might always be and act in such a way that we are able to approve and agree completely. But in God's name let us not forget that it is not a merit on our part if he is like that, even less a merit on our part to require this of him—if there is to be any question of merit on our part, which nevertheless is unseemly and an unseemly way to talk with regard to love, it would just be to love equally faithfully and tenderly.[48]

Because preferential love does not love where it does not "approve," it follows that every moment it ostensibly "loves" the one of whom it approves, it is not really related passionately to the person in his or her specificity, but to its criteria for approval. Christian love does not love because it agrees but because it is commanded to do so, which means that the real, visible person remains the object of this love, unclouded by the filter of fantasy. Let us now move to consider this love specifically, such that we might understand more clearly both its total opposition to erotic love on the question of preference, and its unique corresponding capacity to "reconcile" the eternal and the temporal—through the crucifixion of its interest in worldly distinction.

47. Kierkegaard, *Works of Love*, 164. Emphasis in original.
48. Ibid.

Love as the Crucifixion of Preference

Love as Freedom from Despair

Kierkegaard distinguishes Christian love from preferential love primarily in that the former has "undergone the change of eternity by becoming duty and loves because it *shall* love."[49] For Kierkegaard this means that Christian love is free from any determination by preference; it is love transformed in such a way that it cannot be withheld, even when the object of love does not arouse its preferential desire. At first glance, of course, this freedom seems to come at the expense of a fundamental dependence—a refusal to allow our love to go where it will, spontaneously. For Kierkegaard, however, that Christian love "is dependent upon duty" means precisely that it "can never become dependent in a false sense."[50] That is, for a person's love to be a duty "makes a person dependent and at the same moment eternally independent."[51] In the worldly sense, the freedom of love is expressed in its being self-directed, in its ability to move where it wills, putatively freely, until it finds the object of its preferences. But love as a duty stays the same no matter what changes may affect the objects of its love or even the determinations of its preferences. Even when the beloved expressly rejects the lover, Kierkegaard writes, "the person who answers, 'In that case I *shall* still continue to love you'—that person's love is made eternally free in blessed independence."[52]

Love as a duty thus also reveals that preferential love's ostensible freedom is really despair, precisely by securing the dutiful lover against this hidden sickness. Despair, on Kierkegaard's account, is due

> to relating oneself with infinite passion to a particular something, for one can relate oneself with infinite passion—unless one is in despair—only to the eternal. Spontaneous love *is* in despair in this way, but when it becomes happy, as it is called, its being in despair is hidden from it; when it becomes unhappy, it becomes manifest that it was in despair.[53]

Unhappy preferential love is manifestly in despair because its unhappiness is due to its having an "infinite passion" that is not related to an

49. Ibid., 38.
50. Ibid.
51. Ibid.
52. Ibid., 39–40.
53. Ibid., 40.

appropriate object. But happy preferential love signals an equally despairing misrelation insofar as it is dependent, in its very self-directed "freedom," upon a particular, changeable thing. The commandment to love, by contrast, stipulates "that you must not love in such a way that the loss of the beloved would make it manifest that you were in despair—that is, you must not love in despair."[54] In other words, you must not love by virtue of your determination that the beloved suits your preference. This does not mean, of course, that you must not *love* the one you prefer, but that you must not love that one *because* you prefer him or her. Love as a duty stipulates that one shall be related with infinite passion not to preference but to love itself. Such love secures a person against despair, then, not by "comfort—that one must not take something [i.e., a change in the beloved] too hard, etc. . . . No, love's commandment *forbids despair*—by commanding one to love."[55] The eternal command requires the human being to be related in actuality to love as an eternal possibility, such that when preferential love wants to conclude mistrustingly of existence, when it wants to conclude that love is no longer possible in the absence of the preferred beloved, still love as a duty remains *always possible.*

This articulation of love's freedom and its capacity to secure the lover against despair certainly resonates with Milbank's account of Christian life as the unceasing movement of *caritas*, which indicates the crucial ways in which Milbank is indebted to, or at least influenced by, Kierkegaard. For Milbank, to recall, the despairing human being, like the Christian, is related to the future as infinite possibility. The one who is in despair, however, concludes mistrustingly that such a sublime distance to cross from one present moment to the next must make temporal differentiation an infinite disharmony, impossible to live in accordance with an eternalizing love. The Christian wager of ontological peace, by contrast, suggests that the mystery of temporal differentiation does not imply the reality of disharmony. This wager carries with it the concomitant claim that in *any* present situation, no matter how seemingly disharmonious and foreboding its relationship to the future, the possibility of living that distance via charity is always available. For Milbank, therefore, quite like Kierkegaard, it is mistrust rather than any "metaphysical justification" that rules out love as the eternalizing measure of

54. Ibid., 41.
55. Ibid. Emphasis added.

temporal life. Also like Kierkegaard, for Milbank it is ultimately love, as faith's way of being, which saves the individual human being from despair. In Kierkegaard's terms, to have love as a duty is to be secured against mistrust's tendency to conclude of all but the most preferred of present circumstances that love is not a viable possibility.

The critical point for any continuation of the conversation between Milbank and Kierkegaard thus concerns the "how" of the subject's triumph over the possibility of despair. For Milbank, the subject only comes to be suspended over the sublime distance of the future, and therefore only approaches the actuality of living, on the basis of his or her *persuasion* of the possibility of the good. This is why, for Milbank, Christian love cannot be totally differentiated from erotic love, for in the wooing of *eros* by the "charms" of its object we witness the beginning of the subject's suspension toward the future, in the direction of love. We witness, in other words, the beginnings of a subjective movement toward trust in *caritas* as the measure of spiritual life. *Eros* and *caritas* must then be reconciled, via Christianity's rhetorical appeal to the former, but ultimately on behalf of the latter. For Kierkegaard, by contrast, "Christianity has thrust erotic love and friendship from the throne, the love based on drives and inclination, preferential love, in order to place the spirit's love in its stead."[56] This we see, for example, in the fact that "in the whole New Testament there is not a single word about erotic love in the sense in which the poet celebrates it and paganism idolized it."[57] The Christian thinker who seeks to defend Christian love as in some way still sensible to the poet—who seeks, in other words, to gain a hearing with the poet and to persuade him—is tempted to proceed "on the basis that Christianity does indeed teach a higher love but *in addition* praises erotic love and friendship."[58] We can hear echoes of this approach in both Milbank's attempted rhetorical synthesis of *eros* and *caritas* and C. Stephen Evans' analytic attempt to explain the complementary function of neighbor love vis-à-vis all of our selective, "special loves." Kierkegaard prefers to remain dialectically offensive on this point, however, and in no manner invites such reconciliations:

56. Ibid., 44.
57. Ibid., 45.
58. Ibid.

No, if it is certain that Christianity teaches that love for God and the neighbor is the true love, then it is also certain that what has thrust down "every high thing that elevates itself against the knowledge of God and takes every thought captive in obedience" has likewise also thrust down erotic love and friendship.[59]

Love with the middle term of preference therefore has no "point of contact" with Christian love as a duty. What exactly is it about the operation of Christian love that ensures the impossibility of this synthesis?

Rooting out Self-Love by Becoming the Neighbor

In order to articulate the incompatibility of these two forms of love it is most crucial to try to understand the contrasting relationship of each form to self-love. We have shown in various ways above how preferential love is a form of self-love. Yet for a moment we must concede, to the one who wants to praise such love, that the opposite seems to be true; that is, it seems as if neighbor-love both assumes self-love and limits the lover's capacity to overcome it. In the "as yourself" of the Christian commandment, for example, it appears that the ubiquity of self-love is granted, and moreover that self-love is allowed to remain in full force, so long as it is equaled (though the commandment does not seem to require one to exceed it) by love of neighbor. The one who praises erotic love might argue that only a love that wills to love the beloved *more* than itself can really overcome the dominance of self-love in the world.

For Kierkegaard it is true that Christianity presupposes self-love in the human being; thus it does not begin, "as do those high-flying thinkers, without presuppositions, nor with a flattering presupposition."[60] Indeed, the presumed spontaneity of erotic love, on which its putative "independence" turns, is for Kierkegaard in keeping with the absurdity of "presuppositionless" thinking. Just as such thinking intends to transform the thinker into objective thought and so allow him to evade any personal immediacy to the religious task, so too the presupposed spontaneity of erotic love is designed to spatialize the subject as a lover by "objective definition." Preferential love thus does not presuppose the presence of self-love, precisely in order to presuppose its absence, and so to ensure that the lover can remain "defined" as such—i.e., as a lover—

---

59. Ibid. See also 2 Cor 10:5.
60. Kierkegaard, *Works of Love*, 17.

without needing to actualize his love in existence. The presupposition of self-love ensures, by contrast, that any overcoming of self-love will occur *in actuality rather than by "definition."* Christian love presupposes self-love so that it cannot escape the lover's attention; it presupposes it in order to take it on and break it open: "if one is to love the neighbor *as oneself*, then the commandment, as with a pick, wrenches open the lock of self-love."[61]

Why exactly is this commandment so perilous to self-love? Consider that self-love wants to be left alone with itself; in its effort to be alone it will do whatever it can to keep its character as self-love hidden. It will claim that it does not need to hear the phrase "as yourself," that its devotion so far exceeds self-love that to have it "broken open" becomes an irrelevant injunction. Thus erotic love gains a security from the question as to its relation to self-love, and in so doing ensures that self-love remains at its root, since as Kierkegaard puts it, "what self-love unconditionally cannot endure is redoubling, and the commandment's *as yourself* is a redoubling."[62] Therefore when *eros* ostensibly devotes itself more lavishly than Christianity's mere "as yourself" would allow, it really devotes itself only to "another I." But the commandment presupposes self-love in order to *insist* upon a redoubling in actuality, since "whether we speak of the *first I* or of the *other I*, we do not come a step closer to the neighbor, because the neighbor is the *first you*."[63]

In order to delay its shattering just a little while longer, however, self-love will now ask, "when will I know I have met the one I am to love in this way?" Jesus' answer to this question, which the lawyer of Luke 10:25 poses to him explicitly, consists in the parable of the Good Samaritan. The Levite and the priest in this parable represent those who know how to *know* who is or is not their neighbor. That is, they allow putatively "reasonable" deliberations about whether or not the wounded man on the side of the road is a proper object of their love to mask their fundamental mistrust that love could bridge the gap, the distance of the road, between themselves and this one who is so obviously not "another I." The Samaritan, by contrast, does not have time for self-protective deliberations about who deserves what. Instead, his dutiful belief that love can bridge any gap of objective differentiation makes him immediate

---

61. Ibid.
62. Ibid., 21.
63. Ibid., 57.

to the task of loving this particular injured man as the neighbor. In the first place, then, Jesus' answer to the question, who is the neighbor? is effectively to say, "quick, you do not have time for this question, for eternity's *shall* wants to propel you forward in love for the neighbor!" Or as Kierkegaard extrapolates, "to choose a beloved, to find a friend, yes, this is a complicated business, but one's neighbor is easy to recognize, easy to find if only one will personally—acknowledge one's duty."[64]

While the parable implicitly demonstrates this answer to the question, Jesus' explicit answer is somewhat less expected. When he is finished telling the story, he asks the lawyer, "Which of these three, do you think, was a neighbor to the man who fell into the hands of the robbers?" (Luke 10:36). This suggests that the question, "who is my neighbor?" constitutes an evasion of the duty of love not only insofar as one fails to see the wounded man as the neighbor, but also insofar as one remains unwilling to have one's own selfhood founded on something other than self-love. Thus, for Kierkegaard, "Christ does not speak about knowing the neighbor but about becoming a neighbor oneself."[65] And what is a neighbor again? As we heard above, the neighbor is the *redoubling* of your own self, your possessed self. To become a neighbor is therefore to become a self according to the movement of this redoubling, according to a differentiation that escapes the self-protective rivalry of which Girard warns. It is to become a self precisely by relinquishing one's grasp upon oneself, and thus relinquishing also one's grasping relation to others.

Even to ask that the neighbor be "distinguished" in one's vision implies one's distance from the actualization of love for the neighbor. Moreover, despite the apparent interest in differentiation and particularity residing in this quest for objective criteria, the question also betrays one's fundamental opposition to any differentiation that might break open the circle of self-protection in which one falsely hopes to find sustenance. In other words, it implies that one is opposed to any genuine difference between oneself and another, whom one wishes to remain but a fascinating mirror-image of one's desire. For Kierkegaard, then, there is no possible synthesis between these loves, but instead an eternal difference:

64. Ibid., 22.
65. Ibid.

> What a difference there is between the play of feelings, drives, inclinations, and passions, in short, that play of the powers of immediacy, that celebrated glory of poetry in smiles or in tears, in desire or in want—what a difference between this and the earnestness of eternity, the earnestness of the commandment in spirit and truth, in honesty and self-denial![66]

This difference indicates the divine authority that "it takes to turn the natural man's conceptions and ideas upside down with this phrase [you shall]!"[67] In other words, here we see something of the suggestion we heard in the *Postscript*, that through the Incarnation the natural man's capacity for Religiousness A is not confirmed by a finally persuasive exemplar, but rather infinitely complicated, since the Incarnation asserts that the eternal is not nascent in the human being's heart, but present in a particular man—Jesus. Similarly, one can become related to eternity's "shall" only in virtue of believing upon the authority of its speaker, which means only by having one's native love-as-inclination totally upended and "thrust down," rather than consummated in a worthily persuasive object: "If, therefore, a person presumes that he is simultaneously able to understand his life with the help of the poet and with the help of Christianity's explanation . . . then he is in error."[68]

Christian Love and Worldly Dissimilarity

On this account, Christian love's redoubling constitutes the exposure of all former love as concealed self-love, and accomplishes the rooting out of such despair through its imperative self-denial. Christian love therefore does not consummate or even "transform" all of the "special loves" that Stephen Evans, for example, is concerned to protect. Instead, neighbor-love is the making of a "new creation," or the making of creation anew as what it truly *is*—a way of being in love. The old must fall away, and here the old means a way of being that is *against* true being, the despairing way of self-protection. Unlike "special relationships" such as friendship and romantic love, then, neighbor-love is totally indifferent, *as love*, to the beloved's "admirable" qualities. "Christianity," Kierkegaard writes, "has never taught that one shall admire the neighbor—one shall

---

66. Ibid., 25.
67. Ibid., 24.
68. Ibid., 50.

love him."⁶⁹ Should the Christian therefore become a monastic in a dark cell, physically removed from "the play of feelings, drives," etc.? Not at all; such a dismissive interpretation, to which all self-lovers are surely prone, misses the precise target of self-denial: "self-denial simply drives out all preferential love as it drives out all self-love."⁷⁰ That is, the object of self-denial's mortification is not feelings, drives, or the appearance of difference as such, but the tendency of human beings to make such plays upon feelings into the "ground" of their love. Therefore, the task of self-denial in relation to the preferred one, such as the friend or beloved, is twofold: "for the unfaithful self-love that wants to shirk, the task is: devote yourself; for the devoted self-love the task is: give up this devotion."⁷¹ In no case, in other words, does Christian love's upending of *eros* mean that one must cease loving the admired one, nor even cease admiring the one you love, but rather it stipulates that you must *love* the one you admire, without loving *because* you admire her.

The superlative freedom present in love as duty hereby becomes clear, in that one whose love is secured by duty becomes *freer* than the preferential lover to notice and to celebrate distinction in the worldly sense, precisely because he or she is not *tied* to that distinction by love's infinite passion. Indeed, the implication of all of this is that worldly distinction can only be seen for what it is when it is precluded from becoming the object of a fetishizing love. The freedom of Christian love is thus a freedom from obsession with the preferred, and by extension a freedom *for* the world as it truly appears. Such is Christianity's unique relationship to worldly distinctions: it does not eliminate such distinctions in a worldly sense, but *deactivates* them as eternally significant, *in order to secure love*. This point is reemphasized in Kierkegaard's discussion of the manner in which Christianity is "the highest." The distinction, "highest," is of course that in which human beings as passionately related to preference will be most intensely interested: "Indeed, is there anything for which the human being as such, anything for which the natural man is more desirous than for the highest!"⁷² In wanting to praise the essentially Christian, then, it is important to clarify its relation to the most "distinguished," in a worldly sense. For Kierkegaard, as with Climacus'

69. Ibid., 54.
70. Ibid., 55.
71. Ibid.
72. Ibid., 58.

"Religiousness B," the essentially Christian is indeed to be praised, but without reference to the world's measure, which means its worthiness of praise ought to have nothing to do with the natural man's conception of the highest: "the essentially Christian is certainly the highest and the supremely highest, but, mark well, in such a way that to the natural man it is an offense."[73] Christianity is an offense to the natural man because it represents a life and a power that is utterly indifferent to such a man's esteem, and nonetheless remains life and power. Thus it is offensive to him because it represents his salvation—if only he will die with Christ to himself and to the world. The cultural alliance of self-lovers is fundamentally responsible for the difference, imperceptible to one in the thrall of cultural esteem, between that which is truly distinguished, as seen with a clear eye, and that which is the object of misdirected and rivaling infinite passion. This is why "no bird that has learned only one single word cries out this word more unceasingly, and no crow its own name more unceasingly, than culture is always crying out *the highest*."[74] Christianity is indifferent to this cultural frenzy of rivaling esteem, for its passion is grounded elsewhere—in duty.

This much implies that true love's blindness to preference is at the same time the opening of the subject's eyes. That is, love's transformation by becoming duty means that in love we are "blind" to whether the object of love distinguishes himself or herself in accordance with our preference, but it means also that we cannot blind ourselves to even one single human being *as the neighbor*. Disarmed of our preference and its capacity to become a means of rejection, there is now no one that we are allowed *not* to see, and our duty is to love the very first one that we see, which is therefore also a duty to "see" as such. Thus Kierkegaard suggests that "*one must first and foremost give up all imaginary and exaggerated ideas about a dreamworld where the object of love should be sought and found—that is, one must become sober, gain actuality and truth by finding and remaining in the world of actuality*."[75] Loving via the middle term of preference claims to be especially attuned to the senses, since it purports to be enlivened by its sensitivity to the appearance, in actuality, of its preferences. At the same time, however, because preference is its middle term, such love is prone to becoming passionately related to an increas-

---

73. Ibid.
74. Ibid., 59.
75. Ibid., 161. Emphasis in original.

ingly idealized picture of its preferences themselves, rather than to the beloved who was first "seen" to accord with them. Such a lover "does not love the person he sees but again something unseen, his own idea or something similar."[76] The blindness of Christian love, which implies the lover's blindness to preference as his ground, thus institutes a uniquely sober attunement to the senses, one that refuses to allow the senses, via self-love, to elevate particular attractions to the level of an obsession with a fantastical "idea."

Therefore, Christianity in no way supposes that a Christian can live "without the dissimilarity of earthly life that belongs to every human being in particular by birth, by position, by circumstances, by education etc.—none of us is pure humanity."[77] Indeed, Christianity is entirely opposed to the speculative supposition of a pure humanity, and instead "wants only to make human beings pure."[78] At this point we might want to suggest, however, that this love's indifference to earthly dissimilarity in fact constitutes an evasion of the difficulty of a truly Christian ethic, whose end must be to make all those who are indeed spiritual equals also equals in material circumstance. But for Kierkegaard, the goal of eliminating worldly dissimilarity raises a twofold problem. In the first place, the goal is impossible to achieve. Never mind the material difficulties of orchestrating objective equality, consider also that the diversity of human beings will ensure that even in similar material circumstances different people will have varied capacities for happiness. For Kierkegaard, therefore, "even if this struggle is continued for centuries, it will never attain the goal."[79] The second problem is that, achievable or not, material similarity is "by no means Christian equality."[80] Given the impossibility of achieving such equivalence, this difference in genus is Christianity's blessed relief, since "aided by the shortcut of eternity, [Christianity] is immediately at the goal: *it allows all the dissimilarities to stand but teaches the equality of eternity.*"[81] The task of Christian love therefore stipulates that "everyone is to *lift himself up above* earthly dissimilarity,"[82]

76. Ibid., 164.
77. Ibid., 70.
78. Ibid., 70.
79. Ibid., 72.
80. Ibid.
81. Ibid. Emphasis added.
82. Ibid.

which means the task of the one who would love the neighbor is not to "equalize" that neighbor in an earthly sense, but to love him toward an equality that transcends and "deactivates" his particular distinction, even while it does not remove him from it. Such a person, unconcerned "with removing this or that dissimilarity . . . devoutly concerns himself with permeating his dissimilarity with the sanctifying thought of Christian equality."[83] Yet in this way such a person also quite easily "becomes like someone who does not fit into earthly life . . . Everywhere he looks, he naturally sees the dissimilarities; and those who in a worldly way have clung firmly to a temporal dissimilarity, whatever it may be, are like ravenous wolves."[84]

The dissimilarity of lowliness and that of distinction both can become temptations to despair. This seems obvious only in relation to distinction, given that we have already discussed culture's frenzied fascination with "the highest." Moreover it is easy to recognize that an identification of yourself with *what you possess* is most tempting for the wealthy. Yet the temptation in relation to lowliness is the same, for one who cries out at the injustice of worldly inequality from the position of lowliness also risks engaging in a sort of clinging to dissimilarity that is only too ready to reject Christian love. Just as the rich person will find it difficult to hear that what he or she has is wonderful in its demonstration of the variety of earthly life, and yet is of no ultimate significance, so too the lowly one has a difficult time hearing the injunction of Christian love to "be lifted up" in equality, insofar as the ground of this elevation takes a shortcut past exactly what he is tempted to invest himself in—his lack of worldly distinction. Therefore Christianity "has not wanted to storm forth to abolish dissimilarity, neither the dissimilarity of distinction nor that of lowliness," but instead "wants the dissimilarity to hang loosely on the individual,"[85] wants to secure him in self-denial rather than through the ravenous tightening of self-love. Only when one refuses to "hold together" with people, to hold onto the handle of a particular worldly distinction—which sounds to the "natural" human being like a refusal of love—only in this way can one finally "exist *for*" all people.[86]

83. Ibid., 73.
84. Ibid.
85. Ibid., 88.
86. Ibid., 86.

Love and Self-Denial

By no means does any of this imply that one ought to abandon one's love for those with whom one may have a particularly determined relationship. To repeat, the commandment to love least of all prohibits or reduces love—it *commands* love. In the case of marriage, then, that your love would undergo "eternity's change by becoming duty" does not mean that you would abandon your preference for your spouse, but that you would allow that preference to be driven out *of your love* for him or her, that you would love your spouse in such a way that his or her preferred qualities would be allowed to "hang loosely." In other words, "your wife must first and foremost be to you the neighbor; that she is your wife is then a more precise specification of your particular relationship to each other."[87]

Even this account of the way neighbor love puts a special relationship like marriage through eternity's change, but without destroying that relationship—after all, as we have seen, the change of eternity is precisely to the end of *securing* love—even this does not spell a "synthesis" between neighbor-love and what Stephen Evans, for example, calls "special loves." As we conclude this section, then, we will do well to recall Kierkegaard's addition of "just one more thing! 'Remember in good time that if you do this or at least strive to act accordingly, you will fare badly in the world.'"[88] Worldly self-denial allies itself with the self-deceived crowd, in order to enclose itself as securely as possible in the circle of self-love. Such self-denial thus ventures only "into the danger where honor beckons to the victor, where the admiration of contemporaries and onlookers already beckons to the one who simply ventures."[89] But Christian self-denial means venturing into a danger where no admiration awaits, even the admiration of those with whom you are closest, for as difficult as it is for you, so shall it be for them—to become the neighbor:

> *Christian self-denial is*: without fear for oneself and without regard for oneself to venture into the danger in connection with which the contemporaries, blinded, prejudiced, and conniving, have or want to have no idea that there is honor to be gained; therefore it is not only dangerous to venture into the danger but

---

87. Ibid., 141.
88. Ibid., 191.
89. Ibid., 196.

is doubly dangerous, because the derision of the onlookers awaits the courageous one whether he wins or loses.[90]

With such a conception of Christianity—as not just dangerous in reference to an economy of reward naturally understood, but as the double danger of a venture that can secure, vis-à-vis the others, only more danger—one must be wary of "enticing." In fact, says Kierkegaard, "we almost prefer to warn."[91] We prefer this because mistrust becomes polemical against living the truth precisely under the cover of a fervor for objective certainty. On the other hand, it is faith's refusal to "conclude"—and therefore the necessarily inexplicable nature of its "resolve"—that keeps it interminably in motion. Thus, "if the discourse is to be about the essentially Christian, it must continually hold open the possibility of offense, but then it can never reach the point of *directly* recommending Christianity."[92]

How can it be that a refusal of direct recommendation is uniquely capable of keeping the subject in motion in existence, according to an eternal measure? As Kierkegaard puts it, "only the possibility of offense (the antidote to the sleeping potion of apologetics) is able to rouse the one who has fallen asleep, is able to revoke the enchantment so that Christianity is itself again."[93] In the next and final section of this chapter, we shall need to explore this connection between Christianity's necessarily indirect form and its unique ability to generate a truly existential subjective continuance. It turns out, as we shall see, that this connection has everything to do with Christian love as a unique mode of expectancy, an obstinate comportment to the future as the possibility of the good.

Love as Expectancy of the Good

Believing What is Hidden

For Kierkegaard, the life of Christian love is irreducibly hidden. Therefore nothing about such love, though faith affirms it to be the mysterious root of all existence, can directly attract the human being to traverse the sublime distance that stands dauntingly before any would-be temporal continuance. To be enchanted, to have the gulf appear attractive,

---

90. Ibid.
91. Ibid., 197.
92. Ibid., 199.
93. Ibid., 200.

is really to be asleep, on Kierkegaard's account, numbed to the necessity of your own enactment of the possibility of love. This is why for him the truth that is alive does not appear in a directly compelling form. As Kierkegaard puts it, in the Christian conception there is "no 'thus and so,' that can unconditionally be said to demonstrate unconditionally the presence of love or to demonstrate unconditionally its absence."[94] It is not to be demonstrated, it is to be *believed*. Therefore "the discourse returns to the first point and says, repeating: Believe in love!"[95] This exhortation must be said in response to both the one who mistrustfully concludes love's impossibility, *and* the one who, confident that love will be "known by its fruits," takes up the mantle of "the expert knower."[96] For Kierkegaard, the point of the New Testament claim that love will be known by its fruits is not to puff up the human being with knowledge, but to suggest that only in love and through loving shall one be known in the eternal sense. Fittingly, then, "the last . . . unconditionally convincing mark of love remains—love itself, the love that becomes known and recognized by the love in another. Like is known only by like; only someone who abides in love can know love, and in the same way his love is to be known."[97] That love shall be known by its fruits thus least of all allows the human being to evade the requirement of *believing* in love. For if he or she could "know" love without yet committing to it, this would suggest that on the path to love, mistrust is allowed to come along for awhile, but perhaps will be surmounted at the end. For Kierkegaard, however, the first and the last thing to say is "Believe in love," which must also mean, do not allow your "discovery" of love to win over your mistrust, but instead banish your mistrust!

Thus the transformation accomplished by love is not that of a measurable political result or even of a singularly effective humanitarian effort; rather it is a transformation in the inner being. Love, Kierkegaard writes, "must first of all *form a heart*."[98] But of course, this transformation in the inner being is nothing else if not a kind of giving birth to a new spiritual life in the human being, and thus we might expect it to become obvious to the observer. Yet for Kierkegaard, the "difference" of this spir-

94. Ibid., 14.
95. Ibid., 16.
96. Ibid., 15.
97. Ibid., 16.
98. Ibid., 12.

itual transformation is akin to the difference between the language of immediacy and the language of metaphor. Words used metaphorically bear no overt difference from words that are used in what Kierkegaard calls a "sensate" manner. Similarly, a spiritual transformation need not "parade a noticeable difference—which is merely sensate, whereas *the spirit's manner is the metaphor's quiet, whispering secret*—for the person who has ears to hear."[99] As in the case of language, then, where the attainment of spiritual discernment does not mean learning an entirely new language but gaining the ears to hear the metaphor's whisper in the very same words, so it is with love, whose task is not to *know* the presence of love in particular worldly significations, but to banish doubt over love's presence by actualizing the duty to love. The first step in actualizing this duty is to "deactivate" the pursuit of a conclusive knowledge about the fruits of others. One can only deactivate this pursuit rooted in mistrust by proceeding *as if* love as duty is already the neighbor's ground—in other words, by loving the other person not as he or she might want to be loved according to self-love, but to love him or her *as the neighbor*. Thus we return to love's primary injunction: believe in love!

Why is a "belief" in love in the character of love itself, which seems more about acting and less about thinking/believing? This aspect of love becomes clearer as Kierkegaard proceeds with his discussion of how love "builds up." To love the neighbor means to build up from the ground, to build up a self according to the movement of a true "redoubling." There is no other ground of this redoubling than love, nor any other agency in this building than love. Thus, "love is the ground, love is the building, love builds up. To build up is to build up love, and it is love that builds up."[100] At first glance, this seems to put the lover in control of the neighbor, to turn the object of love into the lover's "construction project." But Kierkegaard is quick to remind us that "it is God, the Creator, who must implant love in each human being, he who himself is Love."[101] This implies that, whereas conventionally speaking to build up means that one is in control of what one is building, in this case "the one who loves builds up by controlling himself!"[102] He controls himself by banishing his mistrust in the other, and he banishes this mistrust *by lov-*

---

99. Ibid., 210. Emphasis added.
100. Ibid., 216.
101. Ibid.
102. Ibid., 217.

ing the neighbor. Therefore the requirement of self-control determines "only one course of action, to presuppose love."[103] Presupposing love is to love the other person, of whom mistrust would conclude despairingly, instead as *the neighbor*, eternally "held fast" by love.[104] By presupposing love in this way, the lover "draws out the good, he loves forth love, he builds up. Love can and will be treated in only one way, by being loved forth; to love it forth is to build up."[105] Building up in this sense cannot even tempt one to adopt a position of control, for to be so tempted one would have to be willing to contemplate the external "effectiveness" of one's love. The Christian lover has no time for this, for he *shall* love, and this means he shall "be the one who serves."[106] The sensate person would like the building up to register in the external in virtue of his "doing something," while "to build up by conquering oneself satisfies only love; yet this is the only way to build up."[107]

Does it not become more and more absurd, however, to continue presupposing love in certain cases? Perhaps it does, to the sensate mind, but the one who actualizes his duty to love recognizes that the injunction to love this other person *as the neighbor* is no less binding now than it was when it seemed like the presupposition of love might be vindicated externally. The transformation of love into a duty to love the neighbor provides an interminable patience—in the form of a requirement continually to banish one's impatience. One must banish such impatience because it signifies a desire to judge and evaluate the neighbor's worthiness, and "the one who judges, even if he goes at it slowly, the one who judges that the other person lacks love—he takes away the foundation; he cannot build up, but love builds up by patience."[108] The lover's patience in presupposing love cannot be exhausted if he or she loves in accordance with duty, for then his or her love is secured at every successive moment—not by virtue of the neighbor's congruence with preferred criteria, but by the lover's duty to love this one and all others *as the neighbor*. And as we have said, to love the other as the neighbor is first of all to presuppose that this one is a neighbor—that he or she is like

103. Ibid.
104. Ibid., 65.
105. Ibid., 217.
106. Ibid.
107. Ibid., 219.
108. Ibid., 220.

the good Samaritan whom Jesus praises, whose selfhood is not secured by his passionate relationship to parochial preferences, but by love itself, the only true security. Thus does Kierkegaard conclude his chapter on love as upbuilding by suggesting that "it has now become manifest that *to be loving means: to presuppose love in others.*"[109]

To love the neighbor, or to love the other person as the neighbor, therefore means to presuppose love in them. This also implies the requirement of abandoning any comportment to that person whereby we might conclude, on the basis of a "knowing" experience, that his or her life has some distance to go before it is truly determined by love. Presupposing love has already dispossessed us of a relation to the other person as "known" by externals—he or she has become for us *the neighbor*. Therefore, Kierkegaard says, "experience will teach that it is most sagacious not to believe everything—but *love believes all things.*"[110]

Does this not simply mean, then, that love "knows" nothing, that in relation to knowledge, it is duped? With this question we risk being caught again in the trap of mistrust, since for Kierkegaard, knowledge about actuality is not as secure as mistrust would like to believe. Instead, he calls knowledge "the infinite art of equivocation, or infinite equivocation," and adds that "at most it is simply a placing of opposite possibilities in equilibrium."[111] We might recall here that for Kierkegaard, as Milbank helpfully explains, temporal existence is truthfully characterized not by a series of lines inexorably connecting dots, but by "infinitely many transitions," each one requiring a "leap." Therefore "knowledge" of the actual at its best means a kind of clear thinking that situates the human being in the place, not of certitude, but of what Kierkegaard calls an "equilibrium" of possibilities. Once bringing the human subject to this place, knowledge cannot bridge the gap between the subject and a particular possibility. Only a subjective gesture can do this—be it a gesture of despair or faith. Once the subject is placed in this equilibrium, "and he is obliged or wills to judge, then who he is, whether he is mistrustful or loving, becomes apparent in what he believes."[112] Knowledge therefore does not bring you to a place where either you continue to "know," or else you abandon reason and adopt "faith"; instead, it brings you to a

---

109. Ibid., 224. Emphasis added.
110. Ibid., 226. Emphasis added.
111. Ibid., 231.
112. Ibid.

place where your heart shall be disclosed, either way. Thus, while mistrust claims it opposes faith *on the basis of knowledge*, it is more accurate to say that "knowledge does not defile a person; it is mistrust that defiles a person's knowledge, just as love purifies it."[113]

This account of knowledge as equilibrium resonates with Milbank's suggestion that there is really no "construal" of existence that is metaphysically justified. Thus the narrative of secular reason, according to which the hypostasized "immanent sphere" was the inevitable discovery of a human reason more and more free of religious authority, is but a wager of faith. More specifically, the wager of secular reason is for Milbank a wager of mistrust, the refusal of a mysterious relation of eternal and temporal, which instead "concludes" an irrevocable boundary between them. Such an account is similar also to Karl Barth's characterization of the pursuit of knowledge in the "exact sciences," which he says is not defiling in and of itself to the Christian faith, except where it becomes "dogmatic."[114] The difference of Kierkegaard's account, of course, especially in relation to Milbank, is that unlike Radical Orthodoxy, the Christian wager of belief for Kierkegaard is not decorated with a beauty that itself banishes the self-protective fear of which mistrust is the expression. Here, instead, only the act of believing can banish mistrust. Knowledge's opposites are for Kierkegaard "undecidable" but for the act of deciding: "Mistrustingly to *believe* nothing at all and lovingly to *believe* all things are not a cognition, nor a cognitive conclusion, but a choice that occurs when knowledge has placed the opposite possibilities in equilibrium."[115]

To Hope All Things

The equilibrium of knowledge and the differing gestures of mistrust and love in relation to the opposite possibilities does not concern only how one is to evaluate a static "truth claim." Indeed, existence's paradigmatic situation of equilibrium among undecidable possibilities is the situation of the human being in the present, for whom the impendence of the future a matter of infinite uncertainty. Therefore love, in determining a believing relationship to the possibility of love in the other person

---

113. Ibid., 233.
114. See Barth, *Church Dogmatics III.2*, 24–25.
115. Kierkegaard, *Works of Love*, 234.

(where mistrust would conclude that it "knows" love is absent), also and especially determines a particular comportment to the future. In this part of Kierkegaard's discourse, where the relationship of love to "hope" is crucial, it becomes clearest how a love that is utterly opposed to preferential *eros* might be uniquely well suited to generating a human existence as passionate temporal continuance. This is, of course, also a matter of crucial importance for this book as a whole, since it concerns how a temporal continuance can be preserved by a love that does not "woo" the subject rhetorically across the sublime gap of future possibility, but only commands him or her to love.

When we speak about hope, for Kierkegaard, we indicate a subjective relation to the future, which, in temporality, is also a relation to the eternal. Thus the *how* of one's relationship to the future may become the reconciliation of time and eternity—if it is a relationship of hope. Let us quote Kierkegaard at length here:

> To hope relates to the future, to possibility, which in turn, unlike actuality, is always a duality, the possibility of advance or of retrogression, of rising or falling, of good or evil . . . When the eternal touches the temporal or is in the temporal, they do not meet each other in the *present*, because in that case the present would itself be the eternal. The present, the moment, is over so quickly that it actually does not exist; it is only the boundary and therefore is past, whereas the past is what was present. Therefore, when the eternal is in the temporal, it is in the future (because it cannot get hold of the present, and the past indeed is past) or in possibility.[116]

Only for love and its concomitant hope does the future, and thus the presence of the eternal in the temporal, remain what it is—possibility. That is, love's security in duty implies that no matter what our experience of a person's past course of life may be, we shall believe love. Therefore we shall act as if we are situated in relation to a future that is not determined by what we think we "know" about the past, but comes toward us as an infinite duality of possibility, which thereby always leaves open the possibility of the good. Mistrust concludes in certain cases that future possibilities of love are already annihilated by a "known" lack of love in a person's past, and that therefore time itself is not "touched" by the eternal via the future. For mistrust, then, the future is not possibility but

---

116. Ibid., 249.

a calculable outworking, an "identical repetition" of the past. Mistrust turns everything into the past. But love hopes otherwise, in that it first of all does not pretend to "know" the neighbor's past, and therefore it does not conclude in any particular vision of the future, but *resolves to hope* that the good is *always possible*. The expression for love's presupposition of love in relation to a human existence understood *as existence, in the temporal*, is therefore "hope in relation to the future."

The lover is related to the possibility of the good in an eternal expectancy because no matter what "actuality" may appear to determine the other person, love's duty is such that it *shall love*. Thus is its hope eternally secured, not temporally refutable. By contrast, "to relate oneself expectantly to the possibility of evil is to *fear*."[117] Mistrust in the eternal possibility of the good is rooted in the subject's fear that if he were to give over his security to the eternal security of duty, he would lose his very self. Therefore such fear decides instead to be related to the future not via an expectancy wherein duty maintains its belief in the good, but via an expectancy that pretends to knowledge on the basis of external determinations. Fear leading to mistrust thus constitutes a denial of possibility *as possibility*, for mistrust's conclusion amounts to the reification of a temporal economy removed from the possibility of being "touched" by the eternal via the future. That is, to pretend to know the unworthiness of love in all but those who meet one's criteria of preference is to claim to "know" the future as the determinate (non)possibility of evil. Thus it is to cease to want to be a "self" according to the spiritual movement by which temporal existence, though not eternal in and of itself, nonetheless *participates* in the eternal. Fear hereby becomes a denial of the possibility of an existential or spiritual selfhood whatsoever. By contrast, "love hopes all things," which means that no possibility is closed off to love, since no matter what foreboding signs it may find in a particular past, love *shall believe love*. Therefore it shall hope all things, which means it shall be, unlike fear, always open to the future *as possibility*.

All of this suggests that to hope all things in virtue of one's duty to love is the only way to avoid the reification or spatialization of your "self," and thus to remain in the process of becoming through which Christianity wants to make human beings eternal. As Kierkegaard puts it,

---

117. Ibid.

> By means of the possible, eternity is continually *near* enough to be available and yet *distant enough* to keep the human being in motion forward toward the eternal, to keep him going, going forward. This is how eternity lures and draws a person, in possibility, from the cradle to the grave—provided he chooses to hope... To lure is continually to be just as *near* as *distant*; in this way the one who hopes is always kept hoping, hoping all things, is kept in hope for the eternal, which in temporality is the possible.[118]

Kierkegaard is emphatic that this "luring" of the human being toward the eternal through possibility is not a direct luring—that it is not, in effect, a rhetorical "push" that would contradict his earlier construal of possibility as equilibrium. Therefore the eternal is, in the possibility of the good, incredibly *near*, but this nearness is only "explained" by the next phrase—*if* one chooses to hope. The one who hopes does not "know" the possibility of the good, he is not "convinced" of it; rather, he hopes according to his duty to love, and therefore the possibility of the good remains for him an eternal possibility, which keeps him ever in motion, in existence. On the other hand, "the person in despair... gives up possibility (to give up possibility is to despair) or, even more correctly, he is brazenly so bold as to *assume* the impossibility of the good."[119] Indeed, being unwilling to face up to this gesture as a mere "assumption," such a person even tells himself he "knows" the impossibility of the good—but this is precisely the defeat of possibility.

Unauthenticated Hope

Finally we must ask, *why* does the lover hope in this way? Has he been persuaded by accounts of others who have hoped and have been "vindicated," in a way that appeals enough to his *eros* to "push" him into making the same leap?

For Kierkegaard, unlike Milbank and Radical Orthodoxy, it is crucial that the "why" of hope is not just inexplicable in terms of a "metaphysical" justification; it is also *rhetorically* unauthenticated. That is, knowledge in relation to the future is indeed an equilibrium (metaphysics is impossible); but at the same time, a rhetorical mitigation of equilibrium is also out of the question: "the one who loves, the one who truly loves, does not hope *because* eternity authenticates it to him, but he

---

118. Ibid., 253.
119. Ibid.

hopes *because* he is one who loves, and he thanks eternity that he dares to hope."[120] This "because" opposes thinkers like Milbank on the question of how one may or may not communicate the Christian "venture" and the fruit it acquires. Recall, for example, how Milbank's reading of *Fear and Trembling* turns Abraham into a rhetorical exemplar of faith, suggesting that "for Abraham to make the gesture of sacrificing Isaac is to *know* that he will not sacrifice him, or that Isaac will return."[121] The offering of Isaac is not a sacrifice because it is not undertaken in the service of preserving something; it is not, in other words, the offer of one person for the sake of "the city," which both Milbank and Girard recognize as the violence animating all secular cultures. Rather, in Isaac, the promised descendant, the whole "people" of Israel is relinquished. Therefore Abraham's gesture is one of giving over the whole of the city to God, instead of an act of violence designed to preserve an existing city's precarious self-security. By using Abraham as an *example*, however, through which one would be able to "know" that a full-scale self-denial nonetheless acquires its true self from God, one misses the fact that a person cannot "know" such security unless she undergoes the same ordeal herself. That is to say, the important thing about Abraham, on the logic of Kierkegaard's *Works of Love*, is not that we can portray the ordeal he undergoes in such a way that we will be persuaded to suffer our own, but rather, like the importance of all of Scripture's metaphorical language, it is that we *can be related to Abraham in faith*. That is, Abraham is important when *we believe* that love is the ground and the acquired security of Abraham's gesture of self-denial. But we cannot do this except by undergoing an analogous ordeal ourselves, which Abraham as a written exemplar does not first help us with. For Abraham to function as an exemplar, we must *already* believe in love, which means we must already suffer our own break with the established order, our own "suspension of the ethical."

Kierkegaard does of course speak of faith's venture in a manner that recalls Milbank's own, which is to say that Kierkegaard tells us that love, which "does not seek its own," gives up everything only to get it all back in fullness and freedom. Consider the following: "As Paul says, 'All things are yours,' and as the truly loving one in a certain divine sense says: All is mine. And yet this happens simply and solely by his having no *mine*

---

120. Ibid., 259.
121. Milbank, "Sublime in Kierkegaard," 145. Emphasis added.

at all."[122] In other words, by giving up his "mine," all things come to "belong" to the one who lives by Christian love; all things "work together" for his good. But for Kierkegaard this state of affairs is never directly graspable. Thus he goes on to say of this believer that "the fact that all things are his is a divine secret, since humanly speaking the truly loving one, the sacrificing, the self-giving one who loves, totally self-denying in all things, is humanly speaking the injured one."[123] This is precisely the ordeal that Abraham goes through; the fact that Isaac is returned to him is God's declaration that "all things are his," and yet humanly speaking, he is the injured one. That is to say, he has received Isaac as the neighbor, as one grounded not in Abraham's possessive preference but in the love of God itself; and yet, humanly speaking, he has become the injured party. He has given up his possession of Isaac so that he can love him as the neighbor, and yet one can perhaps begin to imagine what sort of strain this puts upon his "special relationship," for Isaac must surely want to be loved for what he is "worth" to the one who loves him—his father. Isaac himself, in other words, must go through the ordeal of sacrificing what he is as a "possession" in order to come to terms with his father's love. Even being directly present to Abraham's ordeal must have been no salve to his offended sense of worth. Simply to be related to Abraham's gesture in faith, for Isaac as for us, must also mean precisely this—to get everything back only by becoming, humanly speaking, the injured one. For in order to believe love in the case of Abraham, both we and Isaac must lose the very conception of ourselves as something "worth" withholding from God, our true security. We must, in our own relation to the duty of love, gain the courage that "gains God—by losing its soul."[124] To see Abraham sacrifice Isaac is therefore not to "know" anything, for his gain is a divine secret that love must *believe*.

What a glorious truth, from Kierkegaard's perspective, that "the one who loves, who forgets himself, is recollected by love."[125] But what little time to waste, then, in forgetting oneself! For indeed, this glorious truth is not "acquired" except through the loss of oneself; and the one who has lost himself or herself no longer has time to be persuaded, so busy is he or she—hoping all things. The accusation of a rhetorical

122. Kierkegaard, *Works of Love*, 268.
123. Ibid.
124. Ibid., 269.
125. Ibid., 281.

theology at this point, which should sound familiar by now, might be that such a refusal to mitigate the terrifying duality of possibility—that of good or evil—does too little to set love in motion. That is, a refusal to compel the human being out over the distance of future possibility via some rhetorically persuasive appeal consigns that human being to the stasis of fear's conclusion—the conclusion of mistrust that to live as spirit, to live toward the future as the possibility of the good, is, simply put, impossible. To say that only love knows love in this way is not only to forgo the task of apologetics,[126] but also to give up on the character of Christian life as an irreducible temporal *movement*. To say that one cannot give a construal of love that might *persuade* the one who does not "yet" love to do so is, on Radical Orthodoxy's logic, to abstract the truth of love from its site in existence—it is to refer to a love whose indirect appeal means that it cannot actually be *lived*; to an "eternity" with which we can never be *reconciled*; and to a Christianity that can never become *Sittlichkeit*.

I hope we have heard enough by now to assuage this fear on the part of rhetorical theology, that we have seen with sufficient depth the complicity of human *eros* in fear's effort of self-protection to realize why Christianity must remain both anti-metaphysical *and* rhetorically offensive—despite Radical Orthodoxy's supposition that to oppose metaphysics one *must* adopt a rhetorical form of communication. More than this, I hope we have seen that only a Christian hope that is, humanly speaking, offensive—given its foundation in love as duty—is able to keep one's temporal existence in motion as a becoming in relation to the eternal. As a comportment to the future, this hope acquires its fruit by virtue of its continuance, which does not begin when first one is convinced of its fruitfulness, but only when one, in truth and self-denial, "hopes all things." Only such hope is able to keep temporality in motion because it alone does not waste time with persuasions—which already concede too much to mistrust—but busies itself immediately with abiding in love. Only when rhetorical persuasion is not a factor in a person's transformation by Christianity does this transformation acquire the continuance of a genuine reconciliation of the temporal and the eternal. This lover, who hopes all things, is high above any theological construal of actuality, and

---

126. And we have seen how Radical Orthodoxy is not willing even to forgo the necessity of apologetics. See, for example, Ward, "Barth, Hegel, and the Possibility for Christian Apologetics."

therefore his love and hope uniquely cannot be refuted by any "surprising" circumstances. Even when the beloved appears to "prove" the lack of love which mistrust is already willing to conclude—perhaps by breaking the relationship—still "the one who loves says, 'I abide; in this way we are still speaking with each other, since silence also belongs in conversation at times.'"[127] The future and its possibility of the good, as the point at which eternity "touches" the temporal, is the lure by which the eternal keeps being in motion. What joy, then, that love's inexplicable hope can transform even a "bad," even a rhetorically unaccountable past, into the future: "Therefore the one who loves expresses that the relationship, which the other calls a break, is a relationship that has not yet been finished."[128] What joy, finally, that this dutiful lover "knows no past; he is only waiting for the future,"[129] a future of which he, just like mistrust, knows nothing, and yet hopes all things.

Conclusion: Christianity as a "Way"

In this chapter I have offered a rejoinder to Milbank's suggestion that accounts of Christian love which presume to "purify" it of *eros* are subject to the same nihilistic gesture that animates secular reason. Most crucially, I have tried to show that on Kierkegaard's account, Christian love dethrones preferential *eros* while at the same time remaining better attuned than such love to "the person it sees." Here I shall attempt to give a succinct rehearsal of where the chapter has taken us, and say a few words about the destination of the book as a whole.

Our first section devoted to *Works of Love* treated preferential love and what Kierkegaard suggests is its foundation in self-love. There we saw in various ways that preferential love, which claims to be animated by its attunement to the beloved object in all of its visible particularity, in fact expresses the despairing, self-protective effort of a subject who does not want to be secured in the eternal. This subject, who loves according to preference, believes himself to be truly loving. He relates himself passionately to the object in regard to which his love has "spontaneously" arisen. He will do anything for this beloved object, will safeguard it at all costs. But it turns out that his unreserved passion for this one preferred

---

127. Kierkegaard, *Works of Love*, 306.
128. Ibid.
129. Ibid.

object indicates his refusal to have his selfhood founded upon a love that would prise him apart from self-love. He prefers the security of self-possession, which he "proves" by relating himself passionately to the preferred beloved or friend as but "another I," an occasion on which to congratulate himself for preferring what he prefers—himself. Such a love is therefore explicitly removed from love's need to love, for it believes itself to be justified in refusing love to any but those who will confirm the infinite power of its passion for itself. Instead of loving the person it sees, preferential love more often presumes to discover "sin" even where it does not exist, and especially in the one who loves truly—the one who loves the other not by esteeming him as a self-possessed thing, but as the neighbor. Thus we saw that preferential love must become allied with others in a relationship of escalating esteem, such that its sacrifice of "undesirables" will seem justified.

In the next section we considered the honest self-denial of neighbor love, and in particular how its "blindness" to the beloved's possession of preferred criteria brings about a proximity to the real, particular object of love that preferential love cannot begin to imagine. Unlike preferential love, Christian love's commandment presupposes self-love in the human being, but precisely in order to break it open—to ensure, in other words, that the neighbor is not "another I," but a *redoubling*. When you love because you *shall*, therefore, you are not obsessively related to the beloved as an object of your preference; instead, as concerns your love, you become indifferent to that person as a compilation of objective qualities. Hereby, without the clouding of obsession, the one who truly loves is able to see created distinction in the way that it is meant to be seen, as a splendid variation, the greatest heights of which are still not worthy of worship. Only the one whose love is purified of preference—the one who loves without care for the beloved's objective particularities—is therefore sober enough to remain attuned to those distinctions, since his love is secured elsewhere, and his anxiety need not work itself out in relation to those particularities. He is "freed" of his obsession with them, and so they become, to him, freely available.

In the final section we began with the claim that to love ultimately means "to presuppose love in others." We saw that to love the other person *as the neighbor* means to love that person *as if* he or she is already secured in the eternal through love. To love in this way is to court injury, humanly speaking, for it means to treat the beloved as if his distinctions do not matter in an eternal sense. It means to remove oneself from the escalating frenzy of culture's aspiration to *the highest*. But therefore it also means to "love forth" the other's true selfhood, as grounded not in self-protection but in eternity's peaceful differentiation, its movement of redoubling.

In this section we discovered also that in order to really grapple with love's comportment to differentiation, we had to consider existence's fundamental differentiating principle—that of temporality. Thus we moved to a discussion of love's temporal mode as one of "hope," and found we had to confront the ultimate subtlety of the distinction between Kierkegaard and Radical Orthodoxy. We began by recalling Milbank's suggestion that Christian existence constitutes a metaphysically unjustified "suspension" toward the future, which initiates the subject into a traversal of temporality's "gap" that accords with the measure of *caritas*. I tried to show first of all that Kierkegaard, like Girard in his account of Christian sociality as the practice of forgiveness, has an account of Christian existence that is profoundly resonant with Milbank here. That is, for Kierkegaard, the supposed "metaphysical justifications" of immanentism are but covers for a fearful subjective gesture of mistrust in relation to future possibility. Mistrust is opposed to believing that the future is something other than either predictable fate or sublime disharmony, both of which make it nonsensical to relate to the future in love. By contrast, a love that loves because it *shall* determines the subject's relation to the future as an irrevocable hope in the possibility of the good. Like Milbank's account of *caritas*, for Kierkegaard love's hope alone keeps the subject in motion, thus reconciling the temporal and the eternal by drawing the subject toward the future, that point at which, in temporality, the eternal "touches" existence. So unassailable is this hope-secured-by-love that it can even turn the past—which as dead "actuality" becomes to the natural man a harbinger of fate, a refutation of the future as infinite possibility—into the future, can turn an unhappy state of affairs into an unfinished relationship, can turn *everything* into possibility, all because it *shall* love and therefore must "hope all things."

Despite this similarity, our final pages also gave consideration to a crucial distinction between Milbank's rhetorical Radical Orthodoxy and the indirect appeal of Kierkegaard's Christianity. That is, while both have similar accounts of the existentiality of the Christian life—which for Radical Orthodoxy signifies its important distinction from secular reason's "hypostatization" of immanent and transcendent—Kierkegaard finally does not "go further" than presenting the future as an "equilibrium" of possibilities. For Kierkegaard there is ultimately nothing more to say here, for how one chooses in relation to the equilibrium will be the disclosure of one's heart. To rhetoricize the "gap," to make temporal differentiation persuasive as the possibility of love, is not to do the essentially Christian any favors; or rather, it is not to do the subject who wants to relate himself to the essentially Christian any favors. Contrary to Radical Orthodoxy's logic, for Kierkegaard this rhetorical "draw," which seems to move the Christian beyond the objectifying stasis of one who despairs rather than give himself over to temporality's eternalizing movement—which seems, in other words, to keep being in motion—in fact threatens the interminable continuance of a love secured in duty. That is, as soon as an appeal to Christianity becomes intentionally persuasive, it invites its hearer to evaluate the appeal in relation to his preferences, which is already to remove him from the point of immediate and imperative enactment. To introduce rhetoric is therefore not to inspire the subject to life as an interminable spiritual movement, but to keep alive an evaluative conversation that is the sinful subject's preferred delay tactic. "Yes, please," the subject says to the rhetorician, "only take some time to convince me, and then perhaps I shall act." But for Kierkegaard, the essentially Christian takes no time to persuade; it is too earnest about making the subject *alive* in spirit to allow him to spend even one more second *not living*. So the essentially Christian, for Kierkegaard, does not say anything beyond this: "Believe in love!"

Radical Orthodoxy provides an important theological interjection in the current philosophical discourse, especially because it is opposed in illuminating ways to modern and postmodern objectifications of existence, which presume on metaphysical grounds to rule out the possibility of Christian life as a reconciling way of living. But the urgency it ascribes to itself is problematically complicit, as I have argued, in the life-stultifying elements of secular reason it tries so hard to oppose. In the end I think it is important for theology to make distinctions about what Christianity is and is not. But as soon as the articulation of a particularly persuasive account of Christianity acquires a salvific importance in a particular era, lest we be "lost" to the nihilism of our self-justifications, then we are no longer in the realm of the essentially Christian. The essentially Christian recalls to us that our situation is one of fundamental uncertainty, and that all of our life-denying conclusions are but mistrustful subjective resolutions. But it does not then go further and say, Here, see this one who resolves in faith, and perhaps it shall be easier for you to do so. Instead it tells us that it will not be easy, and that even to consider this one in faith, this Abraham for example, you must have already given up your soul. Christianity thus puts us into a state of equilibrium and then moves immediately to the imperative—"hope all things!" So too must we conclude, by insisting that in reading these pages, no one has come closer to becoming a Christian. Yet at the same time we hasten to add that one must strive to be comported in hope toward the possibility that the same reader shall, through the loss of his soul, gain ears to hear the whisper of metaphor. Thus shall this reader attain freedom *for* the world, and yet also freedom *from* it as an object of obsession. So let none be persuaded; but, in the anxious situation of present anxiety, let each become the neighbor and hope all things!

Bibliography

Augustine. *The City of God Against the Pagans*. Edited and Translated by R. W. Dyson. Cambridge: Cambridge University Press, 1998.
———. *The Confessions*. Translated by Maria Boulding. Hyde Park, NY: New City, 1997.
Badiou, Alain. *Saint Paul: The Foundation of Universalism*. Translated by Ray Brassier. Stanford: Stanford University Press, 2003.
Balthasar, Hans Urs von. *The Glory of the Lord: A Theological Aesthetics, Volume I: Seeing the Form*. Translated by Erasmo Leiva–Merikakis. San Francisco: Ignatius, 1982.
———. *The Theology of Karl Barth: Exposition and Interpretation*. Translated by Edward T. Oakes. San Fransisco: Ignatius, 1992.
Barth, Karl. *Christ and Adam: Man and Humanity in Romans 5*. Translated by T. A. Smail. New York: Harper and Brothers, 1956.
———. *Church Dogmatics III.2, The Doctrine of Creation*. Translated by H. Knight, G. W. Bromiley, J. K. S. Reid, and R. H. Fuller. New York: T. & T. Clark, 1960.
———. *The Epistle to the Romans*. Translated by Edwyn C. Hoskyns. London: Oxford University Press, 1968.
———. "A Thank You and a Bow: Kierkegaard's Reveille." *Canadian Journal of Theology* 11:1 (1965) 3–7.
Bauerschmidt, Frederick Christian. "Aesthetics: The Theological Sublime." In *Radical Orthodoxy: A New Theology*, edited by John Milbank, Catherine Pickstock, and Graham Ward, 201–19. New York: Routledge, 1999.
Bellinger, Charles K. *The Genealogy of Violence: Reflections on Creation, Freedom, and Evil*. New York: Oxford University Press, 2001.
Benjamin, Walter. *Illuminations*. Translated by Harry Zohn. New York: Shocken, 1968.
Betz, John R. *After Enlightenment: Hamann as Post-Secular Visionary*. Oxford: Wiley-Blackwell, 2009.
———. "Beyond the Sublime: The Aesthetics of the Analogy of Being (Part One)." *Modern Theology* 21 (2005) 367–411.
Blond, Phillip. "Theology before Philosophy." In *Post-Secular Philosophy: Between Philosophy and Theology*, edited by Phillip Blond, 1–66. New York: Routledge, 1998.
Boulton, Matthew Myer. *God Against Religion: Rethinking Christian Theology Through Worship*. Grand Rapids: Eerdmans, 2008.
Breton, Stanislas. *The Word and the Cross*. Translated by Jacquelyn Porter. New York: Fordham University Press, 2002.

Breyfogle, Todd. "Is There Room for Political Philosophy in Postmodern Critical Augustinianism?" In *Deconstructing Radical Orthodoxy: Postmodern Theology, Rhetoric and Truth*, edited by Wayne J. Hankey and Douglas Hedley, 31–48. Burlington, VT: Ashgate, 2005.

Caputo, John D. *How to Read Kierkegaard*. London: Granta, 2007.

———. "The Poetics of the Impossible and the Kingdom of God." In *The Blackwell Companion to Postmodern Theology*, edited by Graham Ward, 469–81. Oxford: Blackwell, 2001.

Cavanaugh, William. *Being Consumed: Economics and Christian Desire*. Grand Rapids: Eerdmans, 2008.

Chaplin, Adrienne Dengerink. "The Invisible and the Sublime: From Participation to Reconciliation." In *Radical Orthodoxy and the Reformed Tradition: Creation, Covenant, and Participation*, edited by James K. A. Smith and James H. Olthuis, 89–106. Grand Rapids: Baker Academic, 2005.

Deleuze, Gilles. *Difference and Repetition*. Translated by Paul Patton. New York: Columbia University Press, 1994.

Derrida, Jacques. *The Gift of Death*. Translated by David Wills. Chicago: University of Chicago Press, 1995.

———. *Given Time: I. Counterfeit Money*. Translated by Peggy Kamuf. Chicago: University of Chicago Press, 1995.

Diamond, Eli. "Catherine Pickstock, Plato and the Unity of Divinity and Humanity: Liturgical or Philosophical?" In *Deconstructing Radical Orthodoxy: Postmodern Theology, Rhetoric and Truth*, edited by Wayne J. Hankey and Douglas Hedley, 1–16. Burlington, VT: Ashgate, 2005.

Evans, C. Stephen. *Kierkegaard's Ethic of Love: Divine Commands & Moral Obligations*. Oxford: Oxford University Press, 2004.

Ferreira, M. Jamie. *Love's Grateful Striving: A Commentary on Kierkegaard's* Works of Love. Oxford: Oxford University Press, 2001.

George, Peter. "Something Anti-Social about *Works of Love*." In *Kierkegaard: The Self in Society*, edited by George Pattison and Steven Shakespeare. London: Macmillan, 1998.

Girard, René. *The Girard Reader*. Edited by James G. Williams. New York: Crossroad, 1996.

———. *The Scapegoat*. Translated by Yvonne Freccero. Baltimore: Johns Hopkins University Press, 1986.

———. *I See Satan Fall Like Lightning*. Translated by James G. Williams. Ottawa: Novalis, 1999.

———. *Things Hidden Since the Foundation of the World*. Translated by Stephen Bann & Michael Metteer. Stanford: Stanford University Press, 1987.

———. *Violence and the Sacred*. Translated by Patrick Gregory. Baltimore: Johns Hopkins University Press, 1977.

Hall, Amy Laura. *Kierkegaard and the Treachery of Love*. Cambridge: Cambridge University Press, 2002.

Hankey, Wayne J. "Philosophical Religion and the Neoplatonic Turn to the Subject." In *Deconstructing Radical Orthodoxy: Postmodern Theology, Rhetoric and Truth*, edited by Wayne J. Hankey and Douglas Hedley. Burlington, VT: Ashgate, 2005.

Hart, David Bentley. *Atheist Delusions: The Christian Revolution and its Fashionable Enemies*. New Haven: Yale University Press, 2010.

———. *The Beauty of the Infinite: The Aesthetics of Christian Truth*. Grand Rapids: Eerdmans, 2003.
———. "The Laughter of the Philosophers." *First Things* 149 (January 2005) 31–38.
———. "Review Essay." *Pro Ecclesia* IX (3) 367–72.
Hauerwas, Stanley. "The Christian Difference, or Surviving Postmodernism." In *The Blackwell Companion to Postmodern Theology*, edited by Graham Ward, 144–61. Oxford: Blackwell, 2001.
———. *With the Grain of the Universe: The Church's Witness and Natural Theology*. Grand Rapids: Brazos Press, 2001.
Heidegger, Martin. *Being and Time*. Translated by John Macquarrie and Edward Robinson. New York: Harper & Row, 1962.
———. *The Phenomenology of Religious Life*. Translated by Matthias Fritsch and Jennifer Anna Gosetti-Ferencei. Bloomington: Indiana University Press, 2004.
Hemming, Laurence Paul. "*Analogia non Entis sed Entitatis*: The Ontological Consequences of the Doctrine of Analogy." *International Journal of Systematic Theology* 6:2 (2004) 118–129.
Horton, Michael S. "Participation and Covenant." In *Radical Orthodoxy and the Reformed Tradition: Creation, Covenant, and Participation*, edited by James K. A. Smith and James H. Olthuis, 107–32. Grand Rapids: Baker, 2005.
Hütter, Reinhard. "*Desiderium Naturale Visionis Dei—Est autem duplex hominis beatitudo sive felicitas*: Some Observations about Lawrence Feingold's and John Milbank's Recent Interventions in the Debate over the Natural Desire to See God." *Nova et Vetera* 5:1 (2007) 81–132.
Janicaud, Dominique. *The Theological Turn of French Phenomenology*. Translated by Bernard G. Prusak. In *Phenomenology and the 'Theological Turn': The French Debate*. New York: Fordham University Press, 2000.
Janz, Paul D. "Radical Orthodoxy and the New Culture of Obscurantism." *Modern Theology* 20:3 (2004) 363–405.
Kant, Immanuel. *Observations on the Feeling of the Beautiful and Sublime*. Translated by John T. Goldthwait. Berkeley: University of California Press, 1960.
———. *Kant: Political Writings*. Translated by H. B. Nisbet. Cambridge: Cambridge University Press, 1991.
Kierkegaard, Søren. *Christian Discourses*. Edited and translated by Howard V. Hong and Edna H. Hong. Princeton: Princeton University Press, 1997.
———. *The Concept of Anxiety: A Simple Psychologically Orienting Deliberation on the Dogmatic Issue of Hereditary Sin*. Edited and Translated by Reidar Thomte in collaboration with Albert B. Anderson. Princeton: Princeton University Press, 1980.
———. *Concluding Unscientific Postscript* to Philosophical Fragments. Edited and translated by Howard V. Hong and Edna H. Hong. Princeton: Princeton University Press, 1992.
———. *Eighteen Upbuilding Discourses*. Edited and translated by Howard V. Hong and Edna H. Hong. Princeton: Princeton University Press, 1990.
———. *Fear and Trembling/Repetition*. Edited and translated by Howard V. Hong and Edna H. Hong. Princeton: Princeton University Press, 1983.
———. *For Self-Examination/Judge for Yourself!* Edited and translated by Howard V. Hong and Edna H. Hong. Princeton: Princeton University Press, 1990.

———. *Philosophical Fragments/Johannes Climacus*. Edited and translated by Howard V. Hong and Edna H. Hong. Princeton: Princeton University Press, 1985.

———. *Practice in Christianity*. Edited and translated by Howard V. Hong and Edna H. Hong. Princeton: Princeton University Press, 1991.

———. *The Sickness Unto Death: A Christian Psychological Exposition for Upbuilding and Awakening*. Edited and translated by Howard V. Hong and Edna H. Hong. Princeton: Princeton University Press, 1980.

———. *Works of Love*. Edited and translated by Howard V. Hong and Edna H. Hong. Princeton: Princeton University Press, 1995.

Klassen, Justin D. "Heidegger's Paul and Radical Orthodoxy on the Structure of Christian Hope." In *Paul, Philosophy, and the Theopolitical Vision*, edited by Douglas Harink, 64–89. Eugene, OR: Cascade, 2010

Levinas, Emmanuel. *Otherwise Than Being or Beyond Essence*. Translated by Alphonso Lingis. Pittsburgh: Duquesne University Press, 1998.

———. *Totality and Infinity: An Essay on Exteriority*. Translated by Alphonso Lingis. Pittsburgh: Duquesne University Press, 1969.

Løgstrup, Knud E. "Settling Accounts with Kierkegaard's *Works of Love*." In *The Ethical Demand*, edited by Hans Fink and Alasdair MacIntyre, 218–64. Notre Dame: University of Notre Dame Press, 1997.

Luther, Martin. "Heidelberg Disputation." In *Luther's Works*, edited by Harold J. Grimm, vol. 31. E. Philadelphia: Muhlenberg, 1957.

Malantschuk, George M. *Kierkegaard's Thought*. Translated by Howard V. Hong and Edna H. Hong. Princeton: Princeton University Press, 1971.

Marion, Jean-Luc. *God Without Being*. Translated by Thomas A. Carlson. Chicago: University of Chicago Press, 1991.

———. *Crossing the Visible*. Translated by James K. A. Smith. Stanford: Stanford University Press, 2004.

McCracken, David. "Scandal and Imitation in Matthew, Kierkegaard, and Girard." *Contagion* 4 (1997) 146–62.

Milbank, John. "Alternative Protestantism." In *Radical Orthodoxy and the Reformed Tradition: Creation, Covenant, and Participation*, edited by James K. A. Smith and James H. Olthuis, 25–41. Grand Rapids: Baker, 2005.

———. *Being Reconciled: Ontology and Pardon*. London: Routledge, 2003.

———. "Can a Gift Be Given?: Prolegomena to a Future Trinitarian Metaphysics." *Modern Theology* 11:1 (1995) 119–61.

———. "The Invocation of Clio: A Response." *Journal of Religious Ethics* 33:1 (2005) 3–44.

———. "The Sublime in Kierkegaard." In *Post-Secular Philosophy: Between Philosophy and Theology*, edited by Phillip Blond, 131–56. New York: Routledge, 1998.

———. "Sublimity: The Modern Transcendent." In *Religion, Modernity, and Postmodernity*, edited by Paul Heelas, 258–84. Oxford: Blackwell, 1998.

———. "The Theological Critique of Philosophy in Hamann and Jacobi." In *Radical Orthodoxy: A New Theology*, edited by John Milbank, Catherine Pickstock, and Graham Ward, 21–37. New York: Routledge, 1999.

———. *Theology and Social Theory: Beyond Secular Reason*. Oxford: Blackwell, 1990.

———. *Theology and Social Theory: Beyond Secular Reason*. 2nd ed. Oxford: Blackwell, 2006.

———. *The Word Made Strange: Theology, Language, Culture*. Oxford: Blackwell, 1997.

Milbank, John, Catherine Pickstock, and Graham Ward. "Suspending the Material: The Turn of Radical Orthodoxy." In *Radical Orthodoxy: A New Theology*, edited by John Milbank, Catherine Pickstock, and Graham Ward, 1–20. New York: Routledge, 1999.

Nietzsche, Friedrich. *On the Genealogy of Morality*. Translated by Carol Diethe. Cambridge: Cambridge University Press, 1994.

———. *The Antichrist*. In *The Portable Nietzsche*. Translated by Walter Kaufmann. New York: Viking, 1954.

Oden, Thomas C. *The Humor of Kierkegaard: An Anthology*. Princeton: Princeton University Press, 2004.

Pattison, George. *Kierkegaard: The Aesthetic and the Religious*. London: Macmillan, 1992.

Pelikan, Jaroslav. *Human Culture and the Holy: Essays on the True, the Good, and the Beautiful*. London: SCM, 1955.

Pickstock, Catherine. *After Writing: On the Liturgical Consummation of Philosophy*. Oxford: Blackwell, 1998.

———. "Duns Scotus: His Historical and Contemporary Significance." *Modern Theology* 21 (2005) 543–74.

———. "Soul, City and Cosmos after Augustine." In *Radical Orthodoxy: A New Theology*, edited by John Milbank, Catherine Pickstock, and Graham Ward, 243–77. New York: Routledge, 1999.

Plato. *Phaedrus*. Translated by R. Hackforth. In *Plato: The Collected Dialogues*. Edited by Edith Hamilton and Huntingdon Cairns. Princeton: Princeton University Press, 1963.

———. *The Republic of Plato*. Translated by Allan Bloom. New York: Basic, 1968.

Rayment-Pickard, Hugh. "Derrida and Nihilism." In *Deconstructing Radical Orthodoxy: Postmodern Theology, Rhetoric and Truth*. Edited by Wayne J. Hankey and Douglas Hedley. Burlington, VT: Ashgate, 2005.

Ruether, Rosemary Radford. "The Postmodern as Premodern: The Theology of D. Stephen Long." In *Interpreting the Postmodern: Responses to "Radical Orthodoxy,"* edited by Rosemary Radford Ruether and Marion Grau. New York: T. & T. Clark, 2006.

Rumble, Vanessa. "Love and Difference: The Christian Ideal in Kierkegaard's *Works of Love*." In *The New Kierkegaard*, edited by Elsebet Jegstrup, 161–78. Bloomington: Indiana University Press, 2004.

Schwager, Raymund. *Must There Be Scapegoats? Violence and Redemption in the Bible*. Translated by Maria L. Assad. San Francisco: Harper & Row, 1987.

Shakespeare, Steven. "Better Well Hanged Than Ill Wed? Kierkegaard and Radical Orthodoxy." In *Deconstructing Radical Orthodoxy: Postmodern Theology, Rhetoric and Truth*, edited by Wayne J. Hankey and Douglas Hedley, 133–48. Burlington, VT: Ashgate, 2005.

Smith, James K. A. *Speech and Theology: Language and the Logic of the Incarnation*. London, Routledge, 2002.

———. "Will the Real Plato Please Stand Up? Participation versus Incarnation." In *Radical Orthodoxy and the Reformed Tradition: Creation, Covenant, and Participation*, edited by James K. A. Smith and James H. Olthuis. Grand Rapids: Baker, 2005.

Taylor, Charles. *A Secular Age*. Cambridge: Belknap, 2007.

Toole, David. *Waiting for Godot in Sarajevo: Theological Reflections on Nihilism, Tragedy, and Apocalypse*. Boulder: Westview, 1998.

Vattimo, Gianni. "The Christian Message and the Dissolution of Metaphysics." In *The Blackwell Companion to Postmodern Theology*, edited by Graham Ward, 458–66. Oxford: Blackwell, 2001.

Walsh, Sylvia. *Living Poetically: Kierkegaard's Existential Aesthetics*. University Park: The Pennsylvania State University Press, 1994.

Ward, Graham. "Barth, Hegel, and the Possibility for Christian Apologetics." In *Radical Orthodoxy and the Reformed Tradition*, edited by James K.A. Smith and James H. Olthuis, 43–58. Grand Rapids: Baker, 2005.

———. *Cities of God*. London: Routledge, 2002.

———. "The Displaced Body of Jesus Christ." In *Radical Orthodoxy: A New Theology*, edited by John Milbank, Catherine Pickstock, and Graham Ward, 163–81. New York: Routledge, 1999.

———. "Kenosis and Naming: Beyond Analogy and Towards *Allegoria Amoris*." In *Religion, Modernity and Postmodernity*, edited by Paul Heelas, 233–57. Oxford: Blackwell, 1998.

Westphal, Merold. *Kierkegaard's Critique of Reason and Society*. Macon: Mercer University Press, 1987.

———. "Levinas, Kierkegaard, and the Theological Task." *Modern Theology* 8 (1995) 241–61.

Žižek, Slavoj. *The Puppet and the Dwarf: The Perverse Core of Christianity*. Cambridge: MIT Press, 2003.

Žižek, Slavoj, and John Milbank. *The Monstrosity of Christ: Paradox or Dialectic?* Edited by Creston Davis. Cambridge: MIT Press, 2009.

Index

Abraham, 118–20, 123, 157–58, 239–40, 246
Aquinas, Thomas, 163
Aristotle, 23, 44–45
Augustine, 46–47, 49, 159–65, 168, 211

Balthasar, Hans Urs von, 86, 88, 159, 168
Barth, Karl, 13, 170, 235, 241
Bauerschmidt, Frederick Christian, 88
Bellinger, Charles K., 212
Benjamin, Walter, 91
Betz, John R., 110
Blondel, Maurice, 20, 28–32, 53
Boulton, Matthew Myer, 13
Buchez, Pierre, 164

Caputo, John D., 119, 128
Cavanaugh, William, 77

Deleuze, Gilles, 86
Derrida, Jacques, 41, 60–64, 76, 78–80, 84, 201
Descartes, René, 31, 68–71, 163

Eagleton, Terry, 1
Evans, C. Stephen, 205–6, 220, 224, 229

Girard, René, 7, 27, 37, 47–48, 103, 153, 156, 158, 173–95, 197–99, 201–2, 212–14, 223, 239, 244
George, Peter, 204

Hamann, Johann Georg, 20–21, 108, 110, 112
Hart, David Bentley, 1, 4, 6, 55, 59, 60, 63, 85–91, 93–98, 101, 104, 108–10, 112, 114, 141, 143, 154, 248
Hegel, Georg Wilhelm Friedrich, 11, 20, 22–29, 53, 55, 85, 119, 161, 170, 173–74, 187, 189, 241
Heidegger, Martin, 5–6, 37–42, 49–53, 56, 59, 63, 76, 79–84, 87–89, 92–94, 112–13, 149, 200–201
Hemming, Laurence Paul, 98
Herder, Johan Gottfried, 20–21
Hong, Edna H., 148
Hong, Howard V., 148

Isaac, 118–19, 123, 158, 239–40

Jacobi, Friedrich Heinrich, 112
Janz, Paul, 10
Jesus, 6, 22–24, 46–47, 74–75, 95, 100, 106, 111–12, 115–16, 127–29, 137–38, 141, 143–47, 149–50, 152–53, 155, 160, 171, 182–85, 187–90, 194, 207, 209, 222–24, 234

Kant, Immanuel, 14–15, 20–23, 35, 37, 40, 90, 159
Kierkegaard, Søren, 2, 4–8, 17–18, 27, 37, 42, 51, 55, 75, 96, 103, 104–24, 127–29, 132–41, 144–46, 148–50, 152–55, 157, 160, 169, 170, 173, 193, 195, 200, 203–10, 212–27, 229–32, 234–40, 242, 244–45

Lessing, Gotthold Ephraim, 128, 133
Levinas, Emmanuel, 6, 59, 80, 85, 87–93, 113, 123
Løgstrup, Knud E., 204
Luther, Martin, 196–204

Machiavelli, Niccolo, 16
MacIntyre, Alasdair, 11, 43, 46, 54, 84, 113
Marx, Karl, 11, 20, 24–29, 161
Milbank, John, 2, 4–5, 7–8, 9–55, 57, 63, 65, 72, 77, 79–81, 83–85, 94, 103–4, 110–21, 123, 125, 133, 135–37, 146, 149, 153–74, 180–81, 184–87, 189, 191, 193–205, 207–8, 216, 219–20, 234–35, 238–39, 242, 244

Nietzsche, Friedrich, 33–35, 38, 40, 59, 85–86, 94–98, 103, 112–13, 159–60

Oden, Thomas C., 108

Paul, 95, 99, 192, 239
Peter, 75, 188
Pickstock, Catherine, 4–6, 9, 43, 55, 59–87, 93–94, 98–102, 104–8, 110–12, 114, 120–21, 127, 129, 132–33, 138, 140–41, 154, 168–69, 198
Plato, 6, 34, 43–45, 60–64, 105–8, 119–20, 127, 168, 175–76

Rahner, Karl, 29, 88
Ramus, Peter, 67–68

Socrates, 43, 61–64, 68, 73, 84, 105, 107, 124, 133, 135, 204

Taylor, Charles, 1

Ward, Graham, 9, 64, 170, 241
Weber, Max, 5, 14–18, 20, 36, 53, 160, 174, 201, 207
Williams, James G., 195
Williams, Rowan, 77

Žižek, Slavoj, 2, 12, 24, 38, 104, 169

www.ingramcontent.com/pod-product-compliance
Lightning Source LLC
Chambersburg PA
CBHW031726230426
43669CB00007B/258